The Plot to Kill President Kennedy in Chicago

and the Other Traces of Conspiracy Leading to the Assassination of JFK

— A VISUAL INVESTIGATION —

VINCE PALAMARA

THE PLOT TO KILL PRESIDENT KENNEDY IN CHICAGO AND THE OTHER TRACES OF
CONSPIRACY LEADING TO THE ASSASSINATION OF JFK: A VISUAL INVESTIGATION
© VINCE PALAMARA 2024

Published by:
Trine Day LLC
PO Box 577
Walterville, OR 97489
1-800-556-2012
www.TrineDay.com
trineday@icloud.com

Library of Congress Control Number: 2024940507

Palamara, Vince.
THE PLOT TO KILL PRESIDENT KENNEDY IN CHICAGO AND THE OTHER TRACES OF
CONSPIRACY LEADING TO THE ASSASSINATION OF JFK:—1st ed.
p. cm.

Epub (ISBN-13) 978-1-63424-490-9
TradePaper (ISBN-13) 978-1-63424-489-3
1. Kennedy, John F. 1917-1963 Assassination. 2 United States. Secret Service His-
tory 20th century. 3. PRESIDENTS PROTECTION UNITED STATES. 4. United States.
Secret Service Officials and employees. 5. Bolden, Abraham. I. Palamara, Vince.
II. Title

FIRST EDITION
10 9 8 7 6 5 4 3 2 1

Distribution to the Trade by:
Independent Publishers Group (IPG)
814 North Franklin Street
Chicago, Illinois 60610
312.337.0747

www.ipgbook.com

Twas a dark day in Dallas, November '63
A day that will live on in infamy
President Kennedy was a-ridin' high
Good day to be livin' and a good day to die
Being led to the slaughter like a sacrificial lamb
He said, "Wait a minute, boys, you know who I am?"
"Of course we do, we know who you are"
Then they blew off his head while he was still in the car
Shot down like a dog in broad daylight
Was a matter of timing and the timing was right
You got unpaid debts, we've come to collect
We're gonna kill you with hatred, without any respect
We'll mock you and shock you and we'll put it in your face
We've already got someone here to take your place
The day they blew out the brains of the king
Thousands were watchin', no one saw a thing
It happened so quickly, so quick, by surprise
Right there in front of everyone's eyes
Greatest magic trick ever under the sun
Perfectly executed, skillfully done
Wolfman, oh Wolfman, oh Wolfman, howl
Rub-a-dub-dub, it's a murder most foul

– Bob Dylan © Universal Music Publishing Group

"There was more than one assassin on November 22, 1963. I was sub-poenaed to testify before the House Select Committee on Assassinations, which was a lot more valid than the Warren Commission. My basis for knowing there was a conspiracy stems from my own role in the investigation, my extensive experience with firearms, and my own gut feelings on 11/22/63. As soon as I learned some of the details ... " His voice trailed off.

– Maurice Martineau, former Special Agent in Charge of the Chicago Secret Service office in 1963, to the author 9/21/93

CONTENTS

A Book That Had to Be Written

Itruly believed I was done writing about the JFK assassination after my last book from 2021 called *Honest Answers About the Murder of President John F. Kennedy: A New Look at the JFK Assassination* (honest). Keep in mind, that one was my fifth book- the others were *Survivor's Guilt: The Secret Service & The Failure to Protect President Kennedy* (2013), *JFK: From Parkland to Bethesda* (2015), *The Not-So-Secret Service* (2017) and *Who's Who in the Secret Service* (2018). I mean, after five books on the greatest murder mystery of the 20th century and the Secret Service, what else is there to say? In fact, I even went on somewhat of a "retirement" tour, letting everyone know that the well was dry- I had said all I could say and do all I could do on the topic.

Then something happened in 2023 not long before the 60th anniversary of the assassination that became the seed which planted the idea that, without question, another book had to be written related to the subject. That said, the timing wasn't quite right: my wife's grandmother passed away in March 2023. Then an even more traumatic event happened: my suddenly ailing mother passed away on, of all dates, 11/22/2023. Unbeknownst to me at the time, the source (the "seed", so to speak) had also passed away, freeing me to discuss what was before a very unsatisfying anonymous informant. You see, I hate anonymous sources- I want specific names, bona fide credentials, documents, etc. The late Harry Livingstone had gone down that road for his controversial 1993 volume *Killing the Truth*, which used an unnamed person he called "The Source." No one was satisfied and, by the anonymity of the person, the credibility of the information that was conveyed was lost.

As long as my source was going to be anonymous, I frankly wasn't interested in conveying the information the person gave to me. Coupled with the distraction of personal losses, I decided to keep the information to myself. After all, my prior books had always named names and produced evidence. The thought of writing an online post, blog, or article, let alone a book, using an unnamed source filled me with dread. At this late date, who would believe it? It was 60 years later; enough with censorship, anonymous sources and hidden information.

It is now time. It is now the right time.

Vince Palamara
January 24, 2024

* * *

I write this exactly one week after a gunman from my hometown of Bethel Park, PA, 20-year-old Thomas Matthew Crooks, who also worked at the same skilled nursing home that my late mother was staying at in November 2023, came within a millimeter or so of assassinating former President Donald J. Trump, who also happens to be the Republican nominee for President in 2024. This shooting occurred on 7/13/24 about 45 minutes north of Pittsburgh, PA in Butler. There are many signs of alarm regarding the conduct of the Secret Service:

• The shooter, calling attention to himself by holding rangefinder hunting glasses, was acting suspiciously by the magnetometers at the entrance to the rally in Butler, PA before the rally even began and, because of this, was on law enforcement radar at that time. Crooks used an AR-15 style rifle and had explosives in both his car and in his home. Like Lee Harvey Oswald, associates claimed that Crooks was a bad shot (he was even rejected from his high school rifle team).

• Crooks, a registered Republican who voted in the 2022 midterms, appeared in a since-pulled commercial for Blackrock. Other videos appear to debunk the notion by some of his classmates that Crooks was a picked-on loner, as he had jovial interactions with some of his fellow students. As with Oswald, Crooks had a strange and suspicious background, as Crooks also donated to a Democratic cause and some claim he disliked Trump, despite his family being very pro-Trump. In a sinister side note, news outlets stated that some classmates referred to Crooks with the nickname of "school shooter."

• ROOFTOPS: the Secret Service, already aware of Crooks from his earlier behavior at the magnetometers, allowed the sniper with an AR-15 style weapon on a rooftop with a ladder within 140 or so yards from where Trump was speaking. This rooftop was glaring in its presence in front of Trump. It turns out that this building was used as the staging area for the security: local police, state police, and Secret Service. Incredibly, Secret Service Director Kimberly Cheatle claimed that the sloped roof of the building where Crooks shot from was unsafe for law enforcement to have been standing on, yet sloped roofs were exactly where the two Secret Service Counter Sniper Teams were located across from Crooks (not to mention that the White House itself has, as part of its roof, a sloped section).

- Detection canines were not used at the entry to the rally or to detect threats.

- Why didn't the counter sniper team, the other agents, as well as state and local police fail to see the sniper and take decisive action when, as videos demonstrate, the civilians in the crowd were noticing him and yelling for law enforcement attention several minutes before the shooting began? If anything should have finally swayed the agents into action, this was it.

- While it is obviously admirable that the Secret Service counter sniper team took out the sniper, based on the time sequence of the videos at the scene, it appears that the counter snipers spotted the sniper within 40 seconds of the sniper firing shots at Trump and the crowd (although there are reports that law enforcement in general spotted the sniper 20-30 minutes beforehand). With the rifle scopes that the 2 counter assault teams had, they could have counted the freckles on Crooks face, so taking him out would have been relatively easy.

- Why didn't the advance team of agents, along with law enforcement, recognize the obvious danger that this adjacent rooftop posed as they planned security measures weeks in advance? Why wasn't a drone or drones used? Ironically, as news outlets are now reporting, the shooter himself used a drone on the day of the shooting. EVERY rooftop should have been secured within 48 hours of the rally at a bare minimum (the advance teams usually start their work 2-3 weeks before an event). There should have been agents and/or officers stationed ON that rooftop.

- Why wasn't clear bulletproof or bullet resistant glass used? This has often been used in the recent past and is best exemplified by the November 2008 Chicago video when the Obamas stood before the crowd on election night and on that infamous day of the insurrection on January 6th, 2021 when President Trump spoke to the large crowd in Washington, D.C.?

- STATIONARY TARGET: Why did the agents who were near Trump and who surrounded him right after the shots were fired (conspicuous by not seeming to wear earpieces) let Trump, after just being shot and injured, stay an upright and stationary target for several crucial moments after the shooting? There could have been a conspiracy of multiple shooters and there was no way, despite the call that the "shooter was down," that they could have been sure that another accomplice was not lying in wait to finish the job (there were even several reports of yet another shooter on a nearby water tower). News outlets have claimed that the agents were temporary in nature (perhaps even drawn from Homeland Security Investigations) and were relieving Trump's regular detail, as they felt overburdened as of late and felt that they needed a break. The agents allowed Trump to stand there and pump his first in defiance toward the crowd (shouting "USA" and "fight") and seemed more concerned with creating an iconic photo op and following the orders of the protectee (Trump) to let him get his shoes than doing their jobs. Compare this scene to the Reagan assassination attempt on 3/30/81- I spoke to the head of Reagan's detail who pushed him into the limousine, Jerry Parr, and he and his fellow agents did an outstanding job pushing President Reagan into the limousine and keeping him low and unexposed. "Cover and evacuate" is their motto, as Parr told me, and it was not satisfactorily accomplished on 7/13/24 in comparison to 3/30/81.

• NOT STAGED: As a side not, since a spectator was killed and two others were critically wounded, I do not think this assassination attempt was a staged event, despite many people on social media believing this to be the case. I could buy this notion if no one was hurt, but there was too much collateral damage to think this was staged.

• QANON'S FAKE JFK JR, VINCENT FUSCO, was there standing right behind Trump- an interesting and curious anomaly of the day.

• A serious investigation of the Secret Service is warranted, not some whitewash "blue ribbon commission" like the Warren Commission. Trump came within a millimeter or so of being assassinated. Political violence is unacceptable, whether one is a Democrat, Republican or Independent. I believe, had the assassination been accomplished, there would have been a new Civil War in this country with violent acts like the ones that occurred in Los Angeles in 1992 over the Rodney King verdict, but this time all over the country in every state.

• While I am a big admirer of the Secret Service, 7/13/24 came very, very close to being a date infamous like 11/22/63 in the annals of the Secret Service. The plot to kill President Kennedy in Chicago on 11/2/63, and the many prior threats to his life that were in evidence, stands as historical precedent that the Secret Service must be ever vigilant.

Vince Palamara
7/20/24

Chapter One

Finding Nemo

(Actually, Him Finding Me)

Yes, *Finding Nemo* is the name of a blockbuster kid's movie from 2003, but just be patient; it will all make sense soon enough. As I stated in the Introduction, 2023 was a rough year- my wife's grandmother passed away unexpectedly in late March 2023. My beloved mother passed away on, of all dates, 11/22/2023, the 60th anniversary of the JFK assassination. Very ironic and sad, as both my parents got me started down this journey decades ago due to their own interest in President Kennedy's life and his tragic ending (they were married a couple months before the Cuban Missile Crisis of October 1962).

However, in April 2023, shortly after my wife's grandmother's passing, I started receiving many unsolicited calls from Florida. Since my wife's grandmother was from Florida, I started to think there was a connection and perhaps a friend or relative was trying to reach out to talk to us and perhaps pass on their condolences or some personal information to share. I do not like talking on the phone and I almost always avoid any unsolicited calls from strange numbers (in fact, my phone often flags these calls as possible spam calls or political calls).

Finally, after all these off and on strange phone calls, seeing that the spam call warning never came up, I decided to finally answer the phone in early May 2023. The relatively young male caller said, "Is this Mr. Palamara?" He butchered my last name in translation, but I let it slide. I reluctantly responded, "It may be- who is this and what is this all about with all the calls?" He answered, "I have some important information to share with you related to the JFK assassination." My first thought was "Oh, brother-this was a waste of my time. Another nut or well-meaning but off base 'researcher' attempting to pass off bogus information to me in the hopes that I would run with it." Sorry to be so cynical, but I am inundated literally every day online via various social media platforms, You Tube, and my blogs with someone's pet theory or idea, some original ("Governor Connally turned around and shot Kennedy!"), some not so original ("I swear that the driver of the limo killed Kennedy with his own pistol!") and some just downright obscene ("Jackie killed Jack!").

However, right when I was tempted to abruptly hang up and end this ordeal, the man said, "Have you ever heard of a Secret Service agent named Nemo Ciochina?" I paused for a second without saying anything, as the name struck me as immediately familiar. I then responded with a weary "Yes, I have." Biding some time to think about who the agent was from my memory bank, I asked the man what his name was. He said "Jeff; last name not important." I laughed and responded "Alright, cut the crap. Is that really necessary? I have your number." He then laughed and said "I am using my friend's burner phone, so it doesn't matter. I have a couple of these things."

I was once again tempted to hang up but the name "Nemo Ciochina" fascinated me and imbued what appeared to be, at first glance, a dubious conversation with at least some tentative credibility. I quickly told him to hold on a second as I quickly pulled up my list of Secret Service agents during the JFK administration I put together on my one blog on my open and running laptop. Sure enough, the name Nemo Ciochina was a Chicago field Office agent who later served in the Indianapolis, Indiana field office.[1]

I quickly got back on the phone only to hear some very loud and nasty coughing. I asked the man if he was alright and he responded "Oh, that's not me- that's Nemo himself in the background." I replied "Oh, wow- so he is actually there. Can I talk to him directly about whatever this is about?" He answered "No- he is in pretty bad shape. I think it's best if I try to interpret what he is saying. He loses energy fast. He has your one book *Who's Who [in the Secret Service]* and he really respects your work. How old are you?" I replied "56." He came back with "Wow, dude- you do not look it." I mildly chuckled and said, "With all due respect, I don't have much time to talk- can you or Nemo tell me what this is all about now?" "Hold on a New York minute" he replied. In the background came some rustling and mild coughing sounds. Then Nemo himself came on the line: "Hello? Hello? Mr. Palamara?" (also butchering my last name, but that's fine). "Yes, I am here." What follows is the back and forth between both gentlemen:

"Well, I read your book. I liked it very much. You see, I served with a few of these fellows."

"Oh, that is great! Which ones?"

---

1   As it turns out, I had momentarily forgotten that I had written a letter to Nemo Ciochina that went unanswered in 2005, another reason I remembered his name and no doubt another reason that he remembered mine: *Survivor's Guilt: The Secret Service & The Failure to Protect President Kennedy* by Vince Palamara (2013), page 53.

(Avoiding a direct answer) "You know, you are off base about the whole conspiracy in Dallas stuff."

"Really? Why do you say this?"

"You have to check out the visit President Kennedy was going to make in Chicago earlier in that same month. The real conspiracy was there, not in Texas. Oswald did that one; no doubt about it. I was involved in that investigation, so you can end all that stuff. Hold on."

Then came some really unsettling coughing sounds that reminded one of the death rattle. Perhaps Nemo had a lung disease or similar ailment.

Then "Jeff" came back on the line. "Vince, can you hold on one more second? I promise this is important. You aren't recording this, are you, Vince?"

"No," I answered. "I only record with permission. This was all too soon to even think of recording anyway."

"Okay-hold on a sec."

"Yes, I will," I said. Nemo's attempt to debunk the notion of conspiracy in Dallas on 11/22/63 was a turn off, but I must admit I was intrigued by his seeming caveat about 11/2/63 and Chicago.

I heard in the background between coughs something to the effect "Here- read him this. I don't have the strength."

Then "Jeff" got back on the line: "Dude, are you still there?"

"Yes. I am."

"Ok. Nemo wants you to know that you should focus your attention on Puerto Rican persons of interest for that Chicago trip and a man named Lloyd John Wilson."

In the background I could hear Nemo almost shout "That was his main name, his main alias. Tell him to stop writing about Dallas. He needs to look into this."

I responded: "Let me write that name down-Lloyd John Wilson. Is that right?"

"Jeff" replied: "Yeah, that's it, man. Dude, I am sorry to bother you with all this out of nowhere but he really wanted you to have this information. He admires your work."

I responded: "He can't admire it too much if he thinks there was no conspiracy in Dallas."

"Jeff" then said: "Hold on." Then, in a muffled voice away from the receiver of the phone, "Jeff" repeated my words to Nemo: "You can't admire his work too much if you think there was no conspiracy in Dallas."

Then I heard Nemo say: "I wouldn't have you calling him if I didn't think the world of his work. I read some of his thoughts online about some of the fellows I worked with. He did a lot of research to come up with all that data for a younger person. Tell him to hunt down that name and to look at Chicago- the conspiracy was definitely there, not Dallas. He is wasting his time. Oswald acted all alone!"

"Jeff" began to attempt to repeat all that but I cut him off midway: "I heard him, thanks. I really appreciate him and you taking the time to contact me. I almost blew you off because I thought these were robo calls but my wife's grandmother died in Florida and I saw that your number is from Florida."

"Jeff" then responded: "We are in New Port Richey. Do you know where that's at?"

I responded: "I never heard of it. Oh, ok- she was from Ocala [approximately 98 miles away]."

I then heard Nemo loudly in the background: "The medicine nurse is here. We have to go."

"Jeff" then said: "Vince, we have to go. Did you get all that information? He really wants you to have that. He really was a Secret Service agent back then and isn't all full of shit."

I replied earnestly: "Oh, my God- I definitely can vouch for him- he is mentioned in Secret Service reports and I knew the name."

Then came more disturbing coughing in the background. "Jeff" ended the call: "Check that stuff out, man. Thanks for your time. I don't know much about the JFK killing and all but Nemo was in the Secret Service back in the day. Have a good night, man. Bye."

I heard Nemo say "tell him I said good bye!"

"Did you get that?"

"Yes-thanks a lot. Much appreciated. Take care."

I then hung up the phone.

I sat there kind of stunned for a moment, trying to digest the call when the same number called back. This time I picked it up right away after the first ring.

"Hello?"

"Hi, Vince – it's Jeff again. Nemo said please do not use his name in any of this. He is afraid he could still get in trouble."

I mildly laughed and said "But he is long retired now – what could be the harm?"

"Jeff" responded: "Dude-please! He was nice enough to share this information. Please respect his privacy. Consider this off-the-record and background stuff. He is giving you leads to follow."

I responded: "To be honest with you, it is kind of a bummer to not be able to use his specific name as the source. I hate anonymous sources-they come across as bogus to me."

Then Nemo came on the line: "Mr. Palamara, as a favor to a former military man, can you keep my name out of your writings? I give you permission to use the information but I don't want my name in it."

I replied: "Mr. Ciochina…"

"Please call me Nemo."

"Nemo, I really appreciate all this, but anonymous sources are not my thing."

A pause came on the line. Then "Jeff" came on the line instead and said: "Hold on a second, okay?"

"Alright," I responded.

Between some more coughing and grumbling, Nemo himself came back on the line:

"You can use the information after I am gone. I mean, you can use my name after I go. Is that alright?"

"Alright," I said. "Thanks."

Nemo then ended the call with this: "Now I am trusting you because I respect you talking to all these friends of mine for your books and all. I want this out there but I don't want the trouble. After I am gone, I won't know about it. Check that person Wilson out and that trip out. Goodbye."

The line went dead.

Again, I sat in silence.

After a short time, after writing up a briefing paper on the call for my own immediate memory, I sort of soured on the whole thing: potentially great information and all, but I can't share it now unless I don't use his name, so no one will believe it or take it seriously, I thought.

Then a few months passed and life took over- my mother became ill and passed away a few short weeks later (again, on 11/22/2023).

Then, less than 2 months later, I did a random internet search for Nemo Ciochina (and other agent's names, a habit I have done countless times since 1998).

Then, to my surprise came several online obituaries[2]:

---

2   Nemo G Ciochina (1933-2023) - Find a Grave Memorial : Nemo G Ciochina (1933-2023)- Find a Grave Memorial. Nemo CIOCHINA Obituary (2023) - St. Petersburg,

Nemo Ciochina passed away on 6/15/2023!

He had been gone all these months and I didn't know about it. Then again, with my state of mind and all the distractions, I wouldn't have thought to pursue it at the time.

As I stated in the introduction: It is now time. It is now the right time.

Nemo Ciochina in his military days.

CHAPTER TWO

LLOYD JOHN WILSON

Someday I'll meet you [JFK] and if the government hasn't changed by then I'll destroy it along with you...
                                        – Wilson's threat to President Kennedy

While I may have uncovered evidence of the "Puerto Rican persons of interest" that Nemo Ciochina mentioned (more on that later), I definitely hit pay dirt with Lloyd John Wilson, also known as Dwight Allen Wilson, a name I never heard before (and who also went by other names). These documents need to be seen and read in full. Here they are. Although put together not long after the assassination, note the (Chicago and White House Detail) Secret Service agents involved in the investigation and how much of the data began before 11/22/63. These documents have never been published before and the name Lloyd John Wilson is unknown to John Q. Citizen, let alone the vast majority of the research community, as I have never seen it mentioned in any books on the case. I call this a visual investigation because these documents must be seen, not merely described:

CD 222

STANDARD FORM NO. 64

Office Memorandum • UNITED STATES GOVERNMENT
U. S. SECRET SERVICE

TO   : Chief
         Attention PRS

DATE: December 19, 1963

FROM : SAIC Sheridan - Spokane

File: CO-2-33,775

SUBJECT: Lloyd John Wilson
         aka Dwight Allen Wilson

This will confirm my telephone call today to
ASAIC Miller, Protective Research Section,
concerning the above subject who had called
at the FBI office in Chicago.

Norman Sheridan
Special Agent in Charge

NS: JG

Addressed to Chief James Joseph Rowley from the Special Agent in Charge of the Spokane, Washington Secret Service field office, Norm Sheridan, to PRS, the Protective Research Section of the Secret Service that is an intelligence branch of the agency that investigates mortal threats to the President.

CO 212
CO-2-33,775

SAIC Benavides - San Antonio   Nov. 27, 1963

SAIC Hanson   - San Francisco

Lloyd John WILSON

Attached is the entire file on this subject who,
according to M/R of SAIC Sheridan, Spokane, dated
11-7-63, was accepted for enlistment in the U.S.
Air Force on 10-31-63, and transferred to Lackland
AFB, Texas, on 11-2-63.

Form 1639 is included.

                        Tom H. Hanson
                        Special Agent in Charge

Enclosure

cc: Chief(PRS)

Special Agent in Charge of the San Antonio Secret Service field office, Luis Benavides, who helped protect JFK in San Antonio on 11/21/63, receives this report
from the Special Agent in Charge of the San Francisco Secret Service field office
regarding Wilson. Note the dates 10/31/63 and 11/2/63 (the date of JFK's Chicago trip). Note also Wilson's Air Force enlistment and transfer to Texas.

S. B. FORM 1883
7-1-60

C D222

CROSS REFERENCE SHEET   H-609

Filing code for
Cross Reference Sheet ___CC-2- 33,775___

Name or Subject: Lloyd John Wilson, alias, Dwight Allen Wilson,
John Allen Wilson, Lloyd Long.

Regarding: During the last week of August 1963 or the first of September
1963 the subject is alleged to have met Lee Harvey Oswald at the Cow Palace
in San Francisco, California and paid him (Oswald) $1000.00 stating:-
"This is a gift to help you in your mission. Do it in Texas if possible!"

SEE:

Code: CO-2- 24,030 _____

Date: November 22, 1963. _____

Note the shocking self-confessed Lee Harvey Oswald connection in this report dated 11/22/63 regarding Lloyd John Wilson with the aliases Dwight Allen Wilson, John Allen Wilson and Lloyd Long. It was either Oswald or someone setting the real Oswald up to take the fall for the eventual assassination ("Do it in Texas if possible!"). This meeting took place in either late August or early September 1963 at the Cow Palace in San Francisco, California.

OPTIONAL FORM NO. 10
5010-104

UNITED STATES GOVERNMENT

Memorandum

CO-2-33775

U. S. Secret Service

TO : Chief

DATE: December 19, 1963

FROM : Acting SAIC Martineau - Chicago

SUBJECT: Confirmation of Telephone Call

This is to confirm the long-distance collect telephone
call made by Special Agent Joseph E. Noonan, Jr., Chicago,
on 12-19-63, in which SA Noonan advised ASAIC Chester J.
Miller that Lloyd J. Wilson aka Dwight Allen Wilson was
in the custody of the Chicago Police Department on a complaint filed by SA Noonan, and that Wilson was due to
appear in Branch 42, Municipal Court of Chicago, 1121 S.
State Street, Chicago, Illinois, on December 20, 1963.

ASAIC Miller was further advised that SA Noonan will request that Wilson be given a psychiatric examination by
the Chicago police psychiatrist to determine his sanity
and that this action is based on Wilson's statements that
he intends to start his own political movement and that
if President Johnson should try to interfere with him,
he would see to it that President Johnson was assassinated.

Maurice G. Martineau
Acting Special Agent in Charge

Please note Maurice Martineau, the Acting Special Agent in Charge of the Chicago office and Nemo Ciochina's (and Abraham Bolden's) boss. Joseph Noonan was also a Chicago agent who, like Martineau and Bolden, was interviewed by the HSCA (the HSCA did have Ciochina's name and address[3]). Wilson made threats to both JFK and, after the assassination, LBJ.

---

3   Joe Backes, ARRB Summaries: Page 13. - ASSASSINATION ARCHIVES (aarclibrary.org)

CO-2-33775

Time 1: 05 P M

SAIC Bouck   Dec. 19, 1963.

SA Shutz, FBI Htqrs. Wash. D. C.

Lloyd John Wilson - Thr. to Pres. Johnson. - PRS Case.
    Reference is made to Tel. Call from SA Shutz , FBI, to the reporting agent
with the following information :

    This Date, 12/19/63 the Chicago Off. of the FBI interviewed Wilson, who came into
the Chicago Office this A M & said he paid Oswald $1000 to assassinate the President.
He previously had contacted the Chicago Newspapers in Chicago & said he was turning
himself in - Thus their is a Press Interest.
Papers on his person show he was discharged from US Airforce 12/17/63 as a Schizo-
paranoid state - Wilson stated he had saved his money & with organization backing
was to kill Pres. Johnson - He gave himself in to keep himself from killing Pres.
Johnson. Above information given SS Office in Chicago, immediately who are investigating at once. Local Police have been contacted & given this information.

    Information called this Office primarily because of possible Press Inquiries.,
Subject is in our file since 9/10/63 as a threatening Subject.

SA W C Pine - 12/19/63.

Wilson claimed a connection to Oswald and was a threat to both JFK and LBJ. This report involved both PRS Special Agent Walter Pine and the PRS Special Agent in Charge Robert Bouck, one of the agents who told myself, author Christopher Fulton and the ARRB that there was a conspiracy in the death of JFK. Wilson claimed that he paid a thousand dollars (10 thousand dollars in today's money) to assassinate JFK.

Chicago agents Martineau and Noonan are involved in the following report addressed to Special Agent in Charge Fred Backstrom of the Springfield, Illinois Secret Service field office regarding Wilson's Air Force duffle bag. Backstrom had an interesting background- The Illinois State Register interviewed Backstrom the day Kennedy was in Springfield, Illinois on 10/19/62 and the article, headlined "Secret Service Agent Heaves Sigh of Relief: Happy to See JFK Leave Town — Safely," was published the next day, yet no mention was made of a rifle threat to JFK for that trip.4 Instead, Backstrom spoke of the lengths the Secret Service, with his force of two and the "advance men" from Kennedy's detail, went to secure the president's safety. According to the article, potential sniper spots were cleared at the airport and a guard posted before the agents moved onto the rest of the motorcade route. The route, from the airport to Lincoln's Tomb to the Coliseum, where the president gave a speech, was swept for bombs. Even an abandoned mine at the corner of Walnut Street and North Grand Avenue was inspected and sealed, the article stated.

```
                                           C O ⌐ ⌐ ⌐
                          ------
                          CO-2-33775

                          U. S. Secret Service

. IC Backstrom - Springfield              December 20, 1963


Acting AIC Martineau - Chicago


Confirmation of Long-Distance Telephone Call


This is to confirm the long-distance telephone call
made by Special Agent Joseph B. Noonan, Jr. on this
date and received by Clerk Leroy H. Grandidier.

At this time SA Noonan advised that the FBI, in con-
junction with the Air Force OSI, had located a duffle
bag owned by Lloyd John Wilson which they are intending
to open an inventory.

Since there was no agent available at the time in Spring-
field to observe this, SA Noonan requested that the FBI
in the Springfield area be contacted and requested to
supply this Service with a list of the contents of this
duffle bag.

                          Maurice G. Martineau
                          Acting Special Agent in Charge

cc: Chief
FU:sjl
```

The day before Kennedy was in town agents gave out pictures and descriptions of "potential troublemakers" to all police that would be working during the visit.

---

4 Secret Service agent remembers rifle pointed at JFK during 1962 Springfield visit (rrstar.com)

REFER TO FILE NO. J-CO-2-33775

CD222

Chief

TREASURY DEPARTMENT
UNITED STATES SECRET SERVICE
FIELD FORCE

OFFICE Chicago, Illinois
ADDRESS P. O. LOCK BOX NO. 1077

December 23, 1963

Honorable Frank E. McDonald
United States Attorney
Northern District of Illinois
450, U. S. Court House
Chicago, Illinois

Attention: Mr. James B. Sloan
Assistant U. S. Attorney

Sir:

This report relates to an offense committed in your district against the laws relating to the protection of the President of the United States.

NAMES AND ADDRESSES OF DEFENDANTS

Lloyd John Wilson
aka Dwight Allen Wilson
aka John Allen Wilson
aka Lloyd Long

House of Correction
Chicago, Illinois

OFFENSE COMMITTED

Violation of Section 871, Title 18, U. S. Code, to wit: that on December 19, 1963, the defendant did knowingly and willfully make a verbal threat to take the life of the President of the United States, Lyndon B. Johnson.

DETAILS OF OFFENSE

At approximately 8:45 a.m., on 12-19-63, Lloyd John Wilson telephonically contacted a Chicago newspaper to advise that he was then in the FBI building in Chicago, Illinois, and planned to surrender himself to the FBI because of his involvement in the assassination of President John F. Kennedy.

Immediately thereafter Wilson was intercepted by the FBI as he was preparing to enter the Chicago office of that agency.

5-page document: As one can see, Wilson was most certainly a person of interest. Another Chicago Secret Service agent interviewed by the HSCA, Ed Z. Tucker, enters the investigation, along with Martineau and Noonan (the Chief, James J. Rowley, is copied on the report). Interestingly, Tucker had transferred from the White House Detail to Chicago during the summer of 1963. Wilson's threats to both Kennedy and Johnson are duly noted and that, if necessary, he "would assassinate the President of the United States." Wilson was also "discharged as a security risk" by the U.S. Air Force on 12/19/63.

2.

CO-2-33775

Later on the same date, Acting SAIC Martineau, Chicago, U. S. Secret Service, was telephonically contacted by SAC Marlin Johnson, FBI, and advised that the defendant had made statements which concerned the safety of the President of the United States.

On the afternoon of the same date, the defendant was interviewed by the writer and Special Agent Richard Z. Tucker. The defendant was quite open in his conversation and freely stated that he had paid a man named Oswald $1000 to assassinate President John F. Kennedy. He stated also that he intended to return to the state of California where he would reinstitute a political organization of which he was the founder. This organization is called the DAW Organization or The White Resistance.

When questioned regarding his feelings concerning President Lyndon B. Johnson, the defendant stated that he did not know enough of the present President but that should President Johnson continue the same political course as President Kennedy that he, the defendant, would consider the assassination of President Johnson to be necessary for the good of the United States. The defendant was asked if he would pay to have the assassination committed by another person to which he stated that he would do so.

He stated further that he knew persons who were qualified and willing to carry out such an assassination.

The defendant was asked if he would, under any circumstances, assassinate the President of the United States himself, to which the defendant replied that although he did not like violence, if necessary he would assassinate the President of the United States. The defendant stated that his political beliefs held that assassination was an acceptable political maneuver.

The defendant generally agrees with the beliefs and aims of the American Nazi Party and although he does not identify himself with that organization, shows a tendency to follow the fascist line.

The defendant further stated that his form of government would not tolerate free speech or freedom of the press, that this form of government would allow no opposition and would have no hesitancy in killing persons who did not conform to standards of his belief.

It should be noted that this Service first began to have interest in the defendant on 9-10-63 when they were advised by the FBI that the defendant had supposedly written a letter to President Kennedy, a portion of which contained a sentence "Someday I'll meet you, you'll

19

3.

CO-2-33775

knew me well, if the government hasn't changed by then, I'll destroy it along with you".

The defendant was interviewed by SAIC Norman Sheridan, U. S. Secret Service, Spokane, Washington, at which time he acknowledged writing a letter to President Kennedy and admitted the threatening sentence previously listed.

The defendant executed a signed, sworn statement regarding this matter to SAIC Sheridan. A carbon copy of this statement is attached to this report. Also attached to this report is a copy of the letter the defendant had written to President Kennedy which he rewrote at SAIC Sheridan's request. In it is contained the threatening sentence to the President of the United States. This letter is in the defendant's own handwriting.

It should be noted that this letter was never sent to President Kennedy. The defendant stated that he destroyed the letter.

These last paragraphs are added to show the consistent feeling of extreme antagonism the defendant has towards the office of the President of the United States.

LIST OF EXHIBITS

Exhibit A   Signed, sworn statement of the defendant regarding his threat to President John F. Kennedy witnessed by SAIC Norman Sheridan and dated October 29, 1963, a carbon copy of which is attached to this report.

Exhibit B   A letter in the defendant's own handwriting witnessed by SAIC Norman Sheridan which is a copy to the best of the defendant's memory of the original letter written by him which contains a threat to President John F. Kennedy/ This letter was witnessed and written on October 28, 1963, a photostatic copy of which is attached.

WITNESSES AND THEIR TESTIMONY

Dennis Shanahan	Special Agent	FBI
		536 South Clark Street
		Chicago, Illinois

Will testify as to the statements of the defendant regarding the threat to President Lyndon B. Johnson.

4.

CO-2-33775

Robert Malone	Special Agent	FBI
		536 South Clark Street
		Chicago, Illinois

Will testify as to the statements of the defendant regarding the threat to President Lyndon B. Johnson.

Edward Z. Tucker	Special Agent	U. S. Secret Service
		426, U. S. Court House
		219 South Clark Street
		Chicago, Illinois

Will testify that he assisted in the investigation of this case.

Joseph E. Noonan, Jr.	Special Agent	U. S. Secret Service
		426, U. S. Court House
		219 South Clark Street
		Chicago, Illinois

Will testify that he conducted the investigation in this case for the government and will produce all pertinent papers and records necessary in court.

Norman Sheridan	Special Agent	U. S. Secret Service
	in Charge	Room 201
		Post Office Building
		Spokane, Washington

Will testify that he received and witnessed Exhibits A & B and that these statements were freely given by the defendant at the time stated.

CRIMINAL RECORD AND BRIEF PERSONAL HISTORY

Lloyd John Wilson
aka Dwight Allen Wilson
aka John Allen Wilson
aka Lloyd Long

The defendant is a White male, 18 years of age, born 8-16-45 at Santa Cruz, California. He is single and investigation shows that he has worked at menial jobs for short periods of time. On 10-31-63, he enlisted in the

5.

CO-2-33775

U. S. Air Force at Spokane, Washington, and was discharged as a security risk on December 18, 1963. This discharge was termed honorable; however, it was based on a report by the U. S. Secret Service advising the Air Force that the subject had previously threatened the life of President John F. Kennedy and was considered dangerous by this Service.

Examination of the subject by Air Force psychiatrists was effected prior to his discharge and he was termed as a schizophrenic person with strong paranoid tendencies.

The defendant has no known police record.

The defendant's fingerprints were taken by the FBI and to date no report has been received.

Very truly yours,

Joseph E. Koonan Jr.

Joseph E. Koonan, Jr.
Special Agent

APPROVED:

Maurice G. Martineau

Maurice G. Martineau
Acting Special Agent in Charge

cc: Chief ✓

JEN:sjl

Form No. 1586 (Revised)
MEMORANDUM REPORT
(7-1-60)

UNITED STATES SECRET SERVICE CD222
TREASURY DEPARTMENT

San Francisco			
ORIGIN CDS 10-28-63	OFFICE Spokane, Washington		FILE NO. CO-2-33,775
TYPE OF CASE	STATUS	TITLE OR CAPTION	
Protective Research	Previously Closed-Spokane	Person Identified:	
INVESTIGATION MADE AT	PERIOD COVERED	Name: Lloyd John Wilson	
Spokane, Wash.	12-19-63	aka Dwight Allen Wilson,	
INVESTIGATION MADE BY		John Allen Wilson,	
SAIC Norman Sheridan		Lloyd Long	
DETAILS			

SYNOPSIS

FBI, Spokane, advised that the subject was in their
Chicago office on this date and that the subject
claimed he had conspired with Harvey Lee Oswald in
the assassination of the President.

(A) INTRODUCTION:

Reference is made to my report dated November 7, 1963 closing the investigation
at Spokane; also, to my office memorandum of November 27, 1963 to the Chief
transmitting an envelope and original letter received that day from the subject
with a return address of Lackland Air Force Base, Texas.

(B) GENERAL INQUIRIES

On 12-19-63 Special Agent Donald F. Head, FBI Resident Agency, Spokane, called
at our office about 8:45 a.m. SA Head stated he had received a telephone call
from their special agent in charge in Seattle; that the subject was in their
Chicago office on this date. He further advised that the subject had called
on a Chicago newspaper and claimed he had conspired with Harvey Lee Oswald in
the assassination of President Kennedy. He also stated the subject had been
discharged December 18, 1963 from Chanute Air Force Base, Illinois, and that
the subject had said he had been interviewed by me in the Spokane office. SA
Head asserted he did not know whether their Chicago office had advised the
Secret Service office in Chicago. He stated their Chicago office wanted to
verify my interview with the subject in Spokane.

I telephoned ASAIC Martineau, Chicago, who stated the FBI had advised him that
the subject was in their office. ASAIC Martineau also stated he had received
information from SAIC Backstrom, Springfield, that the subject received a
Profile-4 discharge on December 18, 1963 from Chanute Air Force Base, Illinois.

DISTRIBUTION AIRMAIL	COPIES	REPORT MADE BY		DATE
Chief	Orig/A	*Norman Sheridan*		
Chicago	2 cc			
San Francisco	2 cc	Norman Sheridan SPECIAL AGENT in Charge		12-19-63
Spokane	1 cc	APPROVED		DATE
NS:JG		SPECIAL AGENT IN CHARGE		

3-page document: "Suspect (Wilson) claimed he had conspired with Harvey Lee
Oswald in the assassination of the President." SAIC of PRS Robert Bouck's assistant, ASAIC Chester Miller, is noted in this report.

Page 2

CO-2-33,775

SA Head, FBI, Spokane, returned to our office in about a half hour and stated their Chicago office wanted copies of the statement I obtained October 29, 1963 from the subject; also, a copy of the subject's letter which the subject mailed from Lackland Air Force Base, Texas. SA Head was advised that the desired copies of the subject's statement and letter should be obtained from the Chief's office or our San Franbisco, office. SA Head was assured of my cooperation in every way possible in this case; however, I felt inasmuch as the subject Wilson had associated himself with Harvey Lee Oswald I did not have authorization to furnish these copies and that the best source to obtain them would be through our Chief's office where the original statement and letter are filed.

I telephoned ASAIC Miller, PRS, Washington, D. C. and advised him of the FBI's request. I also telephoned Assistant U. S. Attorney Carroll Gray, Spokane, who had previously been furnished a copy of the subject's statement and letter, and advised him that the FBI had been referred to our Chief's office for the above mentioned copies of the subject's statement and letter. He said SA Head of the FBI had not contacted him regarding this case and in the event he did, he would also refer him to our Chief's office for the information requested.

(J) CONCLUSION

The case remains closed at Spokane.

CO222

No. [ ]

RECORD OF Correspondence, Reports Documents, Telephone Conversations, Oral Interviews and conversations	CO-2-34,030 Re: Lee Harvey Oswald Assassination of President

Date & Time Received: 12-23-63

Received by: alr

Received from: Spokane (Via CO Mail)

Comments
(Brief summary of Document conversation, etc.)   CN - 12-19-63 - Spokane

   Re Lloyd John Wilson

Information Passed for Action to:

FORM NO. [OWN (REVISED)]
MEMORANDUM REPORT
(7-1-48)

UNITED STATES SECRET SERVICE
TREASURY DEPARTMENT

CD222.

ORIGIN Field	OFFICE Chicago, Illinois		FILE NO. J-CO-2-33775
TYPE OF CASE	STATUS	TITLE OR CAPTION	
Protective Research	Pending	**PERSON IDENTIFIED:**	
INVESTIGATION MADE AT	PERIOD COVERED	Name : Lloyd John Wilson	
Chicago, Illinois	1-3-64 to 1-9-64	Address: Cook County Jail	
INVESTIGATION MADE BY		Chicago, Illinois	
Special Agent Joseph E. Noonan, Jr.			

DETAILS

SYNOPSIS

Charges against the subject in State Court were dismissed at the request of the U. S. Attorney. Subject appeared before the U. S. Commissioner in Chicago. His hearing was continued until January 10, 1964. Bond was set for $25,000.00.

On January 9, 1964, Judge Abraham L. Marovitz ordered a sanity hearing to be held on January 16, 1964.

The hearing before the U. S. Commissioner was continued pending the outcome of the sanity hearing before Judge Marovitz.

(A) INTRODUCTION:

Reference is made to the M/R of the writer dated 12-23-63 and to the M/R of SAIC Fred H. Backstrom, Springfield, dated 12-30-63.

(B) GENERAL INQUIRIES:

On 1-3-64, the subject appeared before Judge Harry G. Comerford, Branch 42a, Municipal Court of Chicago, at which time the charges pending against him were dismissed in lieu of the federal warrant and the subject was turned over to the U. S. Marshals.

On the same date, the subject appeared before U. S. Commissioner C. S. Bentley Pike, Chicago, who assigned Raymond Smith as the subject's attorney and at Mr. Smith's request continued the hearing until January 10, 1964. The Commissioner set bond at $25,000.00

DISTRIBUTION	COPIES	REPORT MADE BY	DATE
Chief	Original w/Att.	Joseph E. Noonan	
Chicago	2 cc	SPECIAL AGENT Joseph E. Noonan, Jr	1-10-64
		APPROVED	DATE
JEN:sjl		Acting SPECIAL AGENT IN CHARGE Maurice G. Martineau	1-10-64

Chicago Secret Service agent Joseph Noonan (approved by SAIC Martineau) report regarding Wilson.

Form No. 1500 (Revised)
MEMORANDUM REPORT
(7-1-56)

CD222

UNITED STATES SECRET SERVICE
TREASURY DEPARTMENT

Chicago		OFFICE Springfield, Illinois.	FILE NO. CO-2-33,775
ORIGIN 12-20-63 JEN			
TYPE OF CASE	STATUS	TITLE OR CAPTION	
Protective Research	Closed-Springfield	Person Identified:	
INVESTIGATION MADE AT	PERIOD COVERED	Name : Lloyd John Wilson	
Springfield, Illinois.	12-20/30-63	aka Dwight Allen Wilson,	
INVESTIGATION MADE BY		John Allen Wilson,	
SAIC Fred H. Backstrom		Lloyd Long	

DETAILS

SYNOPSIS

This report concerns search of Lloyd John Wilson's duffle bag at Chanute Air Force Base, Illinois, and copy of his "Ode" to President Kennedy.

DETAILS OF INVESTIGATION

This investigation originated with a L/D call to Clerk Grandidier from SA Noonan, Chicago, on December 20, 1963, advising that the FBI had informed the Chicago Office that they had located Wilson's duffle bag at Chanute Air Force Base and were going to open it.

Other Law Enforcement Agencies

SA Manley Hawkes, FBI, Springfield, was contacted and stated he would have Resident Agent Eugene Irwin of their Champaign Office provide us with any pertinent information.

On December 30, 1963, SA Gerald Shanahan, FBI, Springfield, stated the duffle bag contained only personal articles of subject Wilson and that it had been found by Air Police in an alley behind the bus station at Rantoul, Illinois, which is the town immediately adjacent to Chanute Air Force Base. However, in the duffle bag was an Air Training Command "Student Study Guide and Workbook" issued at Lackland AFB, Texas. On the outside back cover Wilson had written a dedication to President Kennedy apparently on November 22, 1963. Xerox copies were made of the front and back cover and are furnished Chief and Chicago. SA Shanahan further advised that a local Chicago Judge had committed Wilson to the Cook County Psychopathic Hospital for observation.

DISPOSITION

Case closed this District.

ATTACHMENTS - Chief & Chicago - Xerox copy of front & back cover of Air Training Command "Student Study Guide and Workbook".

DISTRIBUTION	COPIES	REPORT MADE BY	DATE
Chief ✓	Orig. W/Enc.	*Fred H. Backstrom* SPECIAL AGENT in Charge	12-30-63
Chicago	2 cc. W/Enc.	APPROVED	DATE
Springfield	1 cc.	SPECIAL AGENT IN CHARGE	

(CONTINUE ON PLAIN PAPER)

4-page document-Springfield, Illinois Secret Service Special Agent in Charge Fred Backstrom report on Wilson who was deemed "extremely dangerous." Somewhat hard to read, but included in the document is a copy of Wilson's "Ode to Kennedy."

2.

J-CO-2-33775

On 1-3-64, the writer conferred with Assistant U. S. Attorney James B. Sloan who stated that the States Attorney's Office of Illinois had advised him that the subject was examined by a psychiatrist of the Chicago Police Department and that his findings were that the subject was a pure paranoid which he considered an extremely rare occurrence and that it was his opinion that the subject was extremely dangerous.

On 1-9-64, Assistant U. S. Attorney Sloan appeared before Judge Abraham L. Marovitz, Northern District of Illinois, and requested a sanity hearing to determine if the subject was capable of answering the charges which have been placed against him. Judge Marovitz ordered the sanity hearing to be held on January 16, 1964. Judge Marovitz also ordered that the subject be examined by a psychiatrist prior to the sanity hearing on January 16, 1964.

On the same date, the writer conferred with Assistant U. S. Attorney James B. Sloan and it was ascertained that the Commissioner's hearing which was scheduled for January 10, 1964, had been continued at the request of Judge Marovitz pending the outcome of the sanity hearing on January 16, 1964.

(J) CONCLUSION:

This case is pending judicial action.

Three frame photographs of the subject which were taken by the Chicago Police Department are attached to the original of this report.

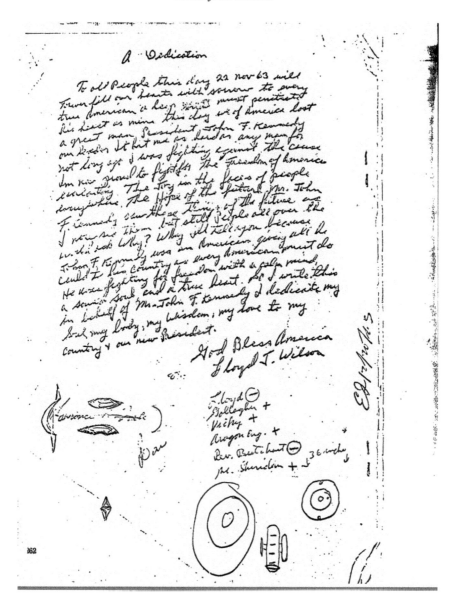

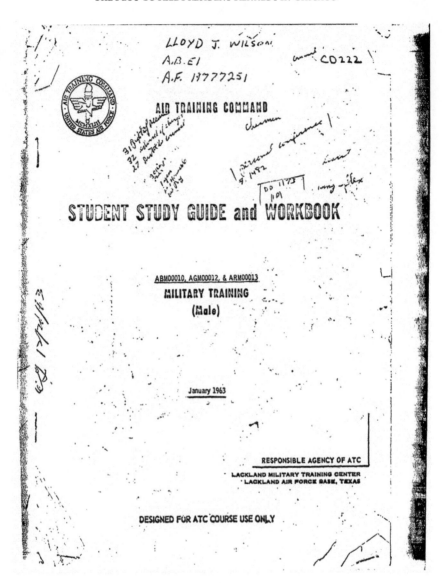

LLOYD J. WILSON
A.B. EI
A.F. 19777251

CO222

AIR TRAINING COMMAND

STUDENT STUDY GUIDE and WORKBOOK

ABM00010, AGM00012, & ARM00013

MILITARY TRAINING
(Male)

January 1963

RESPONSIBLE AGENCY OF ATC

LACKLAND MILITARY TRAINING CENTER
LACKLAND AIR FORCE BASE, TEXAS

DESIGNED FOR ATC COURSE USE ONLY

Form No. *588 (Revised)
MEMORANDUM REPORT
(7-1-53)

'TED STATES SECRET SERVICE
I REASURY DEPARTMENT

ORIGIN Field	OFFICE Chicago, Illinois	FILE NO. J-CO-2-33,775
TYPE OF CASE	**STATUS**	**TITLE OR CAPTION**
Protective Research	Pending	Person Identified:
INVESTIGATION MADE AT	**PERIOD COVERED**	Name : Lloyd John Wilson
Chicago, Illinois	1/30/64	Address: Medical Center for Federal Prisoners Springfield, Missouri
INVESTIGATION MADE BY		
Special Agent Joseph E. Noonan, Jr.		

DETAILS

SYNOPSIS

Lloyd John Wilson was removed to the Medical Center for Federal Prisoners, Springfield, Missouri, on January 24, 1964 for a complete psychiatric evaluation.

This action was at the direction of Federal Judge Abraham Marovitz, Chicago, who issued the order on January 16, 1964.

Assistant U.S. Attorney James B. Sloan, Chicago, has advised that he will endeavor to have Wilson returned to California for treatment in a state hospital.

(A) INTRODUCTION:

Reference is made to the writer's memorandum report dated January 21, 1964.

(I) DISPOSITION:

On January 20, 1964, Acting Special Agent in Charge Maurice G. Martineau, Chicago, received a letter from Mrs. E. Seitsinger, step-mother of Lloyd John Wilson. In this letter, Mrs. Seitsinger advised that if Wilson was convicted in court and if he was sentenced, she would like to put him in a state hospital in California.

On this same date, the subject letter was turned over to Assistant U.S. Attorney James B. Sloan, Chicago, who advised that he would personally write Mrs. Seitsinger and attempt to have Wilson committed to a

DISTRIBUTION	COPIES	REPORT MADE BY	DATE
Chief	Orig.	SPECIAL AGENT Joseph E. Noonan	2/11/64
Chicago	2cc's	**APPROVED**	**DATE**
		Acting SPECIAL AGENT IN CHARGE Maurice G. Martineau	2/11/64
JEN:jmt			

(CONTINUE ON PLAIN PAPER)

2-page document: Chicago Secret Service agent Joseph Noonan, approved by Agent in Charge Maurice Martineau, details Wilson's psychiatric evaluation at the Springfield, Missouri Medical Center for Federal Prisoners, a place where both Abraham Bolden and Richard Case Nagell would sadly end up in.

.2
J-CO-2-33,775

state institution in California. A photograph of Mrs. Seitsinger's
letter is attached to the original of this report for Chief's office.

On January 30, 1964, the writer contacted the U.S. Marshal's office
in Chicago, and was advised that Lloyd John Wilson was removed to the
Medical Center for Federal Prisoners at Springfield, Missouri on
January 24, 1964.

Attached to the original of this report is a Thermo-Fax copy
of the evaluation of Lloyd John Wilson by the Psychiatric Institute
of the Municipal Court of Chicago. This report is dated December 20, 1963.

Form 1609 was sent to the Medical Center for Federal Prisoners
on February 11, 1964.

CO222

UNITED STATES SECRET SERVICE
TREASURY DEPARTMENT

Form No. 1588 (Revised)
MEMORANDUM REPORT
(7-1-60)

ORIGIN Chief's Office	OFFICE San Francisco, California	FILE NO. CO-2-33,775

TYPE OF CASE	STATUS	TITLE OR CAPTION
Protective Research	Continued	Person Identified:

INVESTIGATION MADE AT	PERIOD COVERED	Name : Dwight Allen Wilson
San Francisco and San Jose, California	9/17/63 - 9/20/63	Address : Unknown

INVESTIGATION MADE BY

Special Agent James H. Giovanetti

DETAILS

SYNOPSIS

Information received through the
Federal Bureau of Investigation
regarding alleged threat by a
Dwight Allen Wilson, who has been
identified but has not as yet
been located.

(A) INTRODUCTION:

Reference is made to Office Memorandum of SAIC Hanson dated September
10, 1963, reporting telephone call received at his residence on September 9,
1963, from the Night Supervisor of the Federal Bureau of Investigation, San
Francisco, advising that he had received a call from an anonymous person
stating that Dwight Allen Wilson, an employee of Arrigoni, Rule and Associates,
2363 Prune Ridge, Santa Clara, California, was in the process of organizing
an anti-Negro group of the Nazi type and that he had written a threatening
letter to the President.

Further reference is made to Protective Research Referral Memorandum
dated September 11, 1963, forwarding Office Memorandum dated September 10,
1963, from Special Agent Sherman of the White House Detail, reporting
essentially the same information as received through the Federal Bureau of
Investigation in San Francisco.

(B) GENERAL INQUIRIES:

On September 17, 1963, Mr. David Arrigoni, owner of Arrigoni, Rule and
Associates, 2363 Prune Ridge, Santa Clara, California, was contacted by
telephone and he advised that they had no employee by the name of Dwight
Allen Wilson. Mr. Arrigoni stated that he had been personally interviewed

DISTRIBUTION	COPIES	REPORT MADE BY	DATE
Chief	Orig	SPECIAL AGENT	9/23/63
San Francisco	2 cc	APPROVED SPECIAL AGENT IN CHARGE	9/23/63

(CONTINUE ON PLAIN PAPER)

4-page document and photo: The following is a particularly important document, as it was written before both the assassination and the Chicago plot. Note the agent's name James Giovanetti – he was previously assigned to Hyannis Port in 1962-1963 and guarded JFK (photo per the briefing book for President Kennedy regarding the agents assigned to him courtesy of the JFK Library). Wilson wrote a threatening note for President Kennedy. Also noted is Wilson's interest in Hitler and White Supremacy.

CO-2-33,775
Page 2

by Special Agent Malcolm Sample of the Federal Bureau of Investigation Office, San Jose.

On September 18, 1963, called at the Federal Bureau of Investigation, San Francisco, and interviewed Special Agent John McNamara. A check of their records disclosed two files, one on a Dwight Wilson and another on Dwight Allen Wilson (which contained the referenced correspondence). A report dated September 9, 1963, on Dwight Wilson disclosed that on August 30, 1963, a Mrs. Lynn Hernandez, 1467 Palmwood Drive, San Jose, reported that she had received information through a friend that a Dwight Wilson had indicated a great interest in the Nazi organization and when questioned by his fellow workers at the Aragon Engineering Company, 940 Shulman Street, Santa Clara, California, about registering with the Selective Service System he stated he had refused to do so.

On September 18, 1963, contacted Special Agent Malcolm E. Sample of the San Jose Federal Bureau of Investigation Office. He advised that he had made inquiry of the Retail Credit Bureau in San Jose which disclosed a record on a Dwight A. Wilson, 853 El Camino Real, Santa Clara, California, employed at the Aragon Engineering Company. Special Agent Sample stated that he interviewed Mr. H. C. Bechtle, President of the Aragon Engineering Company. Mr. Bechtle stated that Wilson had been in their employ since the Summer of 1961 as a handyman and delivery man. He stated that the personnel record of the subject was not available as it was in the hands of his accountant at the present time. He further stated that Wilson resided with his stepmother, Mrs. E. Comstock, at 853 El Camino Real, Santa Clara.

Mr. Bechtle stated that during the middle of July 1963 the subject went to Oklahoma City, Oklahoma, and Houston, Texas, with his stepmother. On July 29, 1963, Mr. Bechtle received a long distance telephone call from Mrs. Comstock at Houston stating that Wilson was ill and in need of $100. Mr. Bechtle asked her to have Wilson call him but he failed to do so. Mr. Bechtle learned that Wilson's stepmother had jumped bail on a drunken driving and driving without a license charge. He reported receiving the long distance telephone call to the authorities and Mrs. Comstock was apprehended and is presently confined to the Santa Clara County Jail at San Jose.

Mr. Bechtle stated that Wilson returned to work during the last week of August 1963 and after receiving his pay on Thursday, September 12, 1963, has not returned to work. Mr. Bechtle stated that he considers Wilson a

CO-2-33,775
Page 3

good worker and is well liked by him.

Special Agent Sample learned that Wilson, since his return from Texas, had been living with a co-worker and his wife, John and Joan Chupp, 1792 Eisenhower Drive, Santa Clara, California. Special Agent Sample is of the belief that it was Chupp who made the anonymous telephone call to the Federal Bureau of Investigation.

When interviewed by Special Agent Sample, Chupp stated that Wilson talked about Hitler and white supremacy and that he was starting an organization with the initials DAW. Chupp stated that he had seen a threatening letter, handwritten by Wilson on tablet paper, addressed to the President. Chupp stated that the last time he had seen Wilson was on September 12, 1963, when he had driven him to a hotel in downtown San Jose near the Mercury News, a San Jose newspaper. Special Agent Sample later learned from Mr. Bechtle that the subject had checked into a hotel on September 12, 1963, and had checked out on September 14, 1963.

Special Agent Sample learned that the whereabout of Wilson's father is unknown; that he was adopted; that his stepfather remarried; and that his stepmother is Mrs. Edith Seitsinger, also known as Comstock, Santa Clara Police Department No. 631230, FBI No. 4361875, Social Security No. 555-10-8263.

Special Agent Sample furnished the following description of Wilson:

> White, male, American, approximately 19 years of age, born Santa Cruz, California, 5-4, 160 pounds, light brown hair, crewcut - close cropped and gives the appearance of being bald, blue eyes, light complexion, stocky build, is interested in wrestling.

> Special Agent Sample learned from Mr. Bechtle that Wilson does not own a car but does have a California Driver's license; further, that he does not possess a gun and has no knowledge of firearms.

On September 18, 1963, Mrs. Lynn Hernandez was interviewed at 1467 Palmwood Drive, San Jose. She stated that she became acquainted with Wilson through Mr. and Mrs. John Chupp and has only seen him three times. She

CO-2-33,775
Page 4

stated that Wilson's stepmother had requested psychiatric help for her son through the San Jose Police Department.

Mrs. Hernandes stated that Wilson appeared to be a very unhappy person; that he had expressed great hatred toward minority races, particularly the Negroes. She stated that he was very interested in the Nazi Party organization and is of the belief that this association gives him a sense of importance. Mrs. Hernandez stated that she had learned through Mrs. Chupp that Wilson had written a letter to the President expressing his hatred for minority groups and requesting that he take action. She further stated that Mrs. Chupp, after she had learned of the letter, requested that Wilson leave her home.

UNDEVELOPED LEADS

Efforts are being made to locate and interview Dwight Allen Wilson.

JHG:mv

JIM GIOVANETTI

Secret Service Agent James Giovanetti who guarded President Kennedy in Hyannis Port in 1962-1963.

CO-2-33,445

U.S. Secret Service

CD222

Chief   Attn: PRS   September 10, 1963

SA Sherman - WHD

Information from FBI re. Dwight Allen Wilson
Alleged threat.

At 2:00 P.M., September 10, 1963, Special Agent William A. Asmus,
WFO, Washington, D.C. telephoned this office to relate information
recently received from the San Francisco FBI Office.

On September 9, 1963, the San Francisco FBI office received an anonymous telephone call from a male who discussed certain facts about an
organization he had been asked to join. The caller stated that he had
become acquainted with a person named Dwight Allen Wilson, who is the
leader of an organization called the DRW (Disposition and Rights of
Whites) also TWR (The White Resistance) and who is a great admirer of
the Nazis and Adolph Hitler.

The caller stated that he had read literature of this organization
and a letter supposedly written by Wilson and addressed to the President, a portion of which he quoted;"Someday I'll meet you, you'll
know me well, believe me, if the government hasn't changed by then,
I'll destroy it along with you."

Further conversation with the caller, stated Asmus, revealed that he
and possibly Wilson are employed by the Argonne Rule and Associates
Engineering Company, Santa Clara, California. Further information could
not be obtained as the caller ended the conversation.

Special Agent Asmus stated that SAIC Tom Hanson, San Francisco Field
Office, was advised of the above facts by the FBI on September 9, 1963.

Anthony Sherman Jr.
Special Agent, 1-16

Approved:
Gerald A. Behn
Special Agent In Charge, 1-16

More pre-assassination and pre-Chicago plot reporting, this time from White House Detail agent Tony Sherman with Special Agent in Charge Gerald Behn's approval. Note Wilson's obscene threat to President Kennedy. Sherman and Behn being involved in this matter is definitely an indication of how serious the threat from Wilson is being taken by the FBI and Secret Service, as there are many hundreds if not thousands of threats reported throughout the country that would not necessarily need to be relayed to the White House Detail in Washington, D.C. Interestingly, Sherman would leave the detail days later in October 1963, while Behn would not be a part of the November trips to Chicago on 11/2/63, Florida on 11/18/63 or Texas on 11/21-11/22/63, the last two trips Behn would miss due to his first vacation since being on the Kennedy Detail. I believe there is something to all the agent transfers that occurred in the Summer and Fall of 1963. Agent Tony Sherman went to the Spokane, Washington field office from the White House Detail in October 1963 right after the Wilson threat report reached him and Behn (to work alongside the Secret Service Special Agent in Charge of the Spokane, Washington field office, Norman Sheridan) and ended up in Dallas after the President's death to assist in the assassination investigation. Agent Charlie Kunkel went to the Dallas office from the White House Detail during the Summer of 1963 and also assisted in the assassination investigation. Agent Ed Z. Tucker went to the Chicago office from the White House Detail during the Summer of 1963 (working alongside the Special Agent in Charge of the Chicago Secret Service field office, Maurice Martineau and fellow former White House Detail agents Joseph Noonan and Abraham Bolden) and was later interviewed by the HSCA (as were Martineau, Noonan and Bolden. Recall that the HSCA had fellow Chicago office agent Nemo Ciochina's address). Agent Jim Giovanetti went from the Hyannis port Detail to the San Francisco office (to work alongside the Special Agent in Charge of the San Francisco Secret Service office, Tom Hanson).

TONY SHERMAN

Gerald A. Behn

White House Detail Secret Service Agents Tony Sherman, gone from the detail in October 1963, and SAIC Gerald Behn, absent from the Chicago, Florida and Texas trips and essentially stripped of power when JFK was murdered on 11/22/63 in Dallas.[5]

---

5   During the author's three interviews with SAIC Jerry Behn on 9/27/92, the subject of his unpublished, still-unavailable executive session testimony before the HSCA came up. Behn told the author that he was asked two things. First, the details about the Florida trip of November 18, 1963. Second, why the motorcade route was changed for the Dallas trip! When the author inquired about the second point, since it is another crucial matter of security, Behn responded, "I know it was changed but why – I've forgotten completely – I don't know." (Behn should know: besides being the SAIC, Win Lawson told the HSCA that the selection of the motorcade route involved Behn [11 HSCA 516]). The author asked Behn if Agent Grant could have been involved with the changing of the route in Dallas, to which Behn said, "Grant wouldn't have the authority to change the route."

Form No. 1500 (Revised)
MEMORANDUM REPORT
(7-1-56)

UNITED STATES SECRET SERVICE
TREASURY DEPARTMENT

CD222

ORIGIN Chief's Office   OFFICE San Francisco, California   FILE NO. CO-2-33,875

TYPE OF CASE	STATUS	TITLE OR CAPTION
Protective Research	Continued	Person Identified:

INVESTIGATION MADE AT   PERIOD COVERED   Name : Dwight Allen Wilson
San Francisco, Calif.   10-25-63   Address : Unknown

INVESTIGATION MADE BY
ASAIC Donald C. Stringfield

DETAILS

SYNOPSIS

Partial file forwarded to the
Spokane Office for interview with
Dwight Allen Wilson.

(A) INTRODUCTION:

Reference is made to the Memorandum Report submitted by SA Giovanetti, San Francisco, dated September 23, 1963.

(B) GENERAL INQUIRIES:

At 4:45pm October 25, 1963, a telephone call was received from Special Agent James Bennett, Federal Bureau of Investigation, San Francisco, Calif. SA Bennett stated that he had received information that the above captioned subject was attempting to join the U. S. Air Force on October 25, 1963, at Yakima, Washington. He was using the name of Lloyd John Wilson and was believed to be staying in an unknown hotel in Yakima. SA Bennett advised that Sgt. Jack Cann, who is attached to the USAF Recruiting Office in Yakima, might be able to furnish the subject's present address.

UNDEVELOPED LEADS

Partial file is being forwarded to the Spokane Office for interview with Sgt. Jack Cann at the USAF Recruiting Office, Yakima, Washington, and for interview with the subject.

ATTACHMENTS

Spokane: Copy of referenced M/R
           Copy of O/M of SA Sherman, WHD, dated 9-10-63.

DISTRIBUTION	COPIES	REPORT MADE BY	DATE
Chief	Orig.	*Donald C. Stringfield*	10-28-63
Spokane	2 cc w/att.	Assistant SPECIAL AGENT in Charge	
San Francisco	2 cc	APPROVED	DATE
		[signature] SPECIAL AGENT IN CHARGE	10-28-63

Yet another pre-assassination Secret Service report. The FBI and Secret Service were hot on the trail of Wilson who was attempting to join the U.S. Air Force.

OPTIONAL FORM NO. 10
MAY 1962 EDITION
GSA GEN. REG. NO. 27

1010-108

C0-2-33,775

UNITED STATES GOVERNMENT – U.S. Secret Service   4-8-601.0

Memorandum

TO   :   Chief   – Attention PRS   DATE. Sept. 10, 1963

FROM   :   SAIC Hanson – San Francisco

SUBJECT: Dwight Allen WILSON

The night supervisor of the FBI, San Francisco, telephoned me at my residence yesterday evening and informed that he had received a call from a man who refused to identify himself, who said that Dwight Allen Wilson, an employee of Arrigoni, Rule & Associates, 2363 Prune Ridge, Santa Clara, Cal., was in the process of organizing an anti-negro group of the Nazi type.

During the course of the conversation the man said that Wilson had written a letter to President Kennedy which appeared to contain a threatening statement. The sentence, as the man recalled, was along the following order:

"Someday I'll meet you and if the government hasn't changed by then I'll destroy it along with you."

The FBI Supervisor said that in his conversation with the man it could not be determined whether or not the letter had actually been mailed, as the informant indicated that he had seen a copy.

The Supervisor stated that the FBI would investigate the possibility that Wilson was actually involved in such a venture as organizing an anti-negro group and that this office would be kep informed.

Please advise if further attention should be given to this matter at this time.

Tom H. Hanson
Special Agent in Charge

9/10/63 PRS Secret Service report regarding Wilson and his threat to JFK. The Special Agent in Charge of the San Francisco Secret Service office, Tom Hanson, is the author of the report.

Form No. 1632 (Revised)
MEMORANDUM REPORT
(7-1-50)

UNITED STATES SECRET SERVICE CD122
TREASURY DEPARTMENT

ORIGIN Chief's Office	OFFICE	San Francisco, California	FILE NO. CO-2-33,775
TYPE OF CASE	STATUS	TITLE OR CAPTION	
Protective Research	Continued	Person Identified:	
INVESTIGATION MADE AT	PERIOD COVERED	Name : Dwight Allen Wilson	
San Francisco, California	9/30/63	Address: Unknown	
INVESTIGATION MADE BY			
Special Agent James H. Giovanetti			

DETAILS

SYNOPSIS

Photograph of subject
obtained. Present
whereabouts still un-
known.

(A) INTRODUCTION:

Reference is made to Memorandum Report submitted by this office dated
San Francisco, California, September 23, 1963.

(B) GENERAL INQUIRIES:

On September 30, 1963, Special Agent Bruce Sample of the Federal Bureau
of Investigation, located at San Jose, California, advised that he had obtained a photograph of the subject from a woman photographer taken while the
subject was attending a wrestling match in San Jose. Several copies of the
photograph were furnished this office.

Special Agent Sample stated that he had interviewed the subject's stepmother, Mrs. Edith Seitsinger, also known as Comstock, at the Santa Clara
County Jail, San Jose, who advised that she has no information as to the
subject's whereabouts; further, that when the subject was a child a doctor
had informed her that he had mental problems.

The Federal Bureau of Investigation in San Jose also ascertained that
the subject checked into the Aconda Hotel, 141 Santa Clara Avenue, San Jose,
on September 12, 1963, and that he had checked out on September 14, 1963;
that he had left behind a tablet and a dictionary; that he registered under
his own name. Special Agent Sample stated that he had again contacted Mr.
and Mrs. John Chupp, 1792 Eisenhower Drive, Santa Clara, but they could

DISTRIBUTION	COPIES	REPORT MADE BY	DATE
Chief	Orig w/att	*James H. Giovanetti* SPECIAL AGENT	10/8/63
San Francisco	2 cc	APPROVED *Tom H. Hanson* SPECIAL AGENT IN CHARGE	10/8/63

CONTINUED ON PLAIN PAPER   U. S. GOVERNMENT PRINTING OFFICE   16-61091-1

2-page document from JFK Hyannis Port Secret Service agent James Giovanetti
dated 9/30/63: It is alarmingly noted that Wilson is nowhere to be found – "Present whereabouts still unknown."

CO-2-33,775
Page 2

furnish no information as to subject's whereabouts.

Special Agent Sample states he also had interviewed Mr. H. C. Bechtle, President of the Aragon Engineering Company, 940 Shulman Street, Santa Clara, former employer of the subject, who advised that he is of the belief the subject will contact him as he still has a day's wages due him. He further advised he will immediately notify the Federal Bureau of Investigation Office in San Jose.

UNDEVELOPED LEADS

Investigation continued.

ATTACHMENT

Photograph of Dwight Allen Wilson

JHG:mv

CO22

Form No. 1046 (Revised)
Memorandum Report
(7-1-58)

UNITED STATES SECRET SERVICE
TREASURY DEPARTMENT

San Francisco
ORIGIN Field DCS 10-__-63   OFFICE Spokane, Washington   FILE NO. CO-2-33,775

TYPE OF CASE	STATUS	TITLE OR CAPTION
Protective Research	Closed - Spokane	Person Identified:
INVESTIGATION MADE AT	PERIOD COVERED	Name: Lloyd John Wilson
Spokane, Wash.	10-26/11-6-63	aka Dwight Allen Wilson,
INVESTIGATION MADE BY		John Allen Wilson,
SAIC Norman Sheridan		Lloyd Long

DETAILS

SYNOPSIS

Subject interviewed at Spokane on October 28 & 29;
recruited in the Air Force October 31 and transferred
November 2, 1963 to Lackland Air Force Base, Texas. His
serial number is AF 19777251.

(A) INTRODUCTION:

Case originated October 26 when Thomas Colarelli, FBI Agent, Spokane, informed me by telephone that the suspect was in Spokane and was wanted for questioning by our San Francisco office regarding an alleged threat against the
President; that our San Francisco office had been advised. He also stated A/1C
Lloyd E. Brown, Jr., Air Force Recruiting Office, Bon Marche Building, Spokane,
could furnish additional information regarding the subject.

(B) GENERAL INQUIRIES:

A/1C Lloyd E. Brown, Jr. was interviewed on Saturday, October 26, at his
residence, 1923 West College, Spokane, Washington. He stated the subject had
applied for recruitment in the Air Force and during their verification of his
date and place of birth the subject's stepmother, Edith Seitsinger, was located
in the county jail, San Jose, California. Mrs. Seitsinger had stated the subject was wanted by the FBI for making a threat against the President. A/1C Brown
stated the subject had passed the physical and written tests for the Air Force
and as soon as his birth could be verified the subject would be eligible for recruitment. He said the subject's grade on the written test was slightly above
average. He also stated that as soon as our investigation had been completed,
the subject would be given further consideration for recruitment providing he
was not arrested. He said the Air Force had arranged accommodations for the subject at the Coeur d'Alene Hotel in Spokane and that the subject would return to
his office on Monday morning, October 28.

DISTRIBUTION	COPIES	REPORT MADE BY	DATE
Chief	Orig/A	*Norman Sheridan*	
San Francisco	2 co/A		
Spokane	1 co	Norman Sheridan SPECIAL AGENT in Charge	11-7-63
		APPROVED	DATE
NS:JG			
		SPECIAL AGENT IN CHARGE	

(CONTINUE ON PLAIN PAPER)

4-page document dated 11/7/63: Incredibly, Wilson was recruited into the U.S.
Air Force on 10/31/63 and transferred to Lackland Air Force Base in Texas on
11/2/63, the date of the Chicago plot. Wilson was wanted by both the FBI and
the Secret Service. Wilson is once again deemed to be dangerous.

2.

CO-2-33,775

(C) PERSONAL INTERVIEW

On October 28, 1963 Lloyd John Wilson was located in the Air Force Recruiting Office at Spokane and he accompanied me to our office where he was interviewed. The subject is single and is described as follows: American; male; white; 18 years of age; born August 16, 1945 at Santa Cruz, California; 5 feet 8 inches; 160 pounds; stocky build; blue eyes; light brown hair worn in crew cut; light complexion; red birth mark the size of a dime on right upper arm; fairly neat in appearance, wearing sport coat and slacks.

The subject stated he is an American citizen, that he was an orphan, and that his name by birth was John Allen Wilson and his true parents are unknown to him. The Air Force recruiting office in Spokane subsequently advised me they had verified the subject's date of birth and that his true name is Lloyd John Wilson, and he was recruited under this name in the Air Force. The subject stated his stepfather, Elmer Seitsinger, is deceased and that his stepmother, Edith Seitsinger, is in the county jail, San Jose, California; that he has no brothers or sisters. He said he had been adopted twice and had used the adopted names of Dwight Allen Wilson and Lloyd Long.

The subject acknowledged that during the latter part of August and the first part of September 1963 at San Jose, California he had prepared notes for an organizatization to be known as "T.W.R", representing "The White Resistance" for the suppresion of what he believed to be "an upcoming Negro revolution." He stated that among his notes was a letter he had composed for the President and that he had never mailed this letter. He wrote this letter in longhand from memory and it contains the following exerpt: "One day Mr. President we'll meet face to face and if the government and you haven't changed to my way of thinking then I'll destroy you as well as the government for I have no feelings whatsoever for anyone who doesn't think the same as I do." The subject explained that he meant he would "destroy" the President politically by infiltration in the government with his organization and by "brain washing." He said he left his notes regarding this organization at a hotel, name not recalled, located in Santa Clara, California, when he checked out of this hotel about September 14, 1963.

I telephoned SAIC Hanson, San Francisco, for odditional details and was advised that the subject had a room at the Aconda Hotel, 141 West Santa Clara, San Jose, California; that only a few scribbled notes by the subject of no importance were found in his room. SAIC Hanson stated their file disclosed some persons interviewed had referred to the subject as a "nut" and that the file was being airmailed to Spokane.

The subject was reinterviewed October 29, 1963 in the Spokane office after the San Francisco file was received. A two-page statement was obtained from the subject and the case was discussed in detail with Assistant U. S. Attorney Carroll D. Gray, Spokane. Mr. Grey then questioned the subject in my presence,

3.

CO-2-33,775

and at the conclusion he declined prosecution. During this interview the
subject stated he had completely eliminated any future thought of forming
his proposed Tolk Organization; that he was trying to forget all about it.
He expressed a great desire to be accepted in the Air Force on a four-year
enlistment and to complete his education and make a career in the Air Force.

(D) CURRENT MENTAL CONDITION:

The subject displayed some emotional reaction of aggressiveness. It is
the opinion of Assistant U. S. Attorney Grey and myself that the subject is
in need of psychiatric treatment. The subject stated he had never been hospitalized for any physical or mental reason. The subject also stated he had
never been arrested.

(E) FAMILY BACKGROUND:

Elmer Seitsinger, stepfather, deceased; Edith Seitsinger, stepmother,
853 El Camino, Santa Clara, California. Relatives through stepmother; Mrs.
Gertie Lottz, aunt, Tarewa Avenue, Houston, Texas; David Gallagher, uncle,
1811 Taft Street, Lawton, Oklahoma.

(F) PREVIOUS ACTIVITIES OR HISTORY:

Education: Completed ninth grade at Washington Junior High School,
Salinas, California.

Employment: One week, October 14-22, 1963, Yakima Fruit & Cold Storage
Company, Yakima, Washington, as a laborer. January 1962 to September 13, 1963,
Aragon Engineering Company, 940 Shulman Avenue, Santa Clara, California, as a
machinist helper. 1958 to January 1962, Gill Lemus, Enco Service Station,
Casteroville, California, part-time work as a service station attendant.

Military Record: Enlisted October 31, 1963 at Spokane in the U. S. Air
Force and transferred November 2, 1963 to Lackland Air Force Base, Texas.

The subject expressed no desire to visit the President. The subject
can not use a typewriter and has no machine available.

The subject furnished specimens of his handwriting and handprinting.

(G) PROTECTIVE INFORMATION:

The subject has had very little experience with firearms and he said the
only gun he possessed was a rifle which he sold about three years ago. He said
he had owned this gun about one year and had used it a few times for hunting.
He stated he had no other experience with firearms and no experience with explosives.

46

4.

CO-2-33,775

The subject displayed no animosity toward the President. He said he agrees with some of the things the President has done and disagrees with others; that he "does not have any intention of going against the President."

The subject has shown an interest in the American Nazi Party. However, he stated he had never been a member of this party and had never contacted any of the members, although he had read some of their literature. He stated he is very much against communism.

(H) MEANS OF SOLUTION:

The subject's address in Spokane was obtained from an FBI agent. Assistant U. S. Attorney Carroll Gray, Spokane, declined prosecution and the subject returned to the Air Force recruiting office in Spokane. A/1C Lloyd E. Brown, Jr., Air Force recruiting office, was advised as to the purpose of our interview with the subject and he was permitted to read the subject's statement dated October 29, 1963. A/1C Brown advised me on November 6, 1963 that the subject had been accepted in the Air Force on October 31 and that he had been transferred to Lackland Air Force Base, Texas.

(J) CONCLUSION:

Two polaroid pictures of the subject were taken in the Spokane office. One picture is transmitted with the original of this report and one is attached for San Francisco. Handwriting and handprinting specimens were obtained and they are transmitted with the original of this report. A verifax copy of the subject's unmailed letter written from memory on October 26 in the Spokane office is attached for San Francisco.

Form 1639 has been executed and one copy is transmitted with the original of this report and one copy is enclosed for San Francisco.

The original statement sworn to by the subject October 29, 1963 is enclosed for the Chief and a copy of this statement is attached for San Francisco.

In view of the subject's questionable mental condition, the subject should be considered dangerous.

State of Washington
County of Spokane   SS
City of Spokane

I, JOHN A. WILSON, aka Dwight Allen Wilson, age 18, being first duly sworn under oath, have been advised that I do not have to make any statement, that any statement I make can be used against me, and that I may have an attorney present before making a statement; but in order that the truth may be known, I hereby make the following statement of my own free will and no threats or promises have been made to me.

While in San Jose, California during September 1963, I read a magazine entitled "See." This magazine offered one million dollars to anyone who would assassinate Fidele Castro. There was a cover picture of Castro on the magazine. I read a story in this magazine entitled "The Upcoming Negro Revolution." I was staying with a friend of mine, John Chupp, on Eisenhower Drive, Agnew, California. I asked Mr. Chupp to read this magazine, and after reading it he agreed with my ideas to form an organization of white people against the Negro leaders, such as Malcom X, leader of the Black Moslum Organization.

I bought a notebook the next day and started jotting down my ideas of what I was going to write and how the organization was to be formed. I had an outline of the cards I was going to have printed for the organization which was to be called "DAW", representing my initials. This organisation was also to be called the TWR, representing "The White Resistence." I made notes of several things I was going to have changed in the United States once my organization gained control. The changes included complete control of all publications, no visitors to the United States, close control over imports and exports, and anyone who did not conform to the new government formed by my organization would be deported or assassinated.

I talked to all the employees at the Aragone Engineering Company in Santa Clara, California and tried to get them interested in my organization. Out of the fifteen employees, three or four of the men agreed with me.

I planned to have posters, cards, and literature printed for the organization but I did not have money for this purpose and I discontinued further activity regarding the organisation after about two weeks.

Included in my notes concerning the organization, of which I subsequently lost, was an outline of a letter to the President of the United States. On October 28, 1963, I wrote this letter from memory in the Secret Service office at Spokane, Washington. The letter was intended for President John F. Kennedy, Washington, D. C., and stated in part: "One day, Mr. President, we'll meet face to face, and if the government and you haven't changed to my way of thinking, then I'll destroy you as well as the government for I have no feeling whatsoever for anyone who doesn't think the same as I do." I intended this statement to mean that by the time I was powerful enough to gain control of the United States by infiltration and

2-page document: 10/29/63 statement by Wilson himself to Secret Service agent Norman Sheridan. The assassination of Fidel Castro, White Supremacy, the threat to JFK and other matters are addressed.

Page 2

brainwashing that there would probably be a different president and his ideas
would possibly be the same as mine. If his ideas were not the same as mine,
I would have to depend on the cabinet members in my organization to change his
mind. If the President did not change his mind to agree with our ideas, it
would be necessary for me to have the President of the United States assassinated.

I never know any member of the Nazi Party, but I planned to locate some of them
for financial backing and advice. At the present time I am trying to forget all
about this organization and I do not have any intention to try and form this
organization in the future.

I obtained my ideas for the DAH and TWR Organization from reading Nazi literature.
I am completely against communism. I am completely against any type of violence
and bloodshed; although it is possible that much killing would occur in order for
my organization to obtain power, once I did obtain such power there would be no
future violence and the United States would be a country of peace and happiness.

The above statement has been read by me and I understand it and have been permitted to make corrections.

John A. Wilson

Sworn to before me this
twenty-ninth day of October, 1963.

Special Agent, U.S. Secret Service

WITNESSED:

11/8/63 PRS Secret Service document regarding Wilson, whose present place of domicile was Lackland Air Force Base in Texas.

Item No. 1098 (Revised)
Memorandum Report
(7-1-50)

CO 222

UNITED STATES SECRET SERVICE
TREASURY DEPARTMENT

ORIGIN Chief's Office	OFFICE San Francisco, California	FILE NO. CO-2-33,775

TITLE OF CASE	STATUS	TITLE OR CAPTION
Protective Research	Closed	Person Identified

INVESTIGATION MADE AT	PERIOD COVERED
San Francisco, Calif.	November 13, 1963

INVESTIGATION MADE BY

Special Agent James H. Giovanetti

Name : Lloyd John Wilson
aka Dwight Allen Wilson
John Allen Wilson
Lloyd Long

DETAILS

- SYNOPSIS -

PRS subject interviewed at Spokane,
Washington. U. S. Attorney's Office
at Spokane declined prosecution.
Subject is now in the U. S. Air Force.

(A) INTRODUCTION:

Reference is made to Memorandum Reports submitted by this office dated San Francisco, California, September 23, 1963 and October 8 and 28, 1963. Further reference is made to Memorandum Report submitted by our Spokane office dated November
7, 1963, as to results of interview with subject, Lloyd John Wilson, also known
as Dwight Allen Wilson.

(J) CONCLUSION:

In view of the fact that the subject, Lloyd John Wilson aka Dwight Allen Wilson,
was personally interviewed by our Spokane office on October 28, 1963, and inasmuch as the U. S. Attorney's Office at Spokane, Washington, declined prosecution
of the subject the case is being considered closed in the San Francisco office.
Our Spokane office advised that the subject has been accepted in the U.S. Air
Force, Serial No. AF 19777251, and has been transferred to Lackland Air Force
Base, Texas.

DISTRIBUTION	COPIES	REPORT MADE BY	DATE
Chief	Orig.	*[signature]* SPECIAL AGENT	11-13-63
San Francisco	2 cc's	APPROVED *[signature]* SPECIAL AGENT IN CHARGE	11-13-63

11/13/63 Secret Service document by agent Giovanetti regarding Wilson. Case closed, prosecution declined, and Wilson resumes duty in Texas with the U.S. Air Force. Incredible!

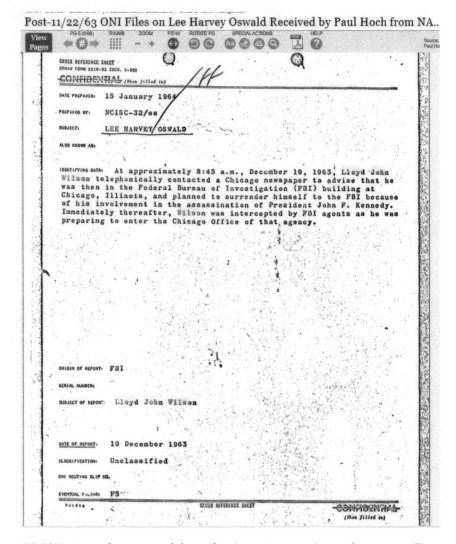

Post-11/22/63 ONI Files on Lee Harvey Oswald Received by Paul Hoch from NA..

12/19/63 report: Over a month later, despite no prosecution and a return to Texas and the Air Force, Wilson surrenders to the FBI in Chicago regarding his involvement in the assassination of JFK. Date report prepared: 1/15/64. Subject: Lee Harvey Oswald.

OFFICE OF THE DIRECTOR

Commission No. *1192*

UNITED STATES DEPARTMENT OF JUSTICE

FEDERAL BUREAU OF INVESTIGATION

WASHINGTON, D.C. 20535

June 29, 1964

BY COURIER SERVICE

Honorable J. Lee Rankin
General Counsel
The President's Commission
200 Maryland Avenue, N. E.
Washington, D. C.

Dear Mr. Rankin:

      Reference is made to our letter dated January 21, 1964, dealing with Lloyd John Wilson. Our letter of reference advised that we were following the disposition of the case involving Wilson in Chicago, and that you would be advised in this regard.

      In this connection there are enclosed two copies each of two reports in the Lloyd John Wilson case dated May 14 and May 20, 1964, at Chicago, Illinois. The enclosed material concludes our investigation of Lloyd John Wilson, and we do not intend to conduct further inquiry concerning his claimed association with Lee Harvey Oswald.

      Sincerely yours,

J. Edgar Hoover

Enclosures (4)

11-page document: 6/29/64 FBI Director J. Edgar Hoover to the Warren Commission's J. Lee Rankin summary of the entire case regarding Wilson. Despite Nemo Ciochina's concern, the case against Wilson was basically dropped and covered up. The government tried to paint Wilson as merely a mental case, albeit one they considered dangerous at one time, yet he was able to pass mental and physical examinations in order to enlist in the U.S. Air Force and come across very much coherent in his statements. Please note the last 4 pages and Wilson's connection to Oswald.

UNITED STATES DEPARTMENT OF JUSTICE
FEDERAL BUREAU OF INVESTIGATION

Commission No. 1192 a

Copy to: 1 - USA, Chicago

Report on: DENNIS W. SHANAHAN   Office: CHICAGO
Date: 5/14/64

Field Office File #: 157-269   Bureau File #: 157-1024

Title: LLOYD JOHN WILSON

Character: RACIAL MATTERS

Synopsis: On 5/1/64, WILSON appeared before USDC Judge ABRAHAM LINCOLN
MAROVITZ, Northern District of Illinois, Chicago, at which
time, based on psychiatric report furnished by Medical
Center for federal persons, Springfield, Missouri. Judge
MAROVITZ ordered that WILSON was competent, at this time,
to understand the nature of the proceedings against him
and to assist his counsel in his defense. On 5/5/64,
WILSON appeared before USC, Chicago, at which time charges
against WILSON were dismissed at government request. WILSON
will return to Venice, California to reside with relatives
and is prepared to undertake psychiatric treatment as out
patient at Agnews State Hospital, San Jose, California.

- P -

Honorable J. Lee Rankin

NOTE CONTINUED:

This has been completely disproven and the Commission so advised by letter of reference. Wilson in Chicago also made verbal threats against President Johnson and Secret Service arrested him. The Federal Court, Chicago, held him for psychiatric examination locally and later ordered him to the Medical Center for Federal Prisoners at Springfield for further study. He was found competent to stand trial; however, the Secret Service charges against him in Chicago were dismissed on May 5, 1964, and he has been paroled to relatives in Venice, California. He is to undertake psychiatric treatment as out patient in San Jose, California. There is no further interest in Wilson from the Oswald aspect.

NOTE FOR CIVIL RIGHTS SECTION:

Wilson has history of mental disturbances and has repeatedly indicated desire to associate himself with George Lincoln Rockwell's American Nazi Party. In view of threats against President Johnson, his claimed association with Oswald and his penchant to sympathize with American Nazi Party, it is suggested Civil Rights Section review the Lloyd John Wilson file (157-1084) to see if further investigation from Racial Matter aspect (American Nazi Party activity) is warranted. Secret Service is aware of developments to date.

- 2 -

Copy to:

Report of: SA W. H. WILLIAMS, II   Office: Seattle, Washington
Date: DEC ... 1963

Field Office File No.: 157-996   Bureau File No.: 157-1024

Title: LLOYD JOHN WILSON

Character: RACIAL MATTERS

Synopsis:

Mr. NORMAN SHERIDAN, Special Agent in Charge, Secret
Service, Spokane, Wash., interviewed WILSON on 10/29/63,
and obtained signed statement in which WILSON outlined
movement to resist marches by Negro groups. WILSON wrote
SHERIDAN on 11/27/63, expressing regret over President
KENNEDY's assassination. WILSON interviewed 10/29/63
regarding possible Selective Service violation.

- RUC -

DETAILS:

AT SPOKANE, WASHINGTON

SE 157-296
JEH:oOa

SA DONALD M. HEAD contacted Mr. NORMAN SHERIDAN, Special
Agent in Charge, Secret Service, 337 Post Office Building, Spokane,
Washington, on December 19, 1963.

According to Mr. SHERIDAN the files of that office reveal
that on September 8, 1963, the San Francisco Office of the FBI received an anonymous call to the effect that WILSON was the leader
of an organization known as "Disposition, Rights and Writes," aka
"White Resistance." The caller advised that he had seen a letter
written by WILSON threatening the President of the United States.
SHERIDAN's file revealed that at that time WILSON was employed by
the Aragon Engineering Company, Santa Clara, California.

His mother, Mrs. EDITH SIXTSINGER, aka COMSTOCK, FBI No.
4361875, had been arrested by the Santa Clara County Sheriff's
Office on a drunk charge. While in custody she had indicated
that she had requested psychiatric help for WILSON.

On October 19, 1963, SHERIDAN revealed he had interviewed WILSON and had taken a signed statement from him, during
which time he admitted writing the letter to the President of
the United States in which he said in substance that he had
established a movement to resist the marches by the Negroes,
and had indicated if anyone stood in their way, they would be
hurt, including the President. WILSON denied ever having been
in a mental hospital or receiving any psychiatric care.

Mr. SHERIDAN indicated that he had discussed this matter
with AUSA CARROLL D. GRAY, Eastern District of Washington, Spokane,
Washington, who declined prosecution in the matter.

SHERIDAN's file revealed that on October 31, 1963,
WILSON entered the U. S. Air Force, after having passed a mental
and physical examination and was sent to the Lackland Air Force
Base for his preliminary training.

On November 27, 1963, SHERIDAN received a letter from
WILSON after the President had been assassinated. His letter was
received from Lackland AFB and in it WILSON had expressed concern
over the President being assassinated and expressed regret over
having written the letter previously referred to. He indicated
he was crying due to this and was quite depressed over it.

SHERIDAN advised that in view of WILSON's alleged
association with LEE HARVEY OSWALD, he thought it most desirable

- 2 -

CO 317 m.

2
SC 157-296
JEN:eon

that his headquarters be contacted in Washington, D.C. to
provide the detailed results of the Secret Service investigation.

The information appears in Secret Service file
CO-2-33775. This file contains the original letters written by
WILSON.

- 3 -

58

Date __November 1, 1953__

JOHN A. WILSON, Room 416, Coeur d'Alene Hotel (temporary address), was interviewed in the office of the Secret Service, Spokane, and after being advised that he did not have to make a statement, that any statements he did make could be used against him in a court of law, and that he had the right to consult an attorney, furnished the following information:

On Thursday, October 24, 1953, he was in Yakima and consulted a Sergeant CASE CASE, an Air Force recruiter, about joining the Air Force. CASE advised him that he must be registered with Selective Service before he could be considered for enlistment. This is the first he knew that he was required to register immediately after attaining his eighteenth birthday. He had no intention of evading the draft. In fact, he had planned on making the military his career and did not realize that he had to register with Selective Service if he intended to enlist anyway. After being so advised by CASE, he went to the Local Board in Yakima and told them he planned to enlist in the Air Force and wanted to register. The Local Board in Yakima gave him some forms to fill out and advised him that these forms would be forwarded to California.

After he had registered, he was sent to Spokane to complete his induction process into the Air Force. He talked with a Sergeant WILLIAMS, an interviewer, with the Air Force Recruiting Office on the 9th floor of the Bon Marche Building upon his arrival in Spokane and this individual can verify his registration with Selective Service in Yakima. He noted that the Air Force is presently awaiting the results of his interview with Secret Service before completing his induction.

He does not know his real parents, but believes their last name was WILSON. He used the name JOHN A. WILSON to enlist as that is the name he has used most, but he has used the names of DWIGHT ALLEN WILSON and DWIGHT ALLEN LONG. His foster mother, EDITH WHITFIELD, presently confined in the San Jose County Jail, San Jose, California, was once married to a man named LONG. He has never used the name LLOYD JOHN WILSON. His last permanent address was 505 El Camino Real, San Jose, California.

The following is a description of the subject obtained through interview and observation:

On _10/28/53_ at _Spokane, Washington_ File # _SS 25-16505_

by _SA IRENE L.____ ____ :nlk_ Date dictated _10/30/53_

2

CG   157-269

During this same period, the latter part of
August, 1963, WILSON wrote a threatening letter to
President JOHN F. KENNEDY but never mailed this letter.

At about this same time, WILSON learned from
two unidentified friends, AJP members, in San Francisco,
California, that a man named OSWALD, first name unknown,
was deeply antagonistic toward President KENNEDY and had
stated intentions of assassinating the President. Those
individuals further advised WILSON that OSWALD was
"communistic" and therefore was not completely sympathetic
to all of the aims of the AJP. WILSON, desirous of making
contact with OSWALD, got in touch with an unidentified friend
living in San Jose, California. This friend, according to
WILSON, was "pro-CASTRO" and possibly had "communist
sympathies". The friend, upon learning of WILSON's desire
to meet OSWALD, put WILSON in touch with a member of the
Communist Party (CP) at San Francisco, California. This
latter individual advised WILSON that he would arrange a
meeting between WILSON and OSWALD and that OSWALD would be
in the San Francisco area in the near future.

During the last week of August, 1963, or possibly
the first day or two in September, 1963, WILSON was advised
by his friend in San Jose, California, that OSWALD was, in
fact, in San Francisco and a meeting could be arranged
during the course of a wrestling match held at the Cow Palace
in San Francisco. WILSON recalled that the headline wrestlers
on this particular wrestling card were: RAY STEVENS, DON DE
NUCCI (phonetic) or CARL GOTCH (phonetic). WILSON stated that
there is only one wrestling match at the Cow Palace in San
Francisco each month.

On the designated date, WILSON, accompanied by his
San Jose friend, went to the Cow Palace, where the friend
pointed out OSWALD at a point near the north gate. WILSON then
introduced himself to OSWALD and complimented him on his
ambition to assassinate President KENNEDY. WILSON and OSWALD

≏⍀⌁⍀9⍀9⎁

3

CG   157-209

went to the second level balcony of the Cow Palace to
continue their discussion. WILSON gave OSWALD an
envelope containing one $1,000 bill, saying "This is a
gift to help you in your mission. Do it in Texas if
possible." He then told OSWALD that the date and manner
of carrying out the assassination was left to OSWALD's
discretion. Immediately thereafter, OSWALD departed and
WILSON states he had had no further contact in any way
with OSWALD since that one meeting.

WILSON indicated he obtained the $1,000 bill
in the following manner: He contributed $250 of his own
money. He secured $350 from his friend in San Jose,
California, and the remaining $400 was given by his two
friends who were members of the ANP at San Francisco.
Because WILSON did not desire to carry a large number of
small denomination bills, he requested and secured from his
ANP friends one $1,000 bill for which he returned the $1,000
in smaller bills.

WILSON continued his employment at the Aragon
Engineering Company, Santa Clara, California, until September
13, 1963. He said that about this time he had decided to
discontinue his efforts in organizing the DAW-White Resistance
Army group since he believed that the formulation of such a
group would inevitably lead to large scale violence which
he indicated he did not desire. WILSON left the San Francisco
area in the middle of September, 1963, and went to Yakima,
Washington. At Spokane, Washington, on October 29, 1963,
WILSON was interviewed by a Mr. SHERIDAN of the Secret Service.
He stated that he furnished Mr. SHERIDAN all of the information
concerning his abortive organization but did not tell Mr.
SHERIDAN anything of his meeting with OSWALD or his contribution
of money toward the furtherance of OSWALD's assassination
plans. On the same date, in the Secret Service office, Spokane,
Washington, WILSON was interviewed by an Agent of the FBI
regarding his Selective Service status. WILSON had not

4

CG   1 5 7 - 2 0 0

registered for the Selective Service since he was
planning to enlist in the Air Force and did not realize
he was required to register. Following this interview,
WILSON did register for Selective Service in Yakima,
Washington, and was sent from there to Spokane, Washington,
to complete his induction into the Air Force. He was
inducted into the Air Force on October 31, 1963, and
immediately went to Lackland Air Force Base, San Antonio,
Texas.

Following the assassination of President KENNEDY,
WILSON requested an interview with his commanding officer,
Major LAWRENCE TATE, 3709 Squadron, Flight 1452. He
requested permission from TATE to attend the funeral of
President KENNEDY and when asked the reason for his request
informed TATE of his prior anti-government feelings and
beliefs, including details concerning the organization
DAW-White Resistance Army. During this interview, WILSON
denied to Major TATE any participation in the assassination
of President KENNEDY.

WILSON advised that he had spoken to the following
Air Force personnel concerning his "troubles in San Francisco"
but had not furnished information concerning his part in the
assassination: P. A. MALLOY, JR., presently attending Air
Police School, Lackland Air Force Base; J. L. HODGE, presently
attending Aircraft Maintenance School, Air Force Base at
Amarillo, Texas; and W. R. MC KAY, whose present whereabouts
are unknown but who was a member of Flight 1453 and a co-trainee
of WILSON.

On December 12, 1963, WILSON, together with several
other men from his detachment, arrived at Chanute Field,
Rantoul, Illinois, for assignment to that base. On
December 13, 1963, WILSON was advised by his commanding
officer at Chanute Field that he was to be sent to the
hospital for certain tests after which he would probably
be given a discharge as a "security risk". WILSON said he

5

OO   157-269

had been admitted to the hospital and examined by several
doctors following which on December 17, 1963, he had been
given an honorable discharge from the United States Air
Force.

WILSON advised that he arrived in Chicago,
Illinois, at approximately 11:00 PM on the night of
December 18, 1963. He said he planned to advise the
FBI office of his contribution to OSWALD on the morning
of December 19, 1963, and because of this decided to have
one last "night on the town."

WILSON advised that on arrival in Chicago he
contacted a cab driver, cab company unknown. This cab driver
directed him to a house in an unidentified part of Chicago
for a charge of $90.00. When WILSON arrived at the house,
driven there by the cab driver, he was directed to a second
floor apartment. In this apartment were two colored
prostitutes and two or more colored men. WILSON spent the
night at this house, paying one of the girls $180.00. On
the following morning, December 19, 1963, he departed from
this house after securing the name of one of the girls as
JEAN and a phone number as VSS-1570. He was told that he could
contact the girls at this house in the future through the
use of this phone number.

During the course of the interview with WILSON,
he indicated that his reason for furnishing the information
to the FBI was to "protect him in the future" if President
JOHNSON were to be assassinated. He said he felt that he
would be released after furnishing the information set forth
above and that should President JOHNSON be assassinated in the
future, the fact that he had voluntarily furnished information
concerning his contribution to OSWALD would tend to preclude
any arrest and/or conviction of him for the assassination
of President JOHNSON.

Needless to say, Nemo Ciochina's concern about Lloyd John Wilson was well founded. It is a damn shame that the case against Wilson and his possible connection to Oswald and the assassination was dropped and covered up. If not for Nemo's and "Jeff's" call in 2023, I wouldn't have known of Wilson and there would be no book. Ciochina would have taken his beliefs to his grave and that would have forever been the end of it. Like Abraham Bolden, I consider Nemo Ciochina to be a true American hero. God Bless his memory.

FBI

Date: 3/25/68

Transmit the following in _____
(Type in plaintext or code)

Via _____ AIRTEL _____
(Priority)

TO: DIRECTOR, FBI

FROM: SAC, CHICAGO (62-6324) (C)

SUBJECT: UNKNOWN SUBJECT: THREAT AGAINST
        SENATOR EUGENE MC CARTHY
        PROTECTION OF THE PRESIDENT

Re Chicago teletype to Bureau and Milwaukee,
3/22/68.

        Enclosed for the Bureau are five copies of a
Letterhead Memorandum (LHM) in captioned matter, and two
copies of FD-376.

        No dissemination is being made locally to
Secret Service as the information was furnished to the
Chicago FBI at 3:51 p.m., on 3/27/68, by Agent NEMO
CIOCHINA, Secret Service.

        One copy of the LHM is designated to the Office
of Deputy Superintendent, Bureau of Field Services,
Chicago Police Department. The information was orally
disseminated to Officer ROBERT MC MAHON, Star Number 4800,
at 4:09 p.m. on 3/22/68.

        One copy of the LHM is designated to Minneapolis
for information as EUGENE MC CARTHY is a U. S. Senator
from Minnesota. A copy is also designated to Milwaukee
as Senator MC CARTHY is currently actively campaigning in
that State.

3 - Bureau (Enc. 7) (RM)
1 - Milwaukee (Info) (Enc.   (RM)
1 - Minneapolis (Info) (Enc. 1) (RM)
1 - Chicago
NHP:mar
(6)

Approved: _____ Sent _____ M Per _____
        Special Agent in Charge

As it turns out, thanks to more newly-discovered documents, Nemo Ciochina was involved in yet another investigation of a threat to kill an official, Presidential Candidate Eugene McCarthy, not long before the assassinations of both MLK and RFK.

```
"BI      DC          ●  (○) FEDERAL BUREAU OF INVESTIGATION     ●  (○)     Mr. Tolson
                            U.S. DEPARTMENT OF JUSTICE                      Mr. DeLoach
                            COMMUNICATIONS SECTION                          Mr. Mohr
                                                                           Mr. Bishop
                                MAR 22 1968                                 Mr. Casper
FBI CHICAGO                     TELETYPE                                    Mr. Callahan
                                                                           Mr. Conrad
62BPM 3-22-68 DEFERRED TAB                                                 Mr. Felt
                                                                           Mr. Gale
TO: DIRECTOR MILWAUKEE                                                      Mr. Rosen
                                                                           Mr. Sullivan
FROM: CHICAGO (62-6324)                                                     Mr. Tavel
                                                                           Mr. Trotter
                                                                           Tele. Room
UNSUB: THREAT AGAINST SENATOR EUGENE MC CARTHY.                             Mrs. Holmes
                                                                           Miss Gandy
PROTECTION OF THE PRESIDENT.

    AGENT NEMO CIOCHINA, U.S. SECRET SERVICE, CHICAGO,

RELAYED FOLLOWING INFORMATION FROM ████████████████

████████████████████████████████

    AT APPROXIMATELY TWO FORTY P.M. TODAY ████████

RECEIVED TELEPHONE CALL AND FEMALE VOICE ASKED IF EUGENE

MC CARHTY WAS THERE. SHE STARTED TO EXPLAIN THAT CALLER HAD

WRONG NUMBER. CALLER SAID TO TELL EUGENE MC CARTHY HE HAD

BETTER NOT ACCEPT NOMINATION OR WE'RE GOING TO KILL HIM AND

HUNG UP.

    CHICAGO PD ADVISED. NO ACTION BEING TAKEN BY SECRET

SERVICE AS ANONYMOUS CALL AND NO APPARENT OVERT ACT. NO

FURTHER ACTION BEING TAKEN BY CHICAGO. LHM FOLLOWS.

BUREAU REQUESTED TO ADVISE SENATOR MC CATHY OFFICE

WASHINGTON DC.

CORR    MC-CARTHY        REC-38  94-40575 8

END                     EX-100      MAR 27 1968

BAP

FBI WASH DC         XEROX
              MAR 28 1968
CC- MR SULLIVAN 1968
```

Chapter Three

Not A Random Act of Fate – Prior Precedent

JFK said to Dave Powers, upon his return from the Florida trip, "Thank God nobody wanted to kill me today!"[6]

"Secret Service Sure All Secure."[7]

"There were many warnings of danger and an antagonistic attitude to be expected in Texas."[8]

Many people understandably tend to view the Kennedy assassination in a vacuum: it was either the act of a lone nut assassin (allegedly Lee Harvey Oswald) or it was a conspiracy. If it was Oswald alone, then it was a freak event. If it was a conspiracy, that too is often viewed as an isolated matter. However, when perusing the many archives of long out of print newspapers from 1961-1963, I was astounded to come across several articles detailing heretofore unknown or long forgotten threats, both singular and plural, to President Kennedy's life. Like the Wilson information, the vast majority of this information has never seen the light of day to the public and the research community since those long-gone days. In a time before the internet and before the assassination, is it any wonder that much of this information would be buried?[9]

---

6   *A Hero For Our Time* by Ralph Martin (New York: Fawcett Crest, 1988), page 503.

7   *Dallas Times Herald* 11/22/63 by Jim Lehrer.

8   Former agent and Chief of the White House Signal Corps Col. George J. McNally wrote on page 216 of his book *A Million Miles of Presidents*.

9   See also chapter 6 from *The JFK Assassination Chokeholds* (2023) by Jim DiEugenio, Paul Bleau, Matt Crumpton, Andrew Iler, and Mark Adamczyk, pages 197-237.

Left: The *Lawrence* (Kansas) *Journal World* 10/12/62 (shortly before the Cuban Missile Crisis) – "The President will be blasted." **Right:** The *Sunday Sun* (Vancouver, B.C.) 4/3/61-JFK's Secret Service guard is doubled due to threats.

Left: *The Lewiston (Idaho) Morning Tribune* 10/11/62-threat to JFK. **Right:** *The Evening Independent (St. Petersburg, Florida), 3/22/62*-a mortal threat to Kennedy.

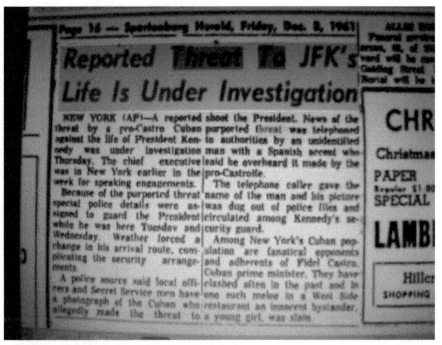

The *Spartanburg* (South Carolina) *Herald* 12/8/61- a pro-Castro Cuban makes a threat.

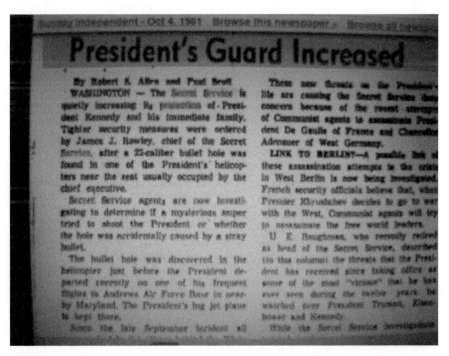

The *Sunday Independent* (South Africa) 10/4/61- a bullet hole in JFK's helicopter.

METROPOLITAN DADE COUNTY · FLORIDA

OFFICE OF METROPOLITAN SHERIFF
1600 N.W. 107TH STREET
MIAMI 38, FLORIDA

FR 7-1911

PUBLIC SAFETY DEPARTMENT

November 19, 1963

LABORATORY REPORT
Case 71498F

Lt. L. J. VanBuskirk
Criminal Intelligence Section
Public Safety Department

On November 18, 1963 Det. Ciacco of our Criminal Intelligence
Section submitted to this office an anonymous typewritten
card addressed to "The Chief of Police, Miami, Fla." This
card was submitted for document examination and study.

Studies of the typewriting on the card reveal that the typewriting was executed on a Royal Typewriter, pica type, with
serial numbers near the 4,000,000 series.

The date of manufacture of such a machine would be before
1952.

Respectfully submitted,

VINCENT E. SEVERS, Criminalist
Crime Laboratory Bureau

VES/ss

2 documents-Death threat made to JFK 11/16/63.[10]

Sat. Nov.16th

The Cuban Commandoes have the BOMBS
ready for killindg JFK and Mayor KING
HIGH either at the AIRPORT at the
Convention Hall.
        A Catholic PADRE is going to givee
instructions at the Cuban WomenS Broadcast
at 8:45 tonight by "RELOJ RADIO" and then
all are invited to Dance at Bayfront Park
Auditorium and take along a BOTTLE of wine,
Wiskey,Etc.,to decide who will throw the
bombs. At King High because he did sign the
Ord.about taxix druivers being only American
Citizens and sending refugees away,Etc. Mary

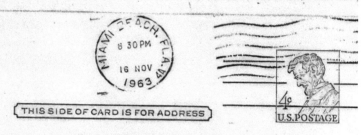

THIS SIDE OF CARD IS FOR ADDRESS

4¢
U.S.POSTAGE

        The Chief of Police
        Miami, Florida.

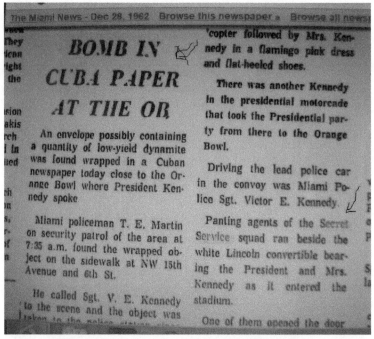

Miami (Florida) *News* 12/28/62-a corroborated threat to Kennedy.

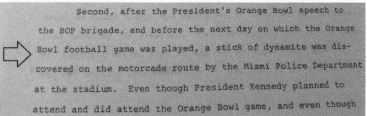

Incredibly, the above dynamite threat was corroborated by Secret Service agent John Marshall, the former Special Agent in Charge of the Miami field office, during his 1978 HSCA interview.

Joseph Noonan, a Chicago office Secret Service agent, told the HSCA that he "participated directly in surveillance involving Tom Mosely and Homer Echevarria ... he and [the] other agents were uneasy that the Cubans might have some ties to the CIA ... a little later they received a call from Headquarters [home of Deputy Chief Paul Paterni, formerly of OSS[11]] to drop everything on Mosely and Echevarria and send all memos, files, and their notebooks to Washington and not to discuss the case with anyone."[12]

11   Julius Mader, *Who's Who in the CIA* (Berlin: Julius Mader, 1968); *Cloak and Gown*, p. 363; Burton Hersh, *The Old Boys: The American Elite and the Origins of the CIA* (New York: Scribner's, 1992), p. 182.

12   4/13/78 HSCA interview with Noonan; RIF#'s: 180-10104-10331; 180-10087-10191; 180- 10099-10491; 180-10078-10493; 180-10082-10453; 1541-0001-10174: Se-

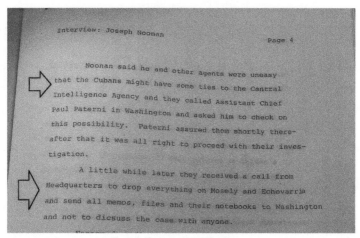

Interview: Joseph Noonan
                                                        Page 4

        Noonan said he and other agents were uneasy
that the Cubans might have some ties to the Central
Intelligence Agency and they called Assistant Chief
Paul Paterni in Washington and asked him to check on
this possibility. Paterni assured them shortly thereafter that it was all right to proceed with their investigation.

        A little while later they received a call from
Headquarters to drop everything on Mosely and Echevarria
and send all memos, files and their notebooks to Washington
and not to discuss the case with anyone.

In Miami, Florida, FBI informant Willie Somersett tapes his conversation with Joseph Milteer on November 9 about plans to kill JFK during a visit to Miami on 11/18/63. This is known by the Secret Service before Dallas, as Special Agent in Charge of the Protective Research Section (PRS) Robert Bouck told the author on 9/27/92 and as Secret Service records reveal.[13]

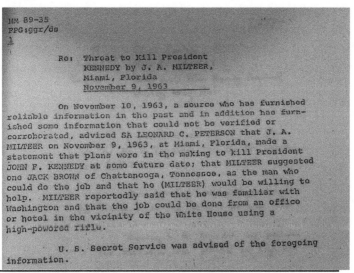

MM 89-35
PPG:ggr/ds
1

            Re: Threat to Kill President
                KENNEDY by J. A. MILTEER,
                Miami, Florida
                November 9, 1963

        On November 10, 1963, a source who has furnished
reliable information in the past and in addition has furnished some information that could not be verified or
corroborated, advised SA LEONARD C. PETERSON that J. A.
MILTEER on November 9, 1963, at Miami, Florida, made a
statement that plans were in the making to kill President
JOHN F. KENNEDY at some future date; that MILTEER suggested
one JACK BROWN of Chattanooga, Tennessee, as the man who
could do the job and that he (MILTEER) would be willing to
help. MILTEER reportedly said that he was familiar with
Washington and that the job could be done from an office
or hotel in the vicinity of the White House using a
high-powered rifle.

        U. S. Secret Service was advised of the foregoing
information.

cret Service shift report.
13   CD 1347, p. 119. See also HSCA Report, page 232-233, as well as 3 HSCA 363-365 (referencing JFK Exhibit F-420: 11/12/63 Secret Service report, Miami SA Robert J. Jamison to Miami SAIC John A. Marshall re: Milteer. The report also states: "This matter has been classified as "Confidential" by SAIC Bouck."). 3 HSCA 447-450: JFK Exhibit F-450 (transcript of conversation between Willie Somersett and Joseph Milteer). See also RIF# 180-10093-10320: 5/31/77 Memorandum from HSCA's Belford Lawson to fellow HSCA members' Gary Cornwell & Ken Klein (revised 8/15/77) & RIF# 180-10074-10393: 2/2/78 HSCA interview with Miami SAIC John Marshall – Marshall and fellow Miami office agent Robert Jamison knew about the Joseph Milteer threat information before Dallas. See

Then something very interesting happens the next day, November 10, 1963, involving the Secret Service (more on this in detail in the next chapter).

The *Nashville Banner* from 1/23/92 carried a report that a threat to President Kennedy's life was hushed up by the Secret Service when JFK visited Nashville, TN, on 5/18/63.[14] The information came from Rep. Bob Clement, the son of former Governor Frank Clement, JFK's host during his 1963 visit to the state (both Clements met JFK on this trip, including a photo from the trip depicting both the elder Clement and his son. At Overton High School, a man approached the president with a gun underneath a sack – he was grabbed by the Secret Service and the incident itself was kept quiet to keep from encouraging similar scares. Bob Clement said, "Back in those days, privacy was easier to accomplish." The paper interviewed the widow of Paul Doster, the former SAIC of the Nashville office – although Paul did not mention the incident to her, she said, "But, you've got to remember, he was pretty secretive, even to me."

Death threats preceded JFK's 1963 Ireland visit: "Police, newspaper received warnings months before president's killing. "The documents indicated that 6,404 police officers were on duty throughout Ireland the night Kennedy arrived, of whom 2,690 lined the U.S. president's route from Dublin airport to the Phoenix Park mansion of Irish President Eamon de Valera. "Costigan wrote that, although the death threats were considered likely to be hoaxes, his officers would use binoculars to monitor rooftops along the route of the presidential motorcade. He said some police would carry firearms, an exceptional measure in a country with a largely unarmed police force, to engage any would-be sniper. "A rifle as well as Thompson guns and revolvers were carried for use against a possible sniper," Daniel Costigan wrote in a post-Kennedy visit memorandum released Friday.[15]

Police were on rooftops in Billings, MT–September 1963: This was confirmed by researcher Deb Galentine's assistant police chief father who worked on the security for this trip, as conveyed to the author on 2/17/14. Deb further wrote: "Weeks before JFK's arrival, my father, who would be in charge of the local police protection, met with Billings' leaders and some of President Kennedy's advance people. JFK's planners wanted the fastest,

also *The JFK Assassination Chokeholds* (2023) by Jim DiEugenio, Paul Bleau, Matt Crumpton, Andrew Iler, and Mark Adamczyk, pages 226-227. See also *From An Office Building With A High-Powered Rifle* (2012) by former FBI agent Don Adams, pages 159, 215-219.
14   See also *The JFK Assassination Chokeholds* (2023) by Jim DiEugenio, Paul Bleau, Matt Crumpton, Andrew Iler, and Mark Adamczyk, pages 199-200.
15   http://www.nbcnews.com/id/16390691/

safest routes possible. They desired routes with no tall buildings and hoped to avoid Billings' Rimrocks as well. The Rimrocks, a natural sandstone formation riddled with caves, paths, and ledges and dotted with pine trees and shrubs, unevenly jut about 500 feet above the city of Billings. Avoiding them would be impossible since Billings' airport lies perched atop them. Three separate routes were available from the airport to the President's venue, and the planners decided to use the one that provided the safest and fastest passage away from the Rimrocks."

6/5/63 El Paso, Texas: the unofficial start of JFK's upcoming Dallas trip in the Fall. LBJ and John Connally were there, as well[16].

U.S. Secret Service
Protective Research Section

CO-2-33,470

EL PASO OFFICE

DATE OF ORIGIN: June 5, 1963

    ORIGIN: Information received telephonically from FBI Headquarters, Washington, D.C.

    DETAILS: An anonymous telephone call was received by the owner of a restaurant in El Paso, Texas. This restaurant is located on the route to be used by the President from the airport on June 5, 1963. The caller stated, "A bomb will go off in your restaurant at 6:30 p.m.," and hung up. The call is one of many referred to the El Paso Police Department which remains unsolved, and no bombs have ever been discovered.

    ACTION: A search was made of the restaurant by local police officers, and they remained in the establishment until the President departed. Nothing was found.

SUBSEQUENT
    ACTIVITY: None

STATUS ON
    11/22/63: The case was closed on June 17, 1963, since no leads were developed.

COMMISSION EXHIBIT 762—Continued

JFK's trip to Duluth, MN 9/24/63: The following appeared on p. 6 in the October 31, 1963 issue of *The Wanderer*, which catered predominantly to right-wingers. Taylor Caldwell that wrote the following letter is the well-known author and John Bircher. Caldwell is replying to Sheldon Emry's letter dated Oct. 17 commenting on the extensive protection that JFK had around him on his trip to Duluth in early October 1963. "President Kennedy in Danger?" By Taylor Caldwell: "I was deeply interested in Sheldon

16   17 H 574.

Emrey's [sic] account [*Wanderer* Forum, October 17th] of Air Force men, soldiers with rifles at the ready, Highway Patrol officers, helicopters, guards, etc., being out in full force day and night when President Kennedy visited Duluth. This account is most extraordinary – but even more alarming, and not for the reasons Mr. Emery [sic] gives: "Mr. Kennedy is now showing a visible power in the soldiers that he had not openly displayed before" … It is possible that Mr. Kennedy is in personal jeopardy from them, a matter which is not being mentioned in the newspapers. Indeed, it is very probable. Presidents have been murdered before in our history, and in less dreadful times.… The very fact that Mr. Kennedy is apparently now being so closely guarded should alarm all of us very deeply, whether or not we agree with the President on political matters. The mere thought of Mr. Kennedy being assassinated should make all of us shudder for the repercussions in America would be most terrible and disorder would result at the very least [emphasis added]." The bubbletop was used on this trip, as well. Researcher Chad Carlson wrote to me regarding this very same trip: "I am friends with a man here who was in charge of JFK's trip to Duluth, MN here in September of 1963. I ask him a lot about JFK. He got to talk one on-one with the President for 30 minutes before he made his rounds and speeches. His name is Larry Yetka, former Minnesota Supreme Court justice. Larry said that he wondered what [Mafia boss] Sam Giancana of Chicago was up to on 11-22-63. I told him that I had been watching the motorcade in Dallas on 11-22-63 and told him it looked very "lax." He said, "Yes it was." So I asked him how was security in Duluth in Sept.1963? He said, "Tight as hell-men were on the rooftops even." So that's the answers I got out of him on that. Vince, that Larry Yetka guy is quite the man. He had met Presidents Truman, Kennedy, and LBJ. He was close friends with former Vice-President Hubert Humphrey of Minnesota. He also met former Vice-President Walter Mondale of Minnesota. Larry went to the 1956 and 1964 Democratic National Conventions … at one of them he exchanged unpleasant words with Texas Gov. John Connally. I'd have to ask him again what happened with that. He was invited to the White House rose garden ceremony under LBJ. The man was a lawyer, and a Minnesota Supreme Court Justice. I think he's around 86 so the time to ask questions is now."

Richard Case Nagell was one of the most important witnesses there was in the JFK case. The following is merely a detailed summary from Dick Russell's book *The Man Who Knew Too Much*:[17] On 9/20/63, Nagell first

---

17   Thanks also to renowned author James DiEugenio for his insights on the newer (2003) edition of this important book.

went to a nearby post office before entering State National Bank in El Paso, Texas. He mailed five hundred-dollar bills to an address in Mexico. He then mailed two letters to the CIA. From the post office, Nagell walked over to the bank. There was a young police officer in plain sight. Nagell walked over to a teller and asked for a hundred dollars in American Express traveler's checks. But before Nagell could retrieve the checks, he turned and fired two shots into a wall right under the ceiling. He calmly returned the revolver to his belt and walked out the front door into the street. He stepped into his car and waited. When no one came out, he pulled his car halfway into the street. He saw the policeman from inside and stopped his car. When the policeman came over to his car with his gun pulled, Nagell put his hands up and surrendered.

The arresting officer was Jim Bundren. When Bundren searched Nagell one of the odd things he found on him was a mimeographed newsletter from the Fair Play for Cuba Committee. When Bundren searched the trunk of Nagell's car, there was a suitcase, two briefcases filled with documents, a 45-rpm record box, two tourist cards for entry into Mexico (one in the name of Aleksei Hidel, amazingly similar to Oswald's alias of Alex Hidell), a tiny Minolta camera, and a miniature film development lab. The personal effects Nagell had bore an uncanny resemblance to Oswald's. A most compelling piece of evidence that Nagell had at the time of his arrest in September of 1963 was this near duplicate of Oswald's Uniformed Services Identification and Privileges Card. In the card seized by the Dallas Police, there is an overstamp that appears which says "October 1963." In the version that Nagell had, the imprint does not appear. Why?

Because Nagell was in jail after September 20, 1963. Also, the photo of Oswald in the Nagell version is different. That photo is from a different ID card. And on that card, Oswald used his Alex J. Hidell alias. As Russell notes, this second card is believed to have been fabricated by Oswald himself, including the added picture. In other words, Nagell had to have been very close to Oswald prior to his September 1963 arrest. For he actually had access to Oswald's identification cards. Some versed in espionage would say that this indicates Nagell might have been either a "control agent" or a "surveillance operative" for Oswald. (The cards are pictured in the photo section of his book.) Nagell had other things in his possession similar to what Oswald had in November: names in their notebooks, Cuba-related leaflets, and miniature spy cameras. After his arrest, on the way to the El Paso Federal Building, Nagell issued a statement to the FBI: "I would rather be arrested than commit murder and treason." At a preliminary hearing for Nagell, the defendant related to the officer the obvious: that he wanted to be caught. To which Bundren replied that he knew Nagell was not out to rob the bank. The following exchange then occurred: Nagell: Well, I'm glad you caught me. I really don't want to be in Dallas. Bundren: What do you mean by that? Nagell: You'll see soon enough. After the assassination and the murder of Oswald by Jack Ruby, Officer Bundren was hit with the ramifications of Nagell's prediction. Bundren stated: "How the hell would he have previous knowledge of it? How would he know what was coming down in Dallas? Nagell knew a lot more about the assassination than he let on, or that the government let on. It's bothered me ever since."

Eugene Dinkin[18] was an Army Cryptographer (an NSA codebreaker) stationed in France who intercepted two secret military codes (one in mid-October 1963 and the other on 11/2/63) about a specific plot to kill Kennedy which was to occur on 11/28/63 and was to be blamed on a Communist or a Negro who would be designated as the assassin. Based on this alarming information, Dinkin wrote a letter to RFK before the assassination but heard nothing back in response. Alarmingly, a declassified CIA document places intelligence operative/assassin Jean Souetre "in Fort Worth on the morning of November 22 and in Dallas in the afternoon," exactly where JFK was at those times. This mortal threat to French President Charles DeGaulle was "expelled from the U. S. at Fort Worth or Dallas eighteen hours after the assassination," according to this document.[19]

Air Force Sergeant David Frederick Christensen,[20] like Dinkin, also intercepted cable traffic of an impending assassination. This information only became public in 2017 thanks to the file releases.[21] Christensen claimed that in the run up to Kennedy's death, he had intercepted an encrypted communication between certain individuals in the Cuban Government and an individual well known in the organized crime world, plotting the assassination. His attempts to get the intercept to NSA were thwarted, causing him (he claimed) to have a mental breakdown, a divorce, etc.

11/17/63: FBI night clerk William S. Walter in the New Orleans Office received a memo via telex warning of a plot to kill JFK: "...a militant revolutionary group may attempt to assassinate President Kennedy on his pro-

18   *They Killed Our President: 63 Reasons to Believe There Was A Conspiracy to Assassinate JFK* by Jesse Ventura (2013), pages 297-300; *Bloody Treason* by Noel Twyman (1997), pages 522-531.

19   See   also: https://www.archives.gov/files/research/jfk/releases/2018/104-10185-10009.pdf.

20   David Frederick Christensen (1942-2008) - Find a Grave Memorial

21   https://wikispooks.com/wiki/David_Christensen.

posed trip to Dallas Texas November twenty two dash twenty three nineteen sixty three."[22] Some have tried to discredit the authenticity of this telex, but a document ignored by the Warren Commission, and since discovered by the author, appears to corroborate it. Originating from the San Antonio, Texas field office and dated 11/15/63, here is the pertinent part of the text: "…a militant group of the National States Rights Party plans to assassinate the President and other high-level officials."[23]

JFK's trip to Miami 11/18/63: Bob Hoelscher worked for the Miami-Dade Police Department for 50 years and was a counter-sniper and observer on the terrace deck of the airport hotel on November 18, 1963, the day Kennedy arrived in Miami. He guarded almost every VIP that came through Dade County from Kennedy to Clinton and started the tactical

U.S. Secret Service
Protective Research Section

CO-2-33,998

SAN ANTONIO OFFICE

DATE OF ORIGIN: November 15, 1963

    ORIGIN: Information received telephonically from FBI Headquarters Washington, D.C.

    DETAILS: Subject interviewed by FBI on November 14, 1963, and stated that he is a member of the Ku Klux Klan; that during his travels throughout the country, his sources have told him that a militant group of the National States Rights Party plans to assassinate the President and other high-level officials. He stated that he does not believe this is planned for the near future, but he does believe the attempt will be made.

BACKGROUND OF
    SUBJECT: Subject was arrested on September 30, 1963, in Piedras Negras, Mexico, with two other men for stealing three automobiles. Information developed by the FBI indicates that the subject was attempting to make some sort of deal with them for his benefit in the criminal case now pending against him. There was no information developed that would indicate any danger to the President in the near future or during his trip to Texas. As of January 27, 1964, subject was still incarcerated pending Federal court action.

EVALUATION OF
DEGREE OF
    DANGER: In view of subject's incarceration, he was considered to be of no danger at this time.

    ACTION: No further action taken.

22   *Encyclopedia of the JFK Assassination* by Michael Benson (New York: Checkmark Books, 2002), pages 276-277, as well as *JFK: The Book of the Film* by Oliver Stone & Zachary Sklar (New York: Applause Books, 1992), page 133.

23   17 H 566. See also *From An Office Building With A High-Powered Rifle* (2012) by former FBI agent Don Adams, page 173, and *Burying the Lead: The Media and the JFK Assassination* by Mel Hyman (2019), pages 136-137.

special weapons team, later known as SWAT, in 1970. Documents reveal a bomb threat against JFK in Miami just days before his death. Hoelscher told CBSMiami.com that he knew of potential threats to the president ahead of his November visit. "I was told that information had been developed that the Cubans might start a protest at an unknown location and they might make an attempt on the life of the President if there was sufficient distraction," Hoelscher said. "I was told to keep this information to myself, watch the periphery and look for anything unusual." While Hoelscher and some others in the police department knew, it was strictly on a "need to know" basis. "The information about the death threat was not shared with the rank and file out of fear that the media would find out," Hoelscher said.

Rose Cherami,[24] real name Melba Christine Marcades, was hospitalized on 11/20/63, two days before the assassination, at Moosa Memorial Hospital in Eunice, Louisiana. Cherami had been en route from Florida to Dallas with two men who looked either Italian or Cuban. All three were part of a drug-smuggling ring but the two men told her that they were going to assassinate the president in Dallas in just a few days. Cherami had been thrown out of the car and, soon after, was hit by another car while hitchhiking. The driver took her to the hospital. After the assassination, Cherami told Dr. Victor Weiss that she knew both Jack Ruby and Oswald and had seen them sitting together on several occasions at Ruby's club. She also said she was acting as a drug courier for Ruby (she was a stripper for Ruby, as well) and that Ruby was involved in the assassination plot.

Tampa (Florida) *Tribune*, November 23, 1963: "Threats on Kennedy Made Here": "Tampa police and Secret Service agents scanned crowds for a man who had vowed to assassinate the President here last Monday, Chief of Police J. P. Mullins said yesterday. In issuing notice to all participating security police prior to the President's motorcade tour in Tampa, Mullins had said: 'I would like to advise all officers that threats against the President have been made from this area in the last few days.' A memo from the White House Secret Service dated Nov. 8 reported: 'Subject made statement of a plan to assassinate the President in October 1963: Subject stated he will use a gun, and if he couldn't get closer, he would find another way. Subject is described as: White, male, 20, slender in build, etc.' Mullins said the Secret Service had been advised of three persons in the area who reportedly

---

24   *Rose Cherami-Gathering Fallen Pedals* by Michael Marcades (2016/2020); *A Rose By Many Other Names: Rose Cherami and the JFK Assassination* by Todd C. Elliott (2013); the JFK movie (1991); *The Assassinations: Probe Magazine on JFK, MLK, RFK and Malcolm X* by James DiEugenio and Lisa Pease, Editors (2003), pages 225-237; from the new file releases: https://www.archives.gov/files/ research/jfk/releases/2018/docid-32261445.pdf.

had made threats on the President's life. One of the three was – and still is – in jail here under heavy bond. Mullins said he did not know if the other two men have followed the Presidential caravan to Dallas. Sarasota County Sheriff Ross E. Boyer also said yesterday that officers who protected Kennedy in Tampa Monday were warned about 'a young man' who had threatened to kill the President during that trip."

White House Detail advance Secret Service agent Lubert "Bert" DeFreese admitted to the HSCA that "a threat did surface in connection with the Miami trip … there was an active threat against the President which the Secret Service was aware in November 1963 in the period immediately prior to JFK's trip to Miami made by a group of people."[25]

In addition to this threat information, and separate from the 11/9/63 Milteer threat above,[26] a CO2 PRS file, released to the HSCA on 5/3/78 and available only recently, reveals yet another threat subject: John Warrington.[27] Secret Service agent Sam Kinney, on both the Florida and Texas trips, told the author, "We had a scare" down there (in Tampa), an unspecified "organized crime" threat related to this same trip.[28] In fact, there were

deFreese interview...Page 5

the "#3-11" meant only that a record about Derber had been made by the local Miami office.

III. Mr. deFreese's Account of An Active Threat

Mr. deFreese acknowledged that there was an active threat against the President of which the Secret Service was aware in November 1963 in the period immediately prior to JFK's trip to Miami. Mr. deFreese indicated that the threat was made by a group of people who were to some extent members of one family, including a "sister and brother." Mr. deFreese was unable to recall the name of any person in the group and he could not recall the original source of his information about the group. His immediate source was local Miami Agent Robert Jamison, who "had touched base with the FBI" and who "briefed me about meetings with other agencies." However, he did remember that the group included "southerners" and originated not ...state," "possibly Alabama

---

25   See also *JFK Revisited* by James DiEugenio (and the documentary with the same name), page 203.
26   For an excellent book all about the Milteer threat, please see *From An Office Building With A High-Powered Rifle* (2012) by former FBI agent Don Adams.
27   RIF#'s 180-10118-10041 and 10033.
28   Author's interview with Kinney, 4/15/94.

six pages of threat subjects and information, including the subjects Orlando Bosch, Pedro Diaz Lanz, Enrique Llaca, Jr., and others.[29] The CIA's Ted Shackley and William Finch assisted the Secret Service on this trip.[30] An HSCA interview with Secret Service agent Robert J. Jamison states: "the threat of November 18, 1963 was posed by a mobile, unidentified rifleman with a high-powered rifle fitted with a scope."[31] In addition, Gilbert Policarpo Lopez is a suspect (a person of interest) regarding the Tampa trip.[32]

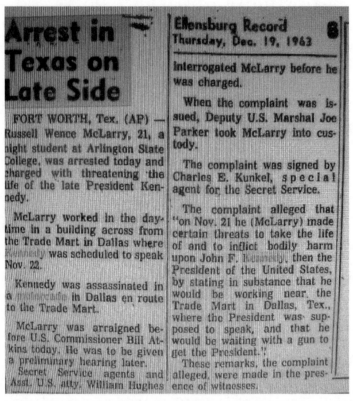

Arrest in Texas on Late Side

FORT WORTH, Tex. (AP) — Russell Wence McLarry, 21, a night student at Arlington State College, was arrested today and charged with threatening the life of the late President Kennedy.

McLarry worked in the daytime in a building across from the Trade Mart in Dallas where Kennedy was scheduled to speak Nov. 22.

Kennedy was assassinated in a motorcade in Dallas en route to the Trade Mart.

McLarry was arraigned before U.S. Commissioner Bill Atkins today. He was to be given a preliminary hearing later.

Secret Service agents and Asst. U.S. atty. William Hughes

Ellensburg Record
Thursday, Dec. 19, 1963

interrogated McLarry before he was charged.

When the complaint was issued, Deputy U.S. Marshal Joe Parker took McLarry into custody.

The complaint was signed by Charles E. Kunkel, s p e c i a l agent for the Secret Service.

The complaint alleged that "on Nov. 21 he (McLarry) made certain threats to take the life of and to inflict bodily harm upon John F. Kennedy, then the President of the United States, by stating in substance that he would be working near the Trade Mart in Dallas, Tex., where the President was supposed to speak, and that he would be waiting with a gun to get the President."

These remarks, the complaint alleged, were made in the presence of witnesses.

Ellensburg (Washington) Record, 12/19/63 (regarding 11/21/63 Texas threat):

29   RIF#154-10002-10422: Miami, FL 11/18/63.

30   RIF#154-10002-10422: Miami, FL 11/18/63.

31   HSCA document 180 – 10074-10394.

32   *Who Really Killed Kennedy?: 50 Years Later: Stunning New Revelations About the JFK Assassination* by Jerome Corsi (2016)- kindle edition; From the newly-released files: https://www.archives.gov/files/research/jfk/releases/104-10419-10352.pdf.

motorcade. Although Secret Service memoranda before him
(some of which were written by Jamison himself) made it clear
that the threat on 11-18-63 was posed by a mobile, unidentified rifleman shooting from a window in a tall building with
a high-powered rifle fitted with a scope, Jamison professed
to "no recall" of these facts even when his recollection was
refreshed by his own memoranda.

9 April 1963

The Honorable James J. Rowley
Chief, United States Secret Service
Department of the Treasury
Washington 25, D. C.

Dear Jim:

Following up on our telephone conversation of this afternoon,
I send you herewith my most recent memorandum to three of my
Deputies on the subject, "The CIA Role in Support of Presidential
Trips Abroad." This is an updating of a memorandum I put out on
8 June 1962, and is designed to tell everybody in the Agency what
their responsibilities are and to whom. You will of course understand that while our responsibilities to the Secret Service are inti-
mate and compelling as covered in paragraph II D of the attached,
we also have responsibilities for pure intelligence aspects and
Presidential briefings which must be covered in detail. If you have
any suggestions as to where we might improve our coverage, I would
be delighted to have them.

This letter also confirms my telephonic invitation to you and
Mr. Campion to have lunch with Lyman Kirkpatrick and me at 12:30
on Friday, 12 April, out here at the pickle factory.

Faithfully yours,

/s/ Pat

Marshall S. Carter
Lieutenant General, USA
Deputy Director

Attachment

Memo to DD/I, DD/P, DD/S from DDCI dtd 8 Mar 63, Subject:
The CIA Role in Support of Presidential Trips Abroad (ER 63-1664)
MSC:blp
Distribution:

A very important document: Kennedy-era correspondence between Deputy Director Marshall Carter and Chief Rowley regarding the CIA's role in support of presidential trips abroad.

Fort Worth (Texas) *Press* 11/22/63:

16 GOOFS ARE CHECKED OUT BY SECRET SERVICE

"A Secret Service man said today 16 persons were "checked out" here last night by agents guarding President Kennedy's life.

"The public doesn't know it," the agent said, "but we checked out 16 goofs." The agent described them as "goofs." "But if they could have gotten close enough, they could have harmed the President."

The agent, who asked not to be quoted by name, declined to elaborate. He would not say whether any of the people investigated were carrying arms.

Police officers said they know a no persons arrested and jailed last night by SS men.

The Secret Service men protected President Kennedy and his wife and Vice President Lyndon Johnson during their reception at Carswell Air Force Base and during their overnight stay at Hotel Texas.

Police officers, sheriff's deputies and federal men roped off Eighth St outside Hotel Texas as the President arrived.

"Everything went smoothly," Police St. S. B. Pruitt, one of dozens of city officers who spent the night at the hotel, said. "We didn't have any trouble at all."

REPORTERS were not allowed in the corridor of the eighth floor where the President and Mrs. Kennedy slept.

SS men and police kept the halls cleared of everybody except those wearing "special badges."

Policemen were stationed on the seventh and ninth floor stairs to keep anybody from going to the floor with the President.

One SS man was stationed outside Vice President and Mrs. Johnson's 13th floor suite.

City firemen stood in the halls on the seventh, eighth and ninth floors and in the hotel kitchens. It was the first time that many of the firemen could remember that such a precaution had been made to protect visiting dignitaries.

"But we don't have the President visit us very often," one fireman said."

11/21/63: U.N. Ambassador Adlai Stevenson and Senator William Fulbright warn JFK not to go to Dallas.[33] DNC advance man Marty Underwood gets "all sorts of rumors," 18 hours before the assassination, that Kennedy was to be killed in Dallas. Marty even conveys this to JFK, who tells him, "Marty, you worry about me too much."[34] Indeed, JFK told San Antonio Congressman Henry Gonzalez, "Henry, the Secret Service told me they took care of everything. There's nothing to worry about."[35] Incredibly, ASAIC Roy Kellerman told the following to FBI agents' James Sibert & Francis O'Neill on the night of the murder of JFK: "The advanced security arrangements made for this specific trip were the most stringent and thorough ever employed by the Secret Service for the visit of a President to an American city."[36]

33 The Death of a President by William Manchester, pages 38-39.
34 Author's interview with Underwood, 10/9/92.
35 High Treason by Robert Groden & Harrison Livingstone (1989), page 127.
36 FBI RIF#124-10012-10239; Kellerman would go on to deny ever saying such a

401

JFK Exhibit F-415

A plot to kill Kennedy from a year before (Secret Service report).

11/12/63 threat:[37]

November 12, 1963. An informant stated there was an international plot to kill the President by Quintin Pino Machado, a Cuban terrorist used by Castro to carry out any Castro action. On November 29, 1963, an informant stated that Machado boosted that he almost succeeded in killing Dr. Enrique Huertos. Huertos was among the invited guests to participate at the dinner honoring J.F.K. on November 18, 1963.

thing: 18 H 707- 708.

37   docid-32277356.pdf (archives.gov)

Twenty-five minutes before John F. Kennedy was assassinated, a British newspaper received an anonymous tip about "some big news" in the United States. The mystery call was made to a senior reporter at the *Cambridge News*, a paper that serves the East Anglia area of eastern England, on Nov. 22, 1963, at 6:05 p.m. local time. Kennedy was shot shortly afterward, as he rode in a presidential motorcade in Dallas, Texas, at 12:30 p.m. CST. Dallas is six hours behind Britain. "The caller said only that the *Cambridge News* reporter should call the American Embassy in London for some big news and then hung up," the memo from the CIA's James Angleton to FBI director J. Edgar Hoover said. The memo, dated Nov. 26, 1963, says: "After the word of the President's death was received the reporter informed the Cambridge police of the anonymous call, and the police informed MI5. The important point is that the call was made, according to MI5 calculations, about 25 minutes before the President was shot. The Cambridge reporter had never received a call of this kind before, and MI5 state that he is known to them as a sound and loyal person with no security record." MI5 is Britain's domestic security agency.

Former Cuban prisoner and anti-Castro activist John Martino[38] accurately predicted that the president would be assassinated in Dallas on 11/22/63. Martino was directly connected not just to the anti-Castro movement (Felipe Vidal Santiago, Gerry Patrick Hemming, Eddie Bayo, Frank Fiorini/Sturgis, David Morales, Rip Robertson, etc.) but to two of Jack Ruby's close associates, R.D. Matthews and Louis McWillie. Martino was also much aware of Amador Odio and his daughters Sarita, Annie and Sylvia.

---

38   *Someone Would Have Talked* by Larry Hancock (2006), numerous.

CHAPTER FOUR:

COVERT SECRET SERVICE MONITORS SUDDENLY APPEAR

"I don't want to do it. I don't want to do it. I'm afraid for my agency."
- Secret Service agent Gerald O'Rourke, on the Texas trip, when asked for more information about fellow agent Glen Bennett.

On November 10, 1963, PRS (Protective Research Section/Intelligence) Secret Service agent Glen Bennett is "temporarily assigned to the White House Detail."[39] From the newly released files courtesy of the Assassination Records Review Board and the JFK Records Act (Bennett's formal date was 11/12/63):

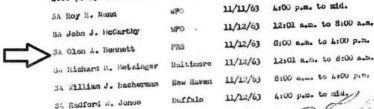

Although Bennett told the HSCA that he "was not on the Florida trip [11/18/63],"[40] the recently released Secret Service shift reports for that trip and the Survey Reports[41] not only state that Bennett was indeed present at all four stops on this trip, but that he rode in the follow-up car on three different occasions: in Palm Beach and in Cape Canaveral, as well as in Tampa.

An excerpt from Bennett's 1978 HSCA interview:

It was not until many years later – 2013, to be exact – that the author

```
        ⟹   He was not on the Florida trip, nor was he scheduled
for the Chicago trip, both in November, 1963.  He stated that he
does not recall any talk or information on alleged threats
in Miami or Chicago.  He doesn't recall any names of persons
to be checked out relative to the Dallas trip, filtering back
through PRS.
                NOTE:  Glen Bennett was accompanied by Secret Ser-
vice legal counsel John Meenan.  Mr. Meenan did not sit in
on the interview, but instead sat outside of our room in case
Glen Bennett wanted to consult with him.  This did not occur.
```

discovered, via photographic confirmation,[42] that PRS Agent Bennett briefly rode on the rear of the limousine, walked beside the limousine, and also rode on the running board of the Secret Service follow-up car in Tampa.[43] Former PRS Secret Service Agent Dale Wunderlich told the author, "Regarding the makeup of the advance team in Palm Beach for the opening of the Ambassador's residence, Glen Bennett was not part of the PRS advance team. He was serving on a temporary assignment on Presidential Protection Division (PPD) and in fact, he was riding on the follow-up car in Dallas when the President was assassinated. Howard [K. Norton] and I were the only two on the advance from PRS."[44] Miami WHD advance agent Bert DeFreese told the HSCA, "In 1963 it was rare for a PRS agent from Washington to accompany an advance agent into the field, and that no PRS

---

40   RIF#180-10082-10452: 1/30/78 HSCA interview of Bennett.
41   Palm Beach, Cape Canaveral, & Tampa: RIF#'s 1541-0001-10064, 1541-0001-10067, 1541- 0001-10078, 1541-0001-10081; RIF#'s 154-10002-10421 and 10422.
42   *Looking Back and Seeing the Future: The United States Secret Service 1865-1990* (1990), page 81. Note: This is a very rare book made for the former members of the Secret Service.
43   RIF#'s 1541-0001-10078, 1541-0001-10064, 1541-0001-10078.
44   E-mail to the author dated 10/9/99.

Press plane departed Tamp (NAL) at 4:10 p.m. (Roberts, Lawton, Zboril, McIntyre, Bennett and Kollar aboard . 4:50 p.m. arrived Miami.

Emory P. Roberts
Special Agent

(Over - More.)

(in charge)
Emory P. Roberts.

Special Agent In Charge:

Gerald A. Behn

Date : Nov. 18, 1963.
Location : Palm Beach, Fla. & return TC
Weather : Clear
Hrs. Today : 8 am - 4 p.m.

AGENTS		REGULAR DUTY	EXTRA DUTY
Roberts		8 am - 4 p.m.	4 .. 12.
Lawton		" "	"
Zboril	(Dror)	" "	"
McIntyre		" "	"
Bennett		" "	"

Section on duty Miami. (See survey report to SA deFreese for details)

9:50 p.m. Roberts, Lawton, Zboril, McIntyre, Bennett, Blaine and Kollar
departed Miami, Fla. via USAF 6972 and arrived Wash., D. C. 11:50 p.m.

..on reported for duty at Amb. Kennedy's Residence, Palm Beach, Fla.
a.m. The President and Gen. McHugh (Boring - Greer) depart Amb. Res.
(F.U. car Roberts, Lawton, Zboril and Bennett - Rybka driving.
a.m. arr. Palm Beach Airport.
a.m. Presidential Plane USAF 26,000 departed Palm Beach
(Boring, Marshall, Roberts, Lawton, Zboril, Bennett, Greer and
Rybka aboard.
a.m. arr. Cape Canaveral.
a.m. Pres. Mr. Webb and Sen. Smathers departed airport - Boring & Greer
came Follow-up Agents.

From Secret Service shift reports only released in the late 1990's via the ARRB-
Bennett was actually on all the stops in Florida-Tampa, Miami, Cape Canaveral
and Palm Beach.

agent accompanied [him] on this trip,"[45] yet Bennett was with DeFreese in
Miami and in Houston[46] on 11/21/63. Bennett further told the HSCA on
1/30/78 that he "was detailed from PRS to the White House Detail for
the Dallas trip [11/22/63]. This was because there was a manpower pull
for the Dallas trip," a statement not backed up by the shift reports. Furthermore, Sam Kinney told the author that Bennett was making his first trip
on 11/22/63.[47] While Kinney's statement is at least orally corroborated by
Bennett's story to the HSCA, it is also contradicted by the shift reports and
Survey reports for the Florida trip of 11/18/63, and Bennett was also on

45   RIF#180-10083-10419: 2/2/78 HSCA interview of de Freese.
46   Sources: RIF#1541000110104;   1541000110064;   1541000110042;
1541000110044 (Daily Shift report, V.P. Detail, 11/21/63); 1541000110031; 180-10083-
10419; 180-10078-10493; 16 H 950-951; 17 H 618; author's 10/9/92 interview with DNC
advance man Marty Underwood; DNC Advance man Jerry Bruno's notes, JFK Library.
47   Author's interview with Kinney, 3/4/94.

the second NYC trip JFK made (11/14- 11/15/63.)[48] Agent Tim McIntyre also told the HSCA that he did not believe he was assigned to either the Miami or the Chicago trips for November 1963.[49] However, like Agent Bennett's seeming amnesia, as proven by the Secret Service Shift Reports released by the ARRB in the 1990's, McIntyre was on both trips. It should be noted that McIntyre, who rode in the follow-up car with Bennett, was also Bennett's roommate in Fort Worth 11/21-11/22/63.[50] Perhaps this was why Bennett felt the need to be accompanied by Secret Service Counsel John Meenan during his HSCA interview.

An excerpt from McIntyre's 1978 HSCA interview. McIntyre was scheduled for both trips.

way to Parkland Hosp—

⇨ McIntyre had heard of Abraham Bolden but did not know him.

The name Conrad Cross sounded familiar.

He did not know the names Vallee and Moseby.

He stated that he does not believe that he was assigned to either the Miami trip or the Chicago trip, both scheduled for November 1963. ⇧

11/11/63: SAIC of PRS Robert Bouck is notified about JFK's upcoming second trip to NYC for 11/14-11/15/63: Bennett was then promptly dispatched to JFK's suite at the Carlyle Hotel, prior to Kennedy's arrival, "to conduct a technical survey."[51] This was not done on any prior trips in November, including the first New York trip, nor on any other trips known to this author. With Bennett's temporary assignment, his denials to the HSCA, and everything above in context, there is something going on here: the timing is everything. Also, by performing these specific duties, Bennett was still wearing his PRS hat, so to speak. In addition, Bennett is listed on the Secret Service shift report of 11/14/63 as "SA-New York City," under the same grouping of agents, six in all, who were advance agents for JFK's upcoming trips to Elkton, Md., Miami, Fl., Austin, Tx., Ft. Worth, Tx., and

---

48   RIF#154-10002-10419.
49   1/31/78 HSCA interview with McIntyre.
50   18 H 682.
51   RIF#154-10002-10419: 2nd New York City trip 11/14-11/15/63.

Tampa, Fl.[52] Was Bennett also part of the advance team in his newfound WHD assignment? Captioned photo from a very rare book[53]:

Advance agent Winston Lawson wrote in his report: "Agent Bennett was

The arrival in Dallas, November 22, 1963. Behind the president are Don Lawton, Win Lawson, Glenn Bennett, and Roy Kellerman; and to the right are Clint Hill and Jack Ready.

reminded that he would work [the] Presidential follow-up car on the movement."[54] 11/22/63: While Bennett rides in the Secret Service follow-up car, scanning the people lining the streets, President Kennedy is murdered right in front of him. After the assassination, Bennett's observations, via his allegedly contemporaneous handwritten notes from 11/22/63[55], were used by Chief Rowley to buttress the notion that Kennedy was struck from the rear, in spite of the films and photos that appear to depict Bennett looking away from JFK. Perhaps HSCA attorney Belford Lawson summed up the

---

52   USSS RIF#1541-0001-10092.
53   *Looking Back and Seeing the Future: The United States Secret Service 1865-1990* (1990), page 81.
54   17 H 631.
55   24 H 541-542 Rowley to Rankin 5/14/64 re: Bennett's alleged 11/22/63 handwritten notes.

situation best: "How could SS Agent Glen Bennett have been able to see JFK, who was 38 feet away and partially concealed by several persons, yet be able to state clearly that the first shot hit JFK four inches down from [the] right shoulder? Why didn't the distance and commotion prevent such an observation? Why [wasn't] Bennett called to testify?"[56] However, this is almost ancillary to the major point: Was PRS agent Glen Bennett monitoring threats to JFK's life, made in the month of November, and was this covered up afterwards? Is this the reason for the conflicting accounts, and the timing, of Bennett's participation in the second New York trip, the Florida trip, and the Texas trip? Did Bennett ride in the follow-up car and participate on these trips for this purpose? Unfortunately, former agent Winston Lawson informed the author that Bennett is now deceased, so no more answers will be forthcoming from the principal person in this mystery.[57] Bennett to the HSCA: "He stated that he does not recall any talk or information on alleged threats in Miami or Chicago. He doesn't recall any names of persons to be checked out relative to the Dallas trip, filtering back to PRS." Incredible.

PRS Secret Service agent Glen Bennett on 11/22/63.

Former PRS agent Frank G. Stoner told the author on 1/17/04 that he didn't know why Bennett, a PRS man, would have been on these trips. Stoner, genuinely puzzled about the matter, thought perhaps Bennett was

---

56   RIF# 180-10093-10320: 5/31/77 Memorandum from HSCA's Belford Lawson to fellow HSCA members' Gary Cornwell & Ken Klein (revised 8/15/77).

57   Letter to author from Lawson dated 1/31/04 Bennett died 4/4/94 in Bradenton, FL at the age of 65.

an "intelligence liaison" in his capacity of riding in the follow-up car. Officially speaking, Bennett was not. Stoner did not elaborate further when pressed on this issue in writing; in fact, he avoided it all together on three different occasions.[58] Former WHD agent J. Walter Coughlin, who assisted fellow agent Dennis R. Halterman on the advance for the San Antonio part of the Texas trip (11/21/63), wrote the author, "I can only add the following – I was not in Dallas so my knowledge is hearsay from good friends who were there. Glen Bennett was on all these trips, not as a member of PRS but as a temporary shift agent in that so many of us were out on advance. This I do know to be a fact and read nothing more into it." Interestingly, Coughlin founded "J. Walter Coughlin & Associates," a security firm based in Dallas.[59] If this was the case, why did Bennett perform PRS functions on the New York trip (what SAIC Bouck referred to as a "technical survey")? These comments by Coughlin sound like Bennett's "manpower pull" comment to the HSCA that was in reference specifically to the Dallas leg of the Texas trip. However, was there also a "manpower pull" for the other trips Bennett was on?[60] Also, the vast majority of the agents who went on these trips did return to Washington, D.C. afterward, ready for further action on future trips. If there was a genuine shortage of men, why not just follow common procedure and add an agent, from the Washington Field Office (WFO), for example?[61] This was the case when WFO agent Roger C. Warner came along to Dallas for his very first Presidential protective mission. Why were Bennett's services needed in the ultra-important follow-up car, of all things? And, to top it off, Bennett just happened to be one of the agents involved in the infamous drinking incident the night of November 21, at both the Fort Worth Press Club and the Cellar. It would seem that Bennett did not take his special duty very seriously.

All this must have touched a nerve in Coughlin. Winston Lawson wrote the author: "I understand from my friend Walt Coughlin that you wondered why Glen Bennett from PRS was on the trip." [Note: The author did

---

58   E-mail to author dated 1/19/04 (in response to my questions. This was the second e-mail in which Stoner avoided any elaboration on this issue, in addition to the author's original letter to the former agent).

59   Letter to author dated 1/15/04.

60   With regard to the Houston trip of 11/21/63, Bennett was on this trip but, like fellow agents' Roberts, Lawton, and McIntyre, his specific duties are not known from the paper record or from testimony. Perhaps he had duties at the Coliseum for Congressman Albert Thomas' dinner.

61   An example of which can be found in one of the shift reports for 11/15/63: "SA [Kent D.] Jordan was on temporary assignment from WFO to WHD for this duty." USSS RIF# 1541-0001-10084.

not tell Coughlin about any contact with Lawson]. "Nothing sinister about it and had nothing to do with threats or intelligence. There were so many trips, MD and FL, just prior to TX and so many stops in TX that the small WH Detail was decimated supplying advance people. A number of temporarily assigned agents were on all 3 shifts in TX ... I believe Walt had been on an advance before he went to his stop in TX." Still, why was Bennett performing PRS functions in New York if he was just another agent? The author decided to make further inquiries to former agent Coughlin in this matter, and asked, "In light of the fact that Bennett, temporarily assigned to the White House Detail on 11/10/63, was on all the stops on JFK's trips [11/11/63-11/22/63] to NY, FL [four], and TX up to Dallas [four; not including Austin], and the fact that he was performing 'technical surveys' on the trip to NY, doesn't his presence concede the seeming fact that he was performing some sort of intelligence function?" [Note: this info on Bennett only came to light because the author ordered the documents from the National Archives. It is far from common knowledge].[62] In response, Coughlin wrote, "Nothing sinister – in 1963 we had about 300 agents and we were not that clever to be sinister. He was there as a temp."[63] Former agent Larry Newman dismissed the author's notion of Bennett's true role, yet said, "What they were starting to do was assign a PI [Protective Intelligence/ PRS] guy to help the advance guy."[64] However, this practice was officially adopted only after 11/22/63 in response to the assassination, unless Newman was also aware of the true roles of Bennett, Norton, and Wunderlich on the trips in November 1963. That said, Newman added that Bennett, who he knew "worked somewhat in on Protective Intelligence," was part of a team and his presence on the trips was in relation to "no specific thing." (It is also important to note that Newman left the White House Detail in October 1963.)[65]

Likewise, former agent Jerry D. Kivett said that members of PRS, later renamed Protective Intelligence, "traveled with us sometimes" and that this was a manpower issue having "nothing to do with – that I know of – special threat levels." However, Kivett added the caveat that the PRS travels were made only "until after" the assassination, as mentioned above. More importantly, when the author asked Kivett if Bennett may have been on the NY, Fl, and Tx trips to monitor threats, the former agent said, "That's

62   Letter to author dated 1/20/04 Lawson reiterated the same information regarding the three shifts in his letter to the author dated 1/31/04.
63   E-mail to author dated 2/22/04.
64   Author's interview with Newman, 2/7/04.
65   Author's interview with Newman, 2/7/04.

very much a possibility."[66] Fellow Texas trip agent Gerald S. Blaine, who had also been on the Florida trip with Bennett, told the author, "I don't know what he had." When asked if Bennett could have been (as PRS agent Stoner claimed) an "intelligence liaison," Blaine said, "I guess. I don't really remember. It's hard to say. I don't know what he was doing. They [PRS agents] operate independently."[67] During a later interview conducted on 6/10/05, Blaine admitted it was "kind of strange" for Bennett to be riding in the follow-up car on the Dallas trip. Former agent Vincent P. Mroz, when asked if Bennett was on these trips to monitor threats, told the author, "Right, uh-huh. It's their job to sort out that information. They go there to work [it] out." Mroz also said that this was "not abnormal."[68] Another agent on all three trips, Samuel E. Sulliman, told the author, "I remember him [Bennett]. He was sort of a quiet guy. I don't know what he was there for." Likewise, Darwin Horn wrote, "I recall Glen Bennett. I don't know what he was doing in Dallas."[69]

Perhaps the biggest surprise of all came from former agent Gerald W. O'Rourke, another Texas trip veteran who also was on the second NY trip and a part of the FL trip. The former agent, who came out on the 40th anniversary of the JFK assassination to reveal his conviction that a conspiracy took the life of President Kennedy,[70] was friendly, cordial, and quite informative in response to the author's first letter of inquiry, answering every question in detail. In fact, O'Rourke ended his letter by stating, "If you have other questions, please feel free to contact me. Jerry."[71] Taking the hint, the author promptly wrote another letter to O'Rourke but did not receive a reply. The author's second letter asked for information about Bennett's role on the NY, FL, and TX trips. When the author phoned O'Rourke on 2/11/04, obviously all was not well on the other end. When asked about Bennett, the former agent said forcefully, "I don't want to do it. I don't want to do it. I'm afraid for my agency." O'Rourke then abruptly ended the conversation.

As the *Rocky Mountain News* reported on 11/20/03: "O'Rourke spent a year in the Secret Service intelligence division [where Bennett worked], which offered him glimpses into the investigation of Kennedy's death. Those glimpses, and the accounts of other [unnamed] agents, have con-

---

66   Author's interview with Kivett, 2/7/04.
67   Author's interview with Blaine, 2/7/04.
68   Author's interview with Mroz, 2/7/04.
69   E-mail to author dated 2/22/04.
70   *Rocky Mountain News*, 11/20/03.
71   Letter to author dated 1/15/04, in response to the author's letter dated 1/7/04.

vinced O'Rourke that Oswald didn't act alone." Bennett was still a member of the USSS, in the Intelligence Division, during the HSCA era. In fact, he initiated a letter to G. Robert Blakey, the General Counsel of the HSCA, regarding the then-current whereabouts of several former agents. Not to be outdone, Clint Hill writes in his memoirs about the formation of the follow-up car agents in Dallas on 11/22/63 and confirms my suspicions: "Glen Bennett from the Protective Research Section, handling intelligence."[72] PRS Agent Dale Wunderlich (in my informed opinion, based on the above) falsely stated in his 10/15/05 Sixth Floor Museum oral history that Dallas was the very first time someone from PRS came to do an intelligence advance. During his oral history given on the same day, former agent Rad Jones claimed that he and Bennett flipped a coin for who would go to Dallas. In any event, as previously mentioned, the newly released Secret Service shift reports for the month of November in the year 1963 do not substantiate the claim that PRS agent Bennett was needed due to an alleged shortage of men or a "manpower pull."[73]

The day he was added to the WHD, 11/10/63, was acknowledged in a shift report with the designation "RDO," or "regular day off," a common abbreviation throughout the November 1963 reports denoting the days a particular agent was not on assignment. For example, Clint Hill was off Friday, November 1, 1963 and Friday, November 8, 1963. So, while the agents from JFK's first trip to New York (11/8-11/9/63) were back in Washington the morning of the 9th (except advance agent Art Godfrey, who stayed in NY for the second trip's advance[74]), Bennett was off duty when he achieved this new (WHD) status on the 10th.[75] Bennett was also given the next day off, Veteran's Day, 11/11/63, along with fellow agents Bacherman, O'Rourke, Metzinger[76], and McCarthy, all of whom were added to the WHD within the same 24-hour time span.[77] It should be noted that

---

72   *Mrs. Kennedy and Me* by Clint Hill, p. 287.

73   USSS RIF#'s 1541-0001-10029 thru 10190, covering all shifts of the WHD from 11/1/63 to 11/23/63, inclusive.

74   In a November 24 1997 letter to the author, advance agent Art Godfrey did not know the reason for the first trip.

75   USSS RIF# 1541-0001-10120.

76   Former agent Walt Coughlin wrote, "Dick Metzinger worked a while with us on the V.P. Detail. I recall he was a temp (maybe permanent) from Baltimore F.O. and resigned early in his career." [E-mail to author dated 2/22/04].

77   USSS RIF#'s 1541-0001-10113 and 1541-0001-10112 Metzinger & McCarthy return to an unnamed field office, probably Baltimore and/ or Washington, on 11/23/63: USSS RIF# 1541-0001-10190 For his part, Bennett was on duty at the Secret Service office in the White House on 11/23/63: USSS RIF# 1541-0001-10189.

William R. Straughn,[78] a WHD agent, was on Godfrey's shift from at least 11/1/63, and probably much earlier, until 11/9/63, then was replaced by one of these men.[79] Jerry Dolan, an agent not mentioned in the released November 1963 shift reports, "did not accompany [JFK] as he had expected. Instead he went on leave to Omaha, Neb., to be with his wife, Josephine, for the birth of their third son."[80] On this date, President Kennedy visited Arlington National Cemetery with a coterie of agents, including Roy Nunn,[81] an experienced WHD agent who had been on JFK's trip to Nashville on 5/18/63. Nunn was also re-added to the WHD on this date, and Radford Jones, another experienced WHD agent who had been on the Kennedy Compound Detail, was added the next day.

So, of the seven agents (some of whom were merely replacements, not new agents, per se), only Bennett came from PRS.[82] President Kennedy's next trip would not be until 11/14/63 when he would visit Elkton, MD for the dedication of the Maryland-Delaware Turnpike (a non-motorcade, ribbon-cutting affair)[83], then to New York once again (11/14-11/15/63). Bennett next appears on the 11/12/63 and 11/13/63 shift reports as part of the 8 a.m. to 4 p.m. shift that "reported for duty at [the] White House."[84] According to these same reports, President Kennedy stayed in the mansion that day, so Bennett evidently stood post in a doorway.[85] Then, as we know, Bennett was a Special Agent on JFK's trips to New York, Florida, and Texas. Of the seven recent WHD additions, only the lone PRS agent, Bennett, is dispatched on all three major trips, and all the major stops on these tours, from 11/14-11/22/63.[86] Again, the question is: why? The covert monitor-

78   Former agent Walt Coughlin wrote the author, "Do not recall Straughan [sic] being on the Detail (maybe a temp) but I recall he spent most of his career in Chicago F.O." [E-mail to author dated 2/22/04].

79   USSS RIF#'s 1541-0001-10182, 1541-0001-10127, 1541-0001-10121.

80   *St. Paul Pioneer Press Dispatch*, Sunday, November 20, 1988.

81   Former agent Walt Coughlin wrote: "Roy (Gene) Nunn lives here in Dallas. Left the SS about '75 and believe he works for FEMA." [E-mail to author dated 2/22/04].

82   Nunn: USSS RIF# 1541-0001-10111; Jones: USSS RIF# 1541-0001-10104 and letter to author dated 1/16/04 The breakdown is as follows: Bennett & Bacherman added to ATSAIC Roberts' shift on 11/10/63; Metzinger & McCarthy (11/10/63), then O'Rourke (11/11/63), added to ATSAIC Godfrey's shift; and Nunn (11/11/63) and Jones (11/12/63) added to ATSAIC Stout's detail.

83   USS RIF# 1541-0001-10092.

84   USSS RIF# 1541-001-10104 and 1541-0001-10099.

85   11/13/63 was also the day the Black Watch Guard performed on the South Grounds of the White House.

86   Bacherman, McCarthy, and Nunn are at Atoka from 11/15/63 until 11/21/63. They were replaced by Zboril, Kollar, and Coughlin on 11/22/63 into 11/23/63: USSS RIF #s 1541-0001-10083, 1541-0001-10073, 1541-0001-10069, 1541-0001-10059, 1541-0001-10052, 1541-0001-10045, 1541-0001- 10038, 1541-0001-10035, 1541-0001-10029

ing of a threat (or threats) to President Kennedy's life remains the most compelling reason.

And, as discovered by the author via a recently released Secret Service shift report, yet another PRS agent, Howard K. Norton, was covertly on the Texas trip, this time in Austin.[87]

According to former PRS Agent Dale Wunderlich, "Howard K. Norton was the first "Security Technician" that was hired by the USSS. He was retired from the Air Force where I believe that he was a Sergeant Major in OSI. He was never a Special Agent but was extremely knowledgeable in the field of electronics and electronic countermeasures. In fact, I was told by a friend of his that he was one of the technicians that discovered the resonance cavity that the Russians planted in the U.S. seal that was given to the U. S. Ambassador to Moscow, Russia. Regarding the makeup of the advance team in Palm Beach for the opening of the Ambassador's residence … Howard and I were the only two on the advance from PRS. Howard was primarily responsible for oversight of the technical sweeps, which I assisted him with, and I was also involved in doing backgrounds on employees, CO-2 cases and contractors that were doing some repairs to the kitchen floor at the Ambassador's residence. CO-2 cases were individuals who were of record with the Protective Research Division of the USSS."[88]

Only from ATSAIC Godfrey's Secret Service Shift Report, not released until the late 1990's via the ARRB, do we even know that Norton was on the Texas trip (in Austin) – his name is unknown until we get to the afternoon of 11/23/63 when, along with fellow PRS employee James Fox,

---

Bacherman & Nunn were listed as "DO" ("Day Off ") for 11/22/63, while Metzinger & McCarthy were listed as "RDO" ("Regular Day Off.") Both would return to a field office, either the Washington or Baltimore office, on 11/23/63, while Bacherman and Nunn would remain with the WHD on 11/23/63: USSS RIF#s 1541-0001-10190, 1541-0001-10189, 1541-0001-10188 Jones was listed as SA: USSS RIF#s 1541-0001-10030, 1541-0001-10031, 1541-0001-10033. Metzinger & Jones both go to New York (11/14-11/15/63) & Florida, but Metzinger, venturing no further than Ambassador Kennedy's residence, departs in the early morning hours of 11/18/63 for Washington, D.C. (USSS RIF# 1541-0001-10065). For his part, O'Rourke went to New York (11/14-11/15/63), and Palm Beach, Florida, departing with Metzinger and a few others at the same time, thus missing Cape Canaveral, Miami, and Tampa, the major stops on the Florida tour where JFK interacted with thousands of citizens during motorcades in these cities. And, while O'Rourke was on the Texas tour, he was NOT on the Houston, San Antonio, or Dallas legs of the trip, in effect missing major stops on two of the three trips from 11/14-11/23/63.

87   USSS RIF# 1541-0001-10033:ATSAIC Godfrey's handwritten shift report for 11/22/63.

88   E-mail to author dated 10/9/99.

he photographs the bloody limousine.[89] Even the Austin Survey Report, released around the same time in the 1990's, does not mention Norton's name. Finally, it should be kept in mind that the Florida Survey Report that does mention Norton was also not released until the late 1990's. PRS Agent Dale Wunderlich wrote the author on 2/6/2009: "I was reading through some of your information on the Internet and in one location where you mention me doing an Intelligence advance in Fort Worth, you indicate that there is no record of me being on that trip. I can assure you that I prepared a report that would have been submitted to SAIC Robert I. Bouck when I returned from Texas. I traveled to Fort Worth from Washington where I joined Bill Duncan and Ned Hall. The advance man for the Vice President was Jerry Kivett. I was the only person from Protective Research Division [Section] and I coordinated the electronic, technical and explosives sweeps with local military agencies at Carswell AFB, the Hotel Texas and for the speech in front of the Hotel Texas the morning of November 22, 1963. I also gathered the names of the people that worked at the Hotel Texas and had them run through Texas state criminal records and NCIC. In addition, it was my job to issue id pins for the employees at the hotel. Although Ned is no longer with us, Bill Duncan, Jerry Kivett and Mike Howard (Dallas FO) and myself have often discussed our advance in Fort Worth. I might comment that Bill Duncan (Lead PPD advance) and I remain very good friends and in fact worked together for several years after leaving the Secret Service. The local DNC advance man from Texas that we worked with was Bedford Winn. He was a lawyer from Dallas. On the day after the funeral, I drove from WDC to Dallas and transported a carload of technical equipment for screening mail that was being sent to Marina Oswald and the Dallas Field Office. I assisted with the investigation in various capacities and also served on Marina Oswalds' protective detail. I returned to DC with Marina Oswald on Sunday February 2, 1964 and I believe she testified before the Warren Commission on the following day."

J. Frank Yeager, a member of the WHD who assisted in the advance of the Austin leg of the Texas tour, wrote, "I do not remember Norton ... I do not remember Bennett."[90] Former agent Joe Paolella, a WHD agent on the New York and Florida trips, wrote, "I am sorry but I do not know why Agent Bennett was on the New York, Florida, or Texas trips in November 1963, nor do I remember Agent Howard Norton."[91] When asked if he re-

---

89   CD 80. See also *Murder in Dealey Plaza* (2000), pages 428-430.
90   Letter to author dated 1/24/04.
91   Letter to author dated 3/24/04.

membered Norton or Bennett, former agent Robert Snow wrote the author, "Why don't you contact the Secret Service, Office of Public Affairs at [number deleted for privacy]--they have all that information."[92] Another former agent on JFK's Austin trip, Gerald Blaine, also twice claimed not to remember Norton.[93] If that weren't enough, another Texas trip veteran, Walt Coughlin, wrote, "I do not recall Norton."[94] When pressed on this matter further, Coughlin responded, "I believe I have answered all your emails!"[95] (Coughlin later relented and resumed responding to the author's inquiries).[96] Yet, four of these men, Yeager, Paolella, Blaine, and Coughlin, were also on the Florida trip with both Bennett and Norton!

When asked if he could provide a thumbnail sketch of what he knew about Norton, former agent Darwin Horn wrote the author, "I do not recall."[97] Former agent Jerry Kivett, yet another Texas trip veteran assigned to then-V.P. Lyndon Johnson, wrote, "I do not recall a PRS Agent named Howard K. Norton. However, that does not mean he did not exist. Nor do I recall him being in Dallas, but again that doesn't mean that he was not there."[98] The author tried yet again with former PRS agent Frank Stoner, asking him, "Do you remember a PRS agent named Howard K. Norton? He was on President Kennedy's trips to Florida and Texas (Austin)?" I also asked Stoner, "Do you remember working with PRS agent Glen Bennett (he was on the NY, FL, and TX trips)?" Stoner answered, "No I did not know any of the agents you named."[99] (Stoner did remember Bennett from the author's previous three inquiries on the matter.) Jerry O'Rourke later responded to the question of his familiarity (or lack thereof) with Norton in this fashion: "No, I do not recall anyone by the name. He could have been in PRS (Protective Research Division), now called Intelligence Division and I wouldn't have known him at the time as I was on the White House Division, now called Presidential Protective Division. Much later, I served, for a short time, at PRS and I don't recall him. Today, the retired agents association are very active and had he retired or served for at least one year, the requirements to belong to the retired agents, I would have heard of him and/or he would be listed on our web site. Is it possible he could have been a political advance man? I do not have a copy of the Warren Commission

---

92   Letter to author dated 3/24/04.
93   Author's interviews with Blaine, 2/7/04 and 6/10/05.
94   E-mail to author dated 2/22/04.
95   E-mail to author dated 2/25/04.
96   E-mail to author dated 2/26/04.
97   E-mail to author dated 2/23/04.
98   Letter to author dated 2/18/04.
99   E-mail to author dated 2/26/04.

Report which would have listed him and his activities. Sorry that I could not have been more help!"

Tim McIntyre, Bob Burke (the lead advance agent for the Austin trip), John Giuffre, John Joe Howlett, Bill Livingood and Floyd Boring would not respond to written inquiries from the author regarding Norton or Bennett. The author wrote to Secret Service Public Affairs Assistant Director George M. Rogers on 7/5/05 asking for tenure dates for Howard K. Norton (Mr. Rogers previously helped the author on other inquiries). In the same message, the author matter-of-factly mentioned Norton's presence on the Austin leg of the Texas trip. Rogers' reply, dated 7/15/05, was surprising: "Dear Mr. Palamara: A search was conducted in response to your electronic message received on July 5, 2005, requesting tenure dates for former Secret Service employee Howard K. Norton…We were unable to locate any reference that provided information regarding the length of time [Norton] spent with the Secret Service." It should also be noted that Rogers did not comment on or dispute the issue of Norton's participation on the ill-fated Texas tour. As for Winston Lawson, when the author sent the former agent a 5-page, detailed account of all the evidence of Bennett's role in President Kennedy's November trips, a substantive answer was not forthcoming. Instead, Lawson wrote, "As for Glen Bennett (now deceased) – I don't remember what stops he was on but probably all of them while assigned temporarily to [the] White House Detail in that time frame. I know one thing though – there could have been no cover up, sinister motive or anything remotely untoward connected with him. He was one of the most dedicated, hard workers and nicest people I've ever known!!"[100] Fair enough, but could Bennett have been an unwitting tool of someone in higher authority? Again, we must keep in mind that Bennett lied to the HSCA concerning his presence on the Florida trip, and nothing was volunteered from the agent regarding his participation on the New York stop, performing PRS functions, of all things. The final answer to these mysteries may have been buried with Bennett. Only time will tell.

Bennett later became head of PRS/the Intelligence Division of the Secret Service and, if that wasn't enough, he maintained the case file on the JFK assassination:

---

100   Letter to author dated 1/31/04; Lawson did not respond to the author's written inquiry regarding Norton.

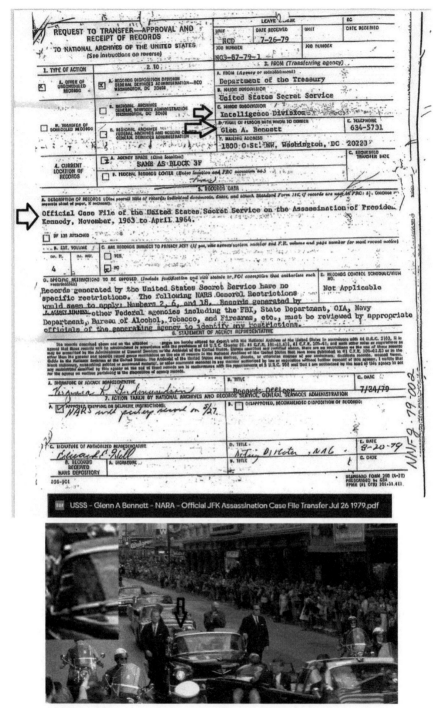

Incredibly, Bennett (enlarged inset) rode in the front passenger seat of the fol-low-up car in San Antonio that was normally reserved for the Shift Leader and commander of the other agents in the car.

AMAZING RECENT FIND: Bennett admits being on the NY, FL, and TX trips. He lied under oath to the HSCA and stated that he was NOT on the Florida trip [he was on every single stop] and did NOT volunteer that he was also on the NY trip (The Daily Reporter, Dover, OH, 11/25/63):

Doverites' Son-In-Law Was With JFK

Glen Bennett, husband of Mrs. Glenna Kline Bennett, former society editor of The Daily Reporter, was a member of the presidential Secret Service detail assigned to guard John F. Kennedy during his Dallas visit.

Bennett was in the agents' car immediately behind the presidential limousine when the fatal shooting occurred. He also accompanied Mr. Kennedy's body back to Washington.

Normally on the White House detail, Agent Bennett recently was assigned to the tour detail and was with Mr. Kennedy when

he spoke in New York, Florida and in the West.

Mrs. Bennett's parents are Mr. and Mrs. George Aebersold of 340 Main St., Dover. They got

TV glimpses of their son-in-law on Mr. Kennedy's arrival in Dallas, when his body was placed aboard the plane and again when it arrived in Washington.

The Doctor Writes:

Stature May Be Inherited

Bennett next to JFK in Tampa 11/18/63 (Tim McIntyre, far right).

SA Tim McIntyre and SA Glen Bennett of PRS walk the front of limousine 11/18/63.

THE TAMPA TRIBUNE

★ ★ ★
Threats On Kennedy Made Here

Tampa police and Secret Service agents scanned crowds for a man who had vowed to assassinate the President here last Monday, Chief of Police J. P. Mullins said yesterday.

In issuing notice to all participating security police prior to the President's motorcade tour in Tampa, Mullins had said: "I would like to advise all officers that threats against the President have been made from this area in the last few days."

A memo from the White House Secret Service dated Nov. 8 reported:

"Subject made statement of a plan to assassinate the President in October 1963. Subject stated he will use a gun, and if he couldn't get closer he would find another way. Subject is described as: White, male, 20, slender build," etc.

Mullins said Secret Service had been advised of three persons in the area who reportedly had made threats on the President's life. One of the three was—and still is—in jail here under heavy bond.

Mullins said he did not know if the other two may have followed the Presidential caravan to Dallas.

Sarasota County Sheriff Ross E. Boyer also said yesterday that officers who protected Kennedy in Tampa Monday were warned about "a young man" who had threatened to kill the President during that trip.

THINGS THAT HAPPENED ON 11/18/63 IN TAMPA THAT DID NOT HAPPEN ON 11/22/63 IN DALLAS:

1. Agents on the rear of the limo (other than Clint Hill, briefly, 4 times before they got to Dealey Plaza; JFK is falsely blamed for the agents not being there).

2. Military aide in front seat between driver and agent in charge (McHugh was asked, for the first time in Dallas, not to ride there!).

3. Press photographer's flatbed truck in front of limo (canceled at last minute at Love Field).

4. Fast speed of cars (slow in Dallas; Greer attempted to blame JFK for the slow speed on the night of the murder after being remorseful all day).

5. ASAIC Boring on trip (SAIC Behn and Boring always accompanied JFK in motorcades. A third-stringer, Kellerman, goes in their place- one of if not the first major trip Kellerman took on his own).

6. Multi story rooftops guarded (officially, no buildings were guarded in Dallas. Eyewitnesses Arnold and Barbara Rowland did see a man with a rifle in the Texas School Book Depository building before the motorcade reached the eventual site of the assassination and, tellingly, thought the man was a Secret Service agent. Rowland later testified to the Warren Commission on his thought process at the time: "I must honestly say my opinion was based on movies I have seen, on the attempted assassination of Theodore Roosevelt where they had Secret Service men up in the building such as that with rifles watching the crowds, and another one concerned with attempted assassination of the other one, Franklin Roosevelt, and both of these had Secret Service men up in windows or on top of buildings with rifles, and this is how my opinion was based and why it didn't alarm me."[101]).

7. Multiple motorcycles running next to JFK in a wedge formation (they repeated this coverage 11/18-11/22/63 [morning in Fort Worth] until Dallas, when the Secret Service reduced the coverage and had the few motorcycles that were remaining drop back from the rear wheels of JFK's limo, rendering them ineffective or, as the HSCA stated, "uniquely insecure").

8. White House Press Photographer Cecil Stoughton riding in follow-up car taking photos (he did 11/18-11/21/63...until they got to Dallas. No satisfactory answer has ever been given as to why Stoughton was not there on 11/22/63).

9. Pierre Salinger on trip (Assistant Malcolm Kilduff makes his first trip on his own to Texas; Salinger said he missed only "one or two trips" with JFK ... Texas was one of them! Agent Bob Lilley told me that Salinger was extremely knowledgeable about motorcade security and planning).

---

101   2 H 174.

10. Dr. George Burkley close to JFK (Burkley protested being placed far away from JFK in Dallas, for this was the only time, save in Rome, this ever happened to him ... and Rome was a model of great security in every other respect).

11. Tampa was the longest motorcade President Kennedy undertook domestically (only the one in Berlin was longer). In contrast, the motorcade in Dallas was far shorter and, thus, more manageable.

```
ORIGINATOR : HSCA
     FROM : MARSHALL, JOHN          02/02/78
       TO : LAWSON, BELFORD
     Twice during the interview, Mr. Marshall mentioned that,
for all he knew, someone in the Secret Service could possibly
have been involved in the assassination. This is not the
first time an agent has mentioned the possibility that a con-
spiracy existed, but it is the first time that an agent has
acknowledged the possibility that the Secret Service could
have been involved.
```

The Special Agent in Charge of the Miami office, John Marshall, had this to say to the HSCA in 1978.

During his 9/18/96 ARRB interview, fellow agent Floyd Boring related the following: "When shown the HSCA summary of its interview with Miami SAIC John Marshall (specifically, Marshall's twice expressed opinion that there may have been a Secret Service conspiracy), Mr. Boring expressed surprise at those sentiments and said he had never heard that opinion expressed by SAIC Marshall (a personal friend of his from their previous association as Pennsylvania State Troopers) before." Marshall served as SAIC of the Miami field office from 1950 until 1971.

At the time of the assassination, the White House Detail was in a weakened condition due to recent resignations and transfers. Nearly one third of the 34 agents on the White House Detail assigned to protect JFK, including a number of experienced agents, had recently resigned or been transferred. Former agent Gerald Blaine wrote: "In the past two months alone, eleven of the most experienced agents on the Kennedy Detail had been replaced. It had been a purely personal choice by the agents – they'd requested, and had been granted, transfers to field offices... Nearly a third of the agents had decided they just couldn't do it anymore. Too many missed birthdays

Left: New White House Detail agent William Straughn introduced to President Kennedy 10/17/63 by Special Agent in Charge Gerald Behn in the background. Right: New White House Detail Secret Service agent Ed Morey chatting with JFK 11/20/63.

Mr. Howard K. Norton, 64, 960 Pilgrim Drive, Titusville, died Wednesday. Born in Saltillo, Miss., he moved to Titusville from Camp Springs, Md., in 1976. He was a retired secret service agent, Protestant and veteran of World War II and the Korean conflict. Survivors: wife, Betty; sons, David, Camp Springs, Terry, Dallas; sister, Mrs. Helen Ingram, Covington, La.; 3 grandchildren. Ott-Laughlin Funeral Home, Winter Haven. *Orlando Sentinel* March 21, 1981

The author could find no photo of PRS agent Howard K. Norton-only his headstone and an article.

Memorandum to Mr. Rosen
RE: LEE HARVEY OSWALD

Item 61   Report of telephonic conversation from Inspector Kelley
in Dallas on 11/24/63 at 8:00 p.m. to Dale Wunderlich relating to
background on Ruth Paine as well as information from John Rice of
Secret Service in New Orleans, Louisiana, on the same date relating
to developments in that area. Report consists of two pages.

Item 62   One-page office memorandum from SA William H. Patterson of
Dallas dated 11/25/63 to the Chief of the U. S. Secret Service
relating to his conversation with an FBI Agent

12/23/63

AIRTEL   AIRMAIL

TO: DIRECTOR, FBI (105-82555),
        SAC, NEW ORLEANS (100-16601)

FROM: SAC, DALLAS (100-10461)

SUBJECT: LEE HARVEY OSWALD, aka:
          IS - R - CUBA

        Enclosed herewith for New Orleans is one copy of
two-page Secret Service memorandum reflecting "Rec'd
11-24-63 L. PM, By Dale Wunderlich", which contains
information from JOHN RICE, SAIC, Secret Service, New
Orleans, Louisiana. This document was furnished to the
Bureau, Washington, D.C. by Secret Service.

        The first paragraph contains information regarding
ELMO BEOPPLE, New Orleans PD, selling tires to a man
calling himself A. J. HIDELL, this being in December, 1962,
or January, 1963. Further, BEOPPLE later saw a picture
of OSWALD on T.V. handing out Fair Play for Cuba literature
and recognized him as HIDELL.

        New Orleans will interview BEOPPLE and resolve,
it being noted Dallas has no information indicating
OSWALD visited New Orleans in December, 1962, or
January, 1963.

3-Bureau
2-New Orleans (ENC. 1)
2-Dallas
REH:mia

Another interesting memo mentioning Dale Wunderlich.

PRS agent Dale Wunderlich:

Exhibit 5 1st   Commission No. 354

Form No. 1586 (Revised)
Memorandum Report
(7-1-60)

UNITED STATES SECRET SERVICE
TREASURY DEPARTMENT

ORIGIN Field	OFFICE Dallas, Texas	FILE NO. CO-2-34,030
TYPE OF CASE PRS	STATUS Continued	TITLE OR CAPTION Assassination of President Kennedy Lee Harvey Oswald
INVESTIGATION MADE AT Dallas, Texas	PERIOD COVERED 1-1/1-29-64	
INVESTIGATION MADE BY SA Roger C. Warner		

DETAILS

SYNOPSIS

Pierce Allman (person believed to be one mentioned by Lee Harvey Oswald as identifying himself as Secret Service Agent at Texas School Book Depository immediately following assassination) interviewed 1-29-64.

DETAILS OF INVESTIGATION

Reference is made to previous reports relative to Lee Harvey Oswald.

Other Investigations

On 11-22-63 the following was reported to SAIC Forrest V. Sorrels, by Captain Will Fritz, Dallas Police Department.

Lee Harvey Oswald in the first interview subsequent to his arrest, stated that as he was leaving the Texas School Book Depository Building, two men (one with a crew cut) had intercepted him at the front door; identified themselves as Secret Service Agents and asked for the location of a telephone.

On 1-1-64 Mr. Jack Brian, Detective, Dallas Police Department, stated that he had interrogated Mr. James Powell, Army Intelligence, who was trapped inside the Texas School Book Depository after the Depository doors had been sealed.

On 1-28-64 Mr. Powell was interviewed relative to his location at the time of the assassination and his actions subsequent to the assassination. Mr. Powell stated that he had been watching the parade from a position near the corner of Houston and Elm Streets, the site of the assassination. Mr. Powell stated further that he heard the shots and he then joined a group of Sheriff's Deputies who were heading toward the rear of the Texas School Book Depository on the basis of information that the assassin had shot from the railroad yards. Mr. Powell

DISTRIBUTION	COPIES	REPORT MADE BY	DATE
Chief	Orig & 2 cc	Roger C. Warner SPECIAL AGENT	2-3-64
Dallas	2 cc	APPROVED Forrest V. Sorrels SPECIAL AGENT IN CHARGE	2-3-64

(CONTINUE ON PLAIN PAPER)   U. S. GOVERNMENT PRINTING OFFICE   16-61423-1

James Powell, Army Intelligence: joined a group of Sheriff's Deputies toward the rear of the TSBD "on the basis of information that the assassin had shot from the railroad yards" Note the Secret Service agent responsible for this report: Roger Warner.

and anniversaries, too many holidays away from home."[102] (This means that despite several known plots to assassinate the president, the Secret Service nonetheless was permitting numbers of its experienced agents to leave the Detail. Shouldn't it have been obvious under the circumstances that allowing so many experienced agents to depart was unwise?). Based on years of intensive research, here are the experienced veteran agents who left in 1963:

---

102   *The Kennedy Detail* by Gerald Blaine, pages 19-20.

Tom Fridley, Bill Skiles, Scott Trundle, Milt Wilhite, Tom Behl, Charlie Kunkel (Summer 1963), Jimmy Johnson (Aug 1963), Ed Z. Tucker (Summer 1963), Jerry Dolan (Fall 1963), Bob Lilley (Fall 1963), Larry Newman (Oct 1963), Anthony Sherman, Jr. (Oct 1963), Thomas B. Shipman (DIED 10/14/63), and Ken Wiesman (10/23/63). The new agents were Robert L. Kollar, Robert R. Burke (Summer 1963), Radford Jones (Summer 1963), George W. Hickey (July 1963), Robert R. Faison (Sept 1963), William T. McIntyre (Fall 1963), Chuck Zboril (Fall 1963), Henry J. Rybka (Fall 1963), William Straughn (10/17/63), Bill Bacherman (11/10/63), Dick Metzinger (11/10/63), John J. McCarthy (11/10/63), Roy "Gene" Nunn (11/11/63), Gerald W. O'Rourke (11/11/63), Kent D. Jordan (11/15/63), Andrew M. Hutch (11/18/63), Ed Morey (11/20/63), Dale Keaner (11/23/63), Ken Thompson (11/23/63), Glenn Weaver (11/23/63) and Bill Livingood (11/23/63). Also, PRS agent Glen Bennett was made a temporary agent of the WHD on 11/10/63.[103]

An important note: "The [HSCA] did obtain evidence that military intelligence personnel may have identified themselves as Secret Service or that they might have been misidentified as such. [Colonel] Robert E. Jones … told the committee that from 8 to 12 military intelligence personnel in plainclothes were assigned to Dallas to provide supplemental security for the President's visit. He indicated that these agents had identification credentials and, if questioned, would most likely have stated that they were on detail to the Secret Service. The committee sought to identify these agents so that they could be questioned. The Department of Defense, however, reported that a search of its files showed "no records … indicating any Department of Defense Protective Services in Dallas. The committee was unable to resolve the contradiction."[104] Jones testified under oath to the HSCA: "Our people were under the control and supervision of Secret Service. We never assumed responsibility for the President's protection….We provided a small force – I do not recall how many, but I would estimate between 8 and 12 – during the President's visit to San Antonio, Texas, and then the following day, on his visit to Dallas, the regions also provided additional people to assist, that is additional people from Region 2…[James W. Powell] was a Captain and also wore civilian clothes and was assigned to Region 2 of the 112 MI Group…Yes he was [on duty the day of the assassination]…"[105]

103   *Who's Who in the Secret Service* by Vince Palamara (2018), pages 237-238.
104   HSCA Report, p 184.
105   Executive session testimony of Col. Robert E. Jones, 4/20/78, HSCA.

This is the same Robert E. Jones who contacted the FBI offices in San Antonio and Dallas and gave detailed information concerning Oswald and A. J. Hidell, Oswald's alleged alias, from the Army Intelligence files. The HSCA rightly felt this information suggested the existence of a military intelligence file on Oswald and raised the possibility that he had intelligence associations of some kind. Jones was directly responsible for counterintelligence operations, background investigations, domestic intelligence, and any special operations in a five-state area.[106] When the Oswald military intelligence file was requested by the HSCA, the Department of Defense relayed that they "destroyed the file as part of a general program aimed at eliminating all of its files pertaining to nonmilitary personnel."[107] James Powell told the ARRB on 4/12/96 that "…I asked for time off, a leave of absence from my regular duties so I could see the motorcade, so I could go out to the airport and see the president. And I was hoping to get a few pictures… [regarding later events in Dealey Plaza, during the assassination] When someone pointed up at the building and said they'd heard shots coming from up there, I wheeled around with my camera and took a picture of the building at that moment."[108] Like PRS Agent Glen Bennett, and the mysterious Mr. Norton, was Powell covertly monitoring a current threat or multiple threats to the president?

THE 76TH AIR TRANSPORT SQUADRON FROM CHARLESTON (S.C.) AIR FORCE BASE, which flew the C-130 transport plane carrying the presidential cars for trips involving President Kennedy, including the Texas trip, consisted of Captain Roland H. Thomason (the pilot),[109] Wayne E. Schake, Hershal R. Woosley, David J. Conn, Stephen A. Bening, Frank E. Roberson, and Vincent J. Gullo, Jr.[110] While two of the men I found (Schake and Woosley) did not respond to my letters, another of the crew I successfully found, Vincent Gullo, did. I wrote: "Sam [Kinney] told me that a) he found the piece of the right rear of President Kennedy's skull on the C-130 while en route back to Andrews Air Force Base after the tragedy and b) that one of you guys got sick from seeing the rear of

---

106   HSCA Report, pp. 221-222.

107   HSCA Report, p. 223; Letter from Department of Defense to House Select Committee on Assassinations, June 22, 1978, pg.6.

108   We can rule out Powell as the "agent" of unknown repute in the plaza: among other reasons, he had a camera, something not noted by any other witness re: the "agent" encounter(s).

109   18 H 730, CD 80, CD 3.

110   Via Sam Kinney and his copy of flight manifest---also found in CD 3 exhibits courtesy of the LBJ Library. This manifest was also referred to in George Hickey's report dated 11/30/63 (18 H 761, 764) but was not included in the volumes.

the limousine with all the blood and gore. Do you remember any of these specific events?" Gullo responded: "I am totally familiar with the facts as you outline them. This was a benchmark in my life and I have shared my thoughts on this incident with few individuals: mostly federal agents. I am sure you can understand my reluctance to entertain your questions given the sensitivity of the matter even to this date."[111] Gullo did not respond to my follow-up letter.

Lt. Col. George L. Whitmeyer, East Texas Section Commander of the Army Reserve, rode in the pilot car in motorcade.[112] "Whitmeyer was simply "along for the ride" with DPD Deputy Chief Lumpkin, who was an Army reserve officer and invited Whitmeyer, his Army advisor, to accompany him. Whitmeyer didn't have very much to say about the events in Dealey Plaza---mostly, he explained what he was doing there."[113] For his part, lead advance agent for Dallas, Winston Lawson, told the HSCA: "Mr. Lawson acknowledged that Lt. Col. George Whitmeyer, who was part of the Dallas District U.S. Army Command, who Lawson said "taught Army Intelligence" and who rode in the pilot car, "wasn't scheduled" to be in the motorcade. [as 17 H 615, Lawson's scheduled motorcade list, bears out]. Mr. Lawson denied that the presence of Col. Whitmeyer had anything to do with Lawson's prior service in the CIC." Whitmeyer's son, George Whitmeyer, Junior, told the author:" My father passed away in 1978 and therefore the answers to your questions are somewhat based on personal recollection of his information given to me. In regard to your first question, my father was invited by Col. George Lumpkin (ret.) (deceased) to ride in the point [sic] car of the motorcade. He was not a scheduled participant. I think that Col. Lumpkin was with the Dallas Police Department at the time. In regard to your second question, the point car in which my father was riding had already passed under the underpass and was turning onto Stemmons freeway when the assassination took place. They only saw the Presidential limousine speeding by on its way to Parkland Hospital. At that time, the car my father was in returned to downtown Dallas and to the area of the Texas School Book Depository. Therefore, he did not see or hear the actual assassination, nor did he go to Parkland Hospital."[114]

---

111   Gullo: 8/27/98 letter to Vince Palamara.
112   WC references: 4 H 170 (Curry: listed as him as "Wiedemeyer"); 21 H 578-579; 24 H 324 (Senkel's report); 24 H 326 (Turner's report). *Deep Politics and the Death of JFK* by Peter Dale Scott (1993), pp. 273-274. *Murder in Dealey Plaza* by James Fetzer (2000), pages 22, 30.
113   1970 interview with Larry Haapanen [3/9/94 letter from Haapanen to author].
114   9/28/98 letter from George Whitmeyer Jr. to Vince Palamara.

Michael Dorman of *Newsday* wrote an article entitled "JFK Plot Leads May Have Been Neglected" from 10/24/97, confirming Chief James Rowley's – and Inspector Thomas Kelley's – knowledge of several threats before 11/22/63. The article states: "In his testimony before the House Select Committee on Assassinations in 1978, James Rowley, Secret Service Chief in 1963, stated several leads to conspiracies to assassinate President Kennedy may not have been checked out. He stated the Secret Service had begun looking into several assassination plots, but stopped when President Johnson ordered the FBI to take over the investigation of the president's murder. The Secret Service was ordered to turn over all relevant information to the FBI. Rowley stated the FBI never informed the Secret Service of any of the leads it turned over. One lead was the Miami Secret Service Report on Joseph Milteer. Milteer, a right-wing activist, was taped by the Secret Service saying Kennedy would be assassinated with a rifle from a window in a downtown business district. Rowley was asked why Milteer was not put on constant surveillance. A reply to this was made by another Secret Service aid, Thomas Kelley. He replied that they didn't have enough manpower."

CHAPTER FIVE:

INTERLUDE – VERY INTERESTING
SECRET SERVICE AGENTS

Deputy Chief Paul J. Paterni, Chief Rowley's direct assistant, was a major behind-the-scenes player in the aftermath of the assassination. Paterni was a member of the OSS, the predecessor of the CIA, during WWII and served in Milan, Italy with fellow OSS men James Jesus Angleton, and Ray Rocca, later liaison to the Warren Commission.[115] Even more alarming is the fact that Chief Inspector Michael Torina wrote to the author stating the following: "Specifically, Paul Paterni (my very good friend) served [in the Secret Service] from late 1930's through mid-1960's."[116] This means that Paterni was a member of the OSS at the same time he was a member of the Secret Service. For his part, former Secret Service agent Rex Scouten wrote: "Paul Paterni was [my] mentor when I entered the Service in the Detroit field office (1948). I learned so very much from him. Paul was most famous for his OSS work during the war and his undercover work (counterfeiting) in New York City. Upon retirement he moved to Missoula, Montana. He died I think around 1980 [Feb. 1984]."[117] Paterni's plate was full in the immediate aftermath of the assassination:

> 1: While at his desk in the White House on 11/22/63, Paterni was asked by Chief James Rowley to arrange with the Immigration Service to close the border.[118]

> 2: He assigned Inspector Thomas Kelley to go to Dallas to speak to Lee Oswald. Kelley would not only end up talking to Oswald moments before Ruby silenced him forever, but would also end up, like Rocca, liaison to the Warren Commission (Kelley would also later

---

115   Julius Mader, *Who's Who in the CIA* (Berlin: Julius Mader, 1968); *Cloak and Gown*, p. 363; Burton Hersh, *The Old Boys: The American Elite and the Origins of the CIA* (New York: Scribner's, 1992), p. 182.

116   Letter to author 12/5/97.

117   Letter to author 5/28/98.

118   5 H 451; See also 3 HSCA 359, 390.

testify to the HSCA – this time as recently-retired Assistant Director).[119]

3: Paterni was involved with Boring in the critical limousine inspection at the White House garage the night of the assassination when skull fragments, bullet fragments, and vehicle damage were "noted" hours before the FBI would get their hands on the car. As we know, some skull fragments disappeared, many questions remain regarding the bullet fragments, and the limousine, which was reported to have had a hole in the windshield, was sent away to be rebuilt.[120] Apparently, Paterni and Boring beat Chief Rowley and Kellerman to the punch regarding overseeing this inspection.[121]

4: Paterni was involved in the investigation of Lee Harvey Oswald's income tax check on 11/22/63.[122]

5: Paterni was given all the information SAIC Forrest Sorrels of the Dallas office had on 11/22/63 regarding Lee Harvey Oswald and his interrogation.[123]

6: Paterni was also involved in the PRS (Protective Research Section) investigation of threats against JFK, which reported no activity in Dallas before the murder.[124]

7: Paterni checked on the CIA connections of assassination suspects Thomas Mosely and Homer Echevarria for the Chicago field office. He had also served in the Chicago office as SAIC in the 1950's.[125] In a possible connection, assassination suspect and Oswald associate W. Guy Bannister had been the SAIC of the Chicago FBI office during the 1950's.[126] The Mosely-Echevarria matter was then unexpectedly dropped by Paterni's headquarters: The field office agents, Joseph Noonan and Ed Tucker, both former White House Detail agents,

---

119   3HSCA357, 454 (referring Kelley's 6/1/64 Affidavit to the Warren Commission).
120   CD 80, pp.2-3 (see also HSCA RIF# 180-10102-10212: 3-page chronology of the presidential limousine); 1/6/64 letter from Chief James J. Rowley to the Warren Commission's J. Lee Rankin re: the presidential limousine; 5H67; 7H354, 403; 13H65; see also *The Day Kennedy Was Shot* by Jim Bishop, pp.511-512, 546, 637; *Best Evidence* by David Lifton, p. 359.
121   Manchester, p. 390. 8/24-8/25/77 HSCA interview of Roy Kellerman.
122   Jerry Rose, "The Feds Spring Into Action," *The Fourth Decade*, May 1996; as Rose states, "Why [was] Deputy Chief Paterni [willing to] indulge [Sorrels] in this curiosity?"
123   7 H 354.
124   3HSCA340.
125   R.I.F. #180-10074-10079: 8/8/78 HSCA interview of Lem Johns. Johns had worked under Paterni from 1957-1959.
126   See, for example, *Oswald and the CIA* by John Newman (1995) pp. 289-290.

Paterni as he appeared on the game show What's My Line 12/8/62.

were to send all memos, files, and notebooks to Washington and not discuss the case with anyone.[127]

Paterni was a leading candidate to become the Chief of the Secret Service after the first Chief under JFK, U.E. Baughman, was "retired." What's more, Paterni was the agent in charge of the Secret Service Chicago office in the 1950's. Guy Banister was the agent in charge of the FBI Chicago office in the 1950's.

Interestingly, Jackson N. Krill, former OSS, Naval Intelligence, and top-ranking JFK/LBJ era Secret Service official (and who was also a Chief Inspector like Michael Torina), was the man who debriefed the agents after the assassination, basically ad-

Secret Service chief resigns

WASHINGTON (UPI) — U. E. Baughman, chief of the U.S. Secret Service since 1948, submitted his resignation today effective Aug. 31.

Treasury Secretary Douglas Dillon accepted "with genuine regret" Baughman's decision to retire after 33 years service.

The Secret Service is responsible for guarding the life of the President and his family. Its major assignment is to stamp out counterfeiting of U.S. currency and coins.

There was no announcement of Baughman's successor. But Treasury sources said the job may go to Paul J. Paterni, deputy chief who was transferred to Washington less than a year ago. He previously headed the agency's Chicago office.

---

127   R.I.F.#180-10104-10331; R.I.F. #180-10087-10137; 3 HSCA 371, 372-379, 383-389.

vising them not to talk.[128] Secret Service agent Robert Jamison admitted during his 2/28/1978 HSCA interview that he was debriefed by Chief Inspector Jackson Krill to not discuss the internal operations of the Secret Service.

Forrest Sorrels, the Special Agent in Charge of the Dallas Secret Service field office, took part in the planning of the motorcade for President Roosevelt in 1936 that took the presidential party in a motorcade through Dallas and Main Street (instead of via Houston and Elm). Sorrels testified to the Warren Commission: "Main Street is right through the heart of the city. It is the best choice for parades. It gives an opportunity for more people – tall buildings on the side of the street – and it is almost invariably – every parade that is had is on Main Street. The one in 1936, when President Roosevelt was there, was the same route in reverse, so to speak."[129]

From an FBI report dated 11/27/63: "At approximately 10:30 p.m. today a telephone call was received from a female individual who refused to furnish her identity. She advised she is a member of the local theatre guild and that on numerous occasions she has attended functions or speeches where Mr. Sorrels, Head of the Secret Service, Dallas, has spoken. She maintained that Mr. Sorrels should be removed from his position as he was incompetent and did not have the ability to protect the president. She stated he was definitely anti-government, against the Kennedy administration, and she felt his position was against the security of not only the President but the United States. During the time this individual furnished the information set out above an effort was made to determine her name and address however she declined." [Signed] Inspector Tom Kelley Secret Service 9:20 a.m. 12/2/63." Here is the 2-page doc on the next page: [130]

Secret Service agent James "Mike" Mastrovito retired in 2004 after a career of some 50 years in law enforcement and intelligence, as an employee of the FBI from June 1958 until June 1959; U.S. Secret Service from July 1959 until July 1979. At the time of his retirement from Secret Service he was special agent in charge of the Intelligence Division at Secret Service Headquarters in Washington, DC. He had served in this Division

128   For example, see 2/28/78 HSCA interview of Agent Robert Jamison. Krill had been in the Kansas City, MO office and was close to President Truman's brother: Rowley Oral History, Truman Library, p. 31.
129   7 H 337.
130   FBI RIF#124-10164-10019.

URGENT 12-2-63   12-37 PM CST EEA
TO DIRECTOR
FROM SAC, DALLAS /89-43
ASSASSINATION OF PRES. KENNEDY, AFO:
INFORMATION HAS BEEN RECEIVED BY DALLAS OFFICE IN THREE
SEPARATE TELEPHONE CALLS, ALL FROM ANONYMOUS FEMALE, INDICATING
THAT CALLER THOUGHT FORREST SORRELS, DALLAS HEAD OF SECRET SERVICE,
SHOULD BE INVESTIGATED. IN FIRST CALL, CALLER STATED SHE IS A
MEMBER OF THE LOCAL THEATER GUILD AND ON NUMEROUS OCCASIONS HAS
ATTENDED FUNCTIONS OR SPEECHES WHERE SORRELS HAD SPOKEN. SHE
MAINTAINS SORRELS SHOULD BE REMOVED FROM HIS POSITION AS HE IS
INCOMPETENT AND DID NOT HAVE THE ABILITY TO PROTECT THE PRESIDENT.
SHE STATED HE WAS ANTI GOVERNMENT, AGAINST THE KENNEDY ADMINISTRATION
AND SHE FELT HIS POSITION WAS AGAINST THE SECURITY OF NOT ONLY
THE PRESIDENT, BUT THE U. S. SHE REFUSED TO FURNISH HER IDENTITY
OR HER ADDRESS.
        ADDITIONAL CALL RECEIVED FROM ANONYMOUS FEMALE, STATING
THAT SORRELS SHOULD NEVER HAVE BEEN PERMITTED TO HAVE THE RESPONSI-
BILITY FOR THE SAFETY OF THE PRESIDENT. THE CALLER COMMENTED THAT
SORRELS WAS ANTI GOVERNMENT, FREQUENTLY MADE REMARKS THAT HE DID
NOT BELIEVE IN ALL THE POLICIES OF THE GOVERNMENT AND HE SHOULD

PAGE TWO
BE INVESTIGATED.
        THE THIRD ANONYMOUS CALL STATED THAT SORRELS SHOULD
BE CHECKED ON. THE CALLER STATED SHE WAS A MEMBER AT ONE TIME
OF THE LEAGUE FOR WOMEN VOTERS, AS WAS THE WIFE OF SORRELS. SHE
CLAIMED MRS. SORRELS, WHEN TAKING HER TURN TO MAKE A BOOK REVIEW,
DID NOT MAKE A BOOK REVIEW AS MOST OF THE MEMBERS DID, BUT INSTEAD
GAVE A REPORT ON OVERTHROWING THE GOVERNMENT. THE CALLER STATED
ON THIS BASIS, SHE THOUGHT MR. SORRELS ACTIVITIES SHOULD BE
CHECKED INTO.
        THE LAST TWO CALLS WERE RECEIVED IN THE DALLAS OFFICE BY
THE SAME AGENT AND THE AGENT IS OF THE OPINION THE SAME WOMAN
WAS CALLING ON BOTH OCCASIONS. IN ALL THREE INSTANCES, THE CALLER
APPEARED TO BE AN INTELLIGENT PERSON AND WAS WELL SPOKEN AT THE
TIME SHE CALLED.
        INFORMATION CONCERNING THE THREE ANONYMOUS TELEPHONE
CALLS RELATIVE TO SORRELS HAS BEEN FURNISHED TO INSPECTOR TOM
KELLEY, SECRET SERVICE OF WASH., WHO IS PRESENTLY IN DALLAS.
END ACK FOR TWO MESSAGES PLS

CC Mr Sullivan
ACK YOUR TWO MSG 1-44 PM OK FBI WA   LA
TU CLEAR

MIKE MASTROVITO

Secret Service (and later CIA) agent James "Mike" Mastrovito.

continuously since 1964. He retired again in 2004 after working as an independent contractor with the CIA and had resided in foreign countries for 20 years prior to his 2004 retirement.131 He became a Deputy in the Intelligence Division (formerly Protective Research Section PRS) for 10 years before becoming the director of the Intelligence Division a few years before he retired from the Secret Service. When Mastrovito took charge of the JFK Assassination file, it consisted of 5 or 6 file cabinets of material. After Mastrovito finished "culling" irrelevant material, the collection was down to one five-draw file cabinet. Mastrovito guessed that his purging of extraneous material took place around 1970. He said that the extraneous material consisted of records of 2000-3000 "mental cases" who called the Secret Service after the Kennedy assassination to claim responsibility for the shooting. Mastrovito offered that Robert Blakey questioned him about this destruction of documents and threatened legal action.

From Mastrovito's ARRB interview: "I asked Mastrovito if he had viewed or obtained any artifacts while he was in charge of the assassination file. Mastrovito replied that he had received a piece of President Kennedy's brain. Mastrovito offered that this item was contained in a vial with a label on it identifying its contents. The vial was the size of a prescription bottle. Mastrovito did not remember if it was glass or plastic. The vial was from the Air Force [sic] Institute of Pathology. [Armed Forces Institute of Pathology] Mastrovito said this vial from the AFIP lab came into his possession "about 3 or 4 years later." i.e. after the assassination. (Later Mastrovito said it was about "1969 or 1970") The label said the vial had been sent from the autopsy at Bethesda; there was no other explanation with it. Mastrovito said he could not see what was special about the portion in the vial. I asked Mastrovito who gave him the vial, and he replied that his supervisor, Walter Young (first Chief of the Intelligence Division), gave it to him when he (Young) resigned from the Secret Service. Young had apparently received it from someone at AFIP. Mastrovito offered that Walter Young died last year. Mastrovito said he destroyed the vial and its contents in a machine that de-

---

131   *Who's Who in the Secret Service* by Vince Palamara (2018), page 85.

stroys food." Mastrovito later commented: "I have been asked several times about my decision to destroy the piece of the President's brain. I make no apologies for this decision. In view of what is being offered for sale on e-Bay these days, I believe I made the correct one."[132]

Secret Service agent Roger C. Warner served in the Secret Service and the CIA, as well as serving in the U.S. Army briefly. A 1957 MSU graduate, Warner served three years for the US Bureau of Narcotics, 20 years in the Secret Service, and 12 years in the CIA.1 Warner was an agent on the Texas trip when JFK was assassinated. It was his very first presidential protective assignment.133

Secret Service (and later CIA) agent Roger Warner.

Warner later accompanied Robert Oswald to his brother's funeral.134 In addition, according to fellow agent Jim Hardin, Warner served on the Treasury Secretary John Connally detail (Connally, a victim of the shooting that day in Dallas, went on to become the boss of the Secret Service during the Nixon era). Warner also served in the Washington, D.C. (as a supervisor) and Jacksonville, Florida field offices. He also served on Vice President Hubert Humphrey's detail (with fellow agents Walt Coughlin, Glen Weaver and others).

Secret Service agent Andy Berger reported CIA presence at Parkland Hospital on 11/22/63:

> Berger reported meeting the following persons at Parkland Hospital shortly after the assassination:
>
> 1. FBI agent Vincent Drain (sent via Hoover); the same agent who would go on to accompany Agent Lawson during the transfer of critical assassination evidence later that weekend.
>
> 2. "A doctor friend of Drain's." This unidentified doctor came with the FBI agent.
>
> 3. An "unidentified CIA agent" who had credentials. Like the FBI man sent by Hoover, how could the CIA agent get to the Dallas hospital so soon after the murder?[135]

---

132   ibid, page 87.
133   Roger Warner, Facebook profile; HSCA interview with Roger Warner, 5/25/78 [RIF# 180-10093-10026].
134   *Four Days in November* (2008) by Vince Bugliosi, page 508.
135   See also *Breaking the Silence* by Bill Sloan (1993), pp. 181-185, *The Man Who Knew Too Much* by Dick Russell (1992), pp. 570-571, and *Who's Who in the JFK Assassination* by Michael Benson (1993), pp. 40-41.

4. An "unidentified FBI agent" who did not have credentials.[136] Berger's report was totally ignored by just about everyone.[137]

Two candidates emerge as the CIA agent: Hugh Huggins a.k.a. Hugh Howell and William Bishop. For his part, Huggins/Howell told author Bill Sloan that he was at both Parkland Hospital and Bethesda. "I talked to some of the doctors and nurses at Parkland, and I talked to Phyllis Bartlett, the chief telephone operator at the hospital, about a call she had allegedly received from Lyndon Johnson while Oswald was in surgery after being shot by Ruby... Bartlett confirmed hat she'd spoken to a man with a loud voice who identified himself as Johnson."[138] Sloan further reported: "Ms. Bartlett... recalled conversing at the time of the assassination with a man fitting Hugh Howell's description. "My little office was overflowing with as many as fifty people at once back then," she said, "but I do remember talking to a short man with a crewcut who identified himself in that capacity [CIA], and I do believe he said his name was Howell."[139]

"Over at Dallas' Parkland Hospital... another military man was standing in the doorway to Trauma Room 1. This was Colonel William Bishop, who had been working for months with the anti-Castro Cuban exiles on behalf of the CIA. "I had been in Palm Beach at the Berkeley Hotel," Bishop told [author Dick Russell] in 1990, "when I received a phone call telling me to be in Dallas on the morning of November 21. I wasn't the only Army officer called, that's all I can say about that. I was flown to Dallas by military aircraft and checked into a Holiday Inn, at which time I received instructions that I was to make sure the press had proper credentials at the Trade Mart when Kennedy came to speak the next afternoon. I was in position and waiting for his arrival, when I heard over a

Secret Service agent Berger.

136   The FBI Agent turned out to be J. Doyle Williams [see *Reasonable Doubt* by Henry Hurt (1985), pp. 71-72 (based on Feb. 1983 interview); see also 18 H 795-796 (Berger), 798-799 (Johnsen); 21 H 261 (Price); RIF#18010082-10454: 1/31/78 HSCA interview of SS agent Tim McIntyre; Also: *Bloody Treason* by Noel Twyman (1997), pp. 90, 91, 93, 96, and 110; 5 H 132, 144; 18 H 96 and *Pictures Of The Pain* by Richard Trask (1994), p. 105: photo of Williams; 22 H 841, 910; 23 H 681; 24 H 523; *No More Silence* by Larry Sneed (1998), pp. 130 and 164.

137   18 H 795.

138   1993 interview (s) with Bill Sloan for *JFK: Breaking the Silence* (1993), Chapter 9, pp. 175-189 [Includes photo of Huggins circa 1962].

139   March 1993 interview with Bill Sloan for *JFK: Breaking the Silence*, p. 185.

squad car parked at the curb that shots had been fired in Dealey Plaza. I commandeered a police car and ordered the driver to take me directly to Parkland Hospital. With the ID I had, that was not a problem. There the Secret Service instructed me to secure the area outside the Trauma Room and make myself available to the First Lady or medical staff."[140]

Gerald Blaine writes on page 233 of his book *The Kennedy Detail*, with regard to Parkland Hospital: "A representative of the CIA appeared a while later." The importance of this is left unstated.

The world at large would not even know of former agent Thomas B. Shipman if not for my early reporting in 1997, my first book *Survivor's Guilt*, my third book *The Not-So-Secret Service*, and my fourth book *Who's Who in the Secret Service*. "October 14, 1963: Died of a heart attack while on a presidential protective assignment at Camp David, Maryland": so reads the official "obituary" for the former agent at the Association of Former Agents of the United States Secret Service (AFAUSSS) website. Out of literally thousands of former agents, officials and personnel who have come and gone from the agency since 1865, only 37 unfortunate souls have passed away in the line of duty … and the only one from the JFK era-and who died at Camp David, of all places – was Shipman. Shipman was one of

Secret Service Agent Dies Of Heart Attack

Was Assigned To Protect JFK

THURMONT, Md. (AP)—Thomas Shipman, 51, one of President Kennedy's Secret Service drivers, died Monday at the presidential retreat at nearby Camp David.

The cause of death was not immediately determined pending a coroner's report.

Shipman, a native of Washington, D.C., was a District of Columbia policeman from 1936 until 1950 when he transferred to the White House police force. He became a Secret Service agent in 1954.

Shipman normally drove the carload of Secret Service agents who follow directly behind the President.

He is survived by his widow.

The Cumberland News (Cumberland, Maryland)
18 Oct 1963, Tue · Page 6

Secret Service agent driver Thomas B. Shipman- the only Kennedy Detail agent to die at the time of Kennedy's presidency and the only person to die at Camp David.

140   5/8/90 interview of Colonel William C. Bishop [deceased 7/92], CIA contract agent, by Dick Russell for *The Man Who Knew Too Much*, numerous--see esp. pages 570-571 [see also *Who's Who in the JFK Assassination* by Michael Benson (1993), pp. 40-41].

President Kennedy's driver agents and one cannot help sincerely wondering if destiny and fate would have been much better for JFK had Shipman, and not William Greer, taken the wheel of the limousine on 11/22/63. Apparently, I am not the only one pondering this situation. Many fellow authors and researchers, as well as Shipman's surviving family, also wonder about this.

Captain Michael D. Groves, MDW Honor Guard, 27 years old (deceased 12/3/63): "Captain Groves, who commanded the JFK Honor Guard for Kennedy's funeral, died under mysterious circumstances seven days after the funeral. While eating dinner, he took a bite of food, paused briefly as a pained look came over his face, then passed out and fell face down into his plate. He died instantly. On December 12th, his possessions and mementos---which had been sent home to Birmingham, Michigan---were destroyed in a fire of mysterious origin. The Honor Guard, for some mysterious reason, had been practicing for a presidential funeral for three days before the assassination. Captain Groves was 27 years old at the time of this death. Cause of death: Unknown. Possibly poison."[141]

From an internet SSN Death listing: Name- MICHAEL GROVES. Born- 19 Aug 1936 Died- Dec 3, 1963. Residence- (No Location Given). Last Benefit- (No Location Given). SSN: ###-##-8313. Issued- (Between 1953 and 1954).

Secret Service agent Elmer Moore should be viewed with deep suspicion. Moore, who told reporter Earl Golz that he was in San Francisco on 11/22/63[142], played a crucial and completely overlooked part in various aspects of the case:

1. Moore guarded Chief Justice Earl Warren.[143]

2. As author David Scheim duly noted,[144] Moore was involved in Jack Ruby's canned alibi: Ruby said, "Does this conflict with my story and yours in great length?" Moore replied, "Substantially the

141   *JFK: The Dead Witnesses* by Craig Roberts and John Armstrong (1995), p. 3. See also *The Death of a President* by William Manchester, p. 638, and *Killing The Truth* by Harrison Livingstone (1993), page 742.
142   *Dallas Morning News*, 8/27/78. That said, according to a Secret Service Memorandum, 8/10/64 Sorrels to Kelley, Moore was temporarily assigned to Dallas from San Francisco, CA office of the Secret Service from 11/30-12/13/63 (14 days) to investigate the JFK assassination. Interestingly, as mentioned above, Deputy Chief Paul Paterni was the SAIC of the San Francisco office during part of the Truman and Eisenhower era.
143   *20 Years in the Secret Service* by Rufus Youngblood, p. 170. *JFK Revisited* by James DiEugenio (and the documentary with the same name), 325.
144   *Contract on America* by David Scheim (1991), pp.186-189, 290, 570.

same, Jack, as well as I remember." Ruby goes on to state, "I may have left out a few things. Mr. Moore remembers probably more ..."[145]

3. On 12/4/63, Moore questions Ruby "regarding his whereabouts and movements" on 11/21/63, the day before the assassination.[146]

4. On 12/3/63, Moore interviews Ruby's roommate, George Senator.[147]

5. Secret Service Report 491: On 12/2-12/5/63, Moore, along with fellow agents Arthur Blake & William Carter, began a series of interviews with the employees of the Texas School Book Depository over a four-day period. Three of the witnesses interviewed, Harold Norman, Bonnie Ray Williams, and Charles Givens, gave totally new evidence to Moore and company that conflicted dramatically with earlier statements made by each of them to the FBI. As Patricia Lambert put it, these new stories "ultimately influenced the Warren Commission's reconstruction of events in Dallas on November 22, 1963."[148] Even the Warren Commission's star witness, Howard Brennan, was influenced by contact with the Secret Service. On the night of the assassination, Brennan could not identify Oswald in a police lineup as the man he claimed to have seen in the sixth-floor window of the Texas School Book Depository.[149] Several days later, Brennan was visited by a Secret Service agent who asked him, "You said you couldn't make a positive identification.... Did you do that for security reasons personally or couldn't you?"[150] Brennan apparently took the hint, and when the FBI visited him about two weeks later on 12/17/63, Brennan told them, "He was sure that the person firing the rifle was Oswald."[151]

6. Parkland doctors: On or around 12/11/63, Moore and another agent, Roger C. Warner, interviewed the Dallas physicians who treated JFK.[152] As the 12/18/63 St. Louis Post-Dispatch wrote, "Secret Service gets revision of Kennedy wound – after visit by agents, doctors say shot was from rear. [The Secret Service] obtained a re-

145   5 H 185, 194, 207 – Ruby's complete testimony can be found 5H 181-213.
146   CE2399; *Contract on America* by David Scheim (1991), p. 290.
147   23 H 459-461; see also Seth Kantor's *The Ruby Cover-up* (1992), p. 121.
148   Lengthy article by Patricia (Billings) Lambert written in the late 1970's obtained via Jim Lesar & the AARC.
149   WR145; 24 H 203; 3 H 148.
150   3 H 148.
151   WR 145.
152   See *Murder in Dealey Plaza*, pp. 115, 165, 256, and especially 272. See also *JFK Revisited* by James DiEugenio (and the documentary with the same name), pages 42, 123-124, 321-326. *Burying the Lead: The Media and the JFK Assassination* by Mel Hyman (2019), pages 91, 361.

versal of their original view that the bullet in his neck entered from the front. The investigators did so by showing the surgeons a document described as an autopsy report from the United States Naval Hospital at Bethesda. The surgeons changed their original view to conform with the report they were shown."[153]

7. Moore told graduate student James Gouchenaur that he "felt remorse for the way he (Moore) had badgered Dr. Malcolm Perry into changing his testimony to the effect that there was not, after all, an entrance wound in the front of the president's neck."[154] Furthermore, Gouchenaur quoted Moore as saying that Kennedy was a traitor for giving things away to the Russians; that it was a shame people had to die, but maybe it was a good thing; that the Secret Service personnel had to go along with the way the assassination was being investigated: "I did everything I was told, we all did everything we were told, or we'd get our heads cut off."[155]

8. According to Gouchenaur, Moore was the "liaison between the staff of the Warren Commission and the Secret Service.[156] As Chief Justice Earl Warren himself said to Jack Ruby, "You know that Mr. Moore is a member of the Secret Service, and he has been a liaison officer with our staff since the Commission was formed."[157]

9. *Dallas Morning News* reporter Earl Golz wrote, "All but one of Sorrels' six Dallas agents in 1963 submitted reports of their whereabouts the day of the assassination: Elmer Moore, the agent who did not submit a report, said he was in San Francisco and did not return to Dallas to join the investigation until a week later."[158] That said, two other agents from the Dallas office, Mike Howard and the late

---

153   See also 2 H 39, 41; *Best Evidence*, pp. 156,166-167, 196, & 286.

154   HSCA 6/1/77 interview transcript RIF#180-10109-10310; See also CD 379; 3 H 363, 364, 387; 6 H 6,7, 17, 27, 44, 50-51, 57,63, & 75. *JFK Revisited* by James DiEugenio (and the documentary with the same name), page 431.

155   During the ARRB's 9/18/96 interview of Floyd Boring, the agent said:" … Mr. Boring was asked whether he was acquainted with SA Elmer Moore, and he indicated that he knew him quite well, and said he was still living in Seattle. Mr. Boring was asked to read and comment on several pages of the HSCA 6/1/77 interview transcript of its interview with former graduate student James Gouchenaur, in which Gochenaur recounted a very long conversation he reportedly had with SA Elmer Moore in 1970 … Mr. Boring said that it would be just like SA Moore to give such a lengthy interview, but that he doubted very much whether agent Moore had really said those things, since he himself had never heard agent Moore say anything like that, nor had he heard any other Secret Service agents say anything like that." *JFK Revisited* by James DiEugenio (and the documentary with the same name), pages 42, 204-205, 323-329.

156   HSCA 6/1/77 interview transcript RIF#180-10109-10310.

157   5 H 210.

158   *Dallas Morning News*, 8/27/78 and Golz notes, AARC.

Charles Kunkel (deceased 6/27/92[159]), also did not submit reports. Howard claimed in a lecture in February 1999 that he was at the Hotel Texas cleaning up when the shooting occurred and that Kunkel was in Washington, D.C on an unspecified investigation at the time. Howard and Kunkel's whereabouts remain unverified.

Name ___ Elmer Moore ___   Telephone ___

Address ___ Bellevue, Washington ___

Type of Contact: X Telephone
                  ___ Person

II. Summary of Contact:

On this date, Elmer Moore, former Secret Service agent temporarily assigned to Dallas following the Kennedy assassination, called to ask why the Committee was interested in him. He said that the Sweiker Com. had already questioned him twice and he had nothing more to say. In fact, he would refuse to answer questions about matters he was already questioned about. He stated that Sweiker's Com. was a waste of tax payers money and that a young lawyer on that Com. had been ready to send him to jail for perjury when Moore had stated he could not remember all the details from several years back. If we want to recontact him, he can be reached at the above number.

III. Recommended Follow-up (if any):
      Interview with kid gloves. or boxing

Moore's refusal to cooperate with the HSCA and the funny note at the bottom ("or boxing").

Secret Service agent Elmer Moore.

Secret Service agent Emory Roberts, while still a member of the agency, also worked for LBJ as his appointment secretary! This was unprecedented and disturbing, to say the least. Roberts, commander of the agents in the follow-up car on 11/22/63, did nothing to protect Kennedy and actually ordered the agents not to move when the shooting began. Roberts had also recalled agents Henry Rybka and Don Lawton away from the presidential limo at Love Field.[160]

White House Is Mum
On LBJ Staff Changes

WASHINGTON (AP) — The White House Wednesday clamped a secrecy lid for the time being on changes in President Johnson's staff, expanding an earlier bar to the disclosure of staff salaries.

The question of the current composition of Johnson's official family came up after a veteran Secret Service agent, Emory Roberts, was seen performing the receptionist chores formerly carried out by David F. Powers, who was a close friend of the late President John F. Kennedy.

Asked about Roberts' day-long appearance at the receptionist's desk in the White House lobby, Press Secretary George E. Reedy said the presidential body guard was carrying out his regular assignment as a Secret Service agent. Reedy referred vaguely to Roberts' checking the passes of people passing through the lobby. Reporters

observed no pass-checking by Roberts, but did see him greeting Japanese Prime Minister Eisaku Sato, and other visitors.

UN Dues Is Rising

UNITED NATIONS, N.Y. (AP) — Secretary-General U Thant conferred separately Wednesday with the chief delegates of the United States and the Soviet Union but apparently failed to make any progress in resolving the crisis over U.N. peacekeeping debts.

Thant met first with U.S. Ambassador Adlai E. Stevenson and then with Soviet Ambassador Nikolai T. Fedorenko.

'RECEPTIONIST'

President Johnson's White House staff, still undergoing a shakedown, has acquired a Secret Service agent to serve as a "receptionist."

Emory Roberts, 50, who has been with the service for 21 years, sat down Wednesday at the big reception desk in the lobby of the west wing which official greeter David Powers has occupied since 1961.

EMORY ROBERTS

them, too.

To you, and Emory Roberts, who I am sorry can't be here today—he greets me every morning and tells me goodby every night—

LBJ said this about Roberts on 11/23/68.

Dallas Secret Service agent Robert Steuart, Special Agent in Charge Forrest Sorrels assistant: He had dangerous knowledge- the statements of former Dallas agent Robert A. Steuart, as revealed in Bill Sloan's 1993 work,

---

160   See *A Coup in Camelot* DVD/ Blu Ray and the author's prior books.

JFK: Breaking the Silence, are short but quite amazing.[161] Although the agent who spoke to Sloan was unnamed in the book, Sloan confirmed to this author the agent's identity based on the firm conviction that this agent had to have been Steuart. Why? Because, as the author told Sloan, the agent used identical phrases during two interviews with Steuart conducted in 1992 and 1993. In any event, Sloan did indeed confirm the author's suspicions. So, just what did Steuart say to Sloan? Sworn to absolute secrecy about the "Kennedy thing," Steuart went on to say, "I can't talk about it. There are so many things I could tell you, but I just can't. I can't tell you anything. I'd like to, but I can't. It was a very heavy deal, and they would know. Someone would know. It's … too dangerous, even now." This from a local agent, stationed at the Trade Mart on November 22, 1963.

Dallas Secret Service agent Robert Steuart.

From Bill Sloan's 1993 book *JFK: Breaking the Silence* – When I first read this, I was stunned … not just by the content, but because it was so familiar to me. As I noted in my first book, although Sloan did not identify WHO the agent was, I was convinced, based on my 1992 and 1993 conversations, that the agent had to be Robert Steuart, SAIC Forrest Sorrels' assistant in the Dallas office. When I wrote Sloan, he confirmed that I was correct!

---

161   *Breaking the Silence* by Bill Sloan (1993), pp. 1-5.

Introduction

A Mystery Frozen in Time

To the casual observer, he was just another slowly fading old man in his middle 80s, frail and gentlemanly and unassuming, and all he asked of life was to be allowed to dig quietly in the garden behind his new duplex and be left alone.

Perhaps it was a lot to ask, under the circumstances, but he and his wife deserved that much, he thought. They had kept the faith. They had given up the stately house in an exclusive Dallas suburb where they had lived for many years. They had sold off the bulk of their treasured possessions in order to fit into the duplex, and now they deserved to be left in peace to finish out their years.

But there was a lurking problem that kept getting in the way. Although the old man had been retired for more than two decades, people somehow kept finding out that he had been a Secret Service agent stationed in Dallas on November 22, 1963, and they kept wanting to find out what he knew about it. They kept wanting to ask questions—questions that he couldn't bring himself to face, much less to answer.

His response to their inquiries was inevitably the same.

"I can't talk about it," he would say. "There are so many things I could tell you, but I just can't."

Along with all the others who had been there and survived to retire from the Service, he said he had been sworn to absolute secrecy about the "Kennedy thing," as they called it. Those in the Service didn't even discuss it among themselves, and he had been told that he was never, ever to talk about it with anyone on the outside. They had made that abundantly clear to him. It was a pledge he had felt he had to make in return for his retirement.

So it gave him a queasy feeling in his stomach the day the writer called. The old man's digestion wasn't that good anymore anyway, and when the writer called, the old man thought for all the world that he was going to be sick.

"I can't tell you anything," he said mildly, trying to control the slight tremor in his voice. "I'd like to, but I can't."

"Not even if I give you my solemn word that I'll never betray your confidence?" the writer pressed. "Not even if I promise I'll never reveal the source of the information to anyone?"

"No, no, I can't. I'm sorry but it's absolutely impossible. It was a very heavy deal, and they would know. Someone would know. It's . . . it's too dangerous, even now."

"Are you actually apprehensive about discussing it? I mean even after all this time?"

"Please. I simply can't say anything. That's all."

And the writer could only wonder why. Why, after close to three decades, is the murder of the thirty-fifth president of the United States still a forbidden subject among those sworn to protect him?

Why? For God's sake, why?

130

Steuart served 32 years with the Secret Service and retired in 1965. Unfortunately, the lengthy conversation I had with him on 10/22/92 never went past human-interest topics, Presidents the agent served, including his fondness for Truman ("A good Democrat") and how some of the agents were crying out at the Trade Mart when they heard the news of JFK's death. Steuart did not want to be quoted about 11/22/63 in any detail. The author attempted to elicit more information from Steuart on 9/21/93 but was unsuccessful. Steuart is the leading candidate for the agent who, as Presidential Aide Ken O'Donnell confided in Jerry Bruno, was the unnamed local Dallas agent who told SAIC Behn that they felt they now could protect JFK at the Trade Mart after all, despite the agency's prior reservations. Steuart was the other Dallas agent who checked out the Trade Mart with SAIC Sorrels. The HSCA rightly stated, "if any local agent did in fact make such recommendations despite Behn's prior decision on November 6 favoring the Women's Building, this would have presented a clear case of a subordinate agent contradicting the SAIC of the WHD."[162]

The *News and Courier* (Charleston, SC 1/30/69) – Assistant Special Agent in Charge Roy Kellerman, who rode in the front passenger seat of the presidential limousine on 11/22/63, later became an FBI agent and was ordered by a judge to testify in the Jim Garrison trial (he ended up not testifying).

Serving as both her interpreters and her captors, Secret Service agents Mike Howard and Charles Kunkel threatened Marina with deportation in subtle (and not-so-subtle) ways if she didn't tow the "official" line that her husband, Lee Harvey Oswald, was the lone-nut assassin of JFK. The *New York Times* of 12/8/63 reported, Secret Service agents suggested to her that it might be safer and easier for her to return to the Soviet Union than to try to live in the United States. This distressed her.... She is now secluded from Oswald's relatives as well as from the public. While Marina originally denied that Oswald had

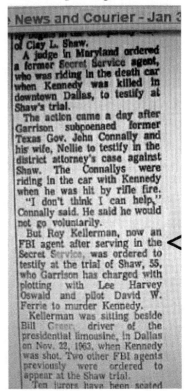

News and Courier – Jan 3

of Clay L. Shaw.
A judge in Maryland ordered a former Secret Service agent, who was riding in the death car when Kennedy was killed in downtown Dallas, to testify at Shaw's trial.
The action came a day after Garrison subpoenaed former Texas Gov. John Connally and his wife, Nellie to testify in the district attorney's case against Shaw. The Connallys were riding in the car with Kennedy when he was hit by rifle fire.
"I don't think I can help," Connally said. He said he would not go voluntarily.
But Roy Kellerman, now an FBI agent after serving in the Secret Service, was ordered to testify at the trial of Shaw, 55, who Garrison has charged with plotting with Lee Harvey Oswald and pilot David W. Ferrie to murder Kennedy.
Kellerman was sitting beside Bill Greer, driver of the presidential limousine, in Dallas on Nov. 22, 1963, when Kennedy was shot. Two other FBI agents previously were ordered to appear at the Shaw trial.
Ten jurors have been seated

The Evening Independent - Apr 2, 1981   Browse this newspaper »   Browse all newspapers »

Assassination Try Stirs Former Agent's Memories

Jimmy Mann is a free-lance writer living in St. Petersburg. My View columnists, invited by editors to contribute regularly, write on subjects of their choice.

JIMMY MANN

Well, it is full circle for Roy Kellerman again

Sometimes the events of that November afternoon in Dallas, Texas in 1963 fade slightly; other times they lean hard on the spirit.

On Monday, March 30, 1981, while living in retirement in the Snell Isle section of St. Petersburg, Roy was watching a little afternoon television when news of the attempted assassination of President Ronald Reagan filled his den with sound and his mind with bitter memories.

On Nov. 22, 1963, Secret Service agent Kellerman was seated in the right front passenger seat of the Lincoln Continental in which John Kennedy was riding when Lee Harvey Oswald opened fire.

Honestly now, from my heart, I have to say that without training, if I heard what I thought were pistol-rifle shots, I would hit the deck fast.

How, Roy, can a man be trained to function normally in the face of an ambush?

"That's the work hour. That is when you go to work. You react to sound. Did you notice that they brought up that firecracker thing again?" Firecrackers or someone's faulty carburetion always receive ink in gunshot stories.

Reflecting back, Kellerman put personal harm aside at the moment Kennedy was shot. He ordered the driver out of the motorcade, grabbed the radio and shouted instructions.

Secret Service agent Tim McCarthy on Monday, March 30, turned toward the gunfire and was struck in the abdomen. Other agents shoved Reagan into the car.

"The reaction Monday was marvelous," said Kellerman. "The service owns the most sophisticated training grounds in the world. Techniques have advanced since the '63 thing."

of the President many times."

The determined ones can do as they please. That is why Secret Service people always have their heads revolving. They are watching for hands. They want to see everybody's hands.

Kellerman reflecting on the assassination after the Reagan assassination attempt on 3/30/81. Kellerman calls it "the '63 thing"? (Evening Independent. St. Petersburg, Florida 4/2/81).

a revolver, a riflescope, or even a rifle, all this would change soon enough after the questioning by these agents.[163]

Russian-speaking agent Leon Gopadze, Marina's interpreter, translated Marina's letter in the following way, in contradiction to the above account: "I am very, very grateful to the Secret Service agents who treated me so well and took such good care of me. Although some of the letters which I received accused these wonderful people of preventing me from seeing others, I am free to do anything I want ... "[164] Perhaps a tad flowery and overdone. In addition, Gopadze, responsible for translating Marina's many FBI interviews and her first Warren Commission appearance[165], was first introduced to Marina by the Secret Service as "Mr. Lee," the very same name Lee Harvey Oswald had used when rooming at a boardinghouse away from his wife in 1963.[166]

---

163   Secret Service interview, Warren Commission document 344, pages 23 & 43; WR 128; 1 H 492; see also *Cover-Up* by Stewart Galanor (1998), p. 92.
164   18 H 642.
165   5 H 588; see also *The Warren Omission* by Walt Brown (1996), p. 238.
166   23 H 385.

Perhaps Oswald's mother, Marguerite, summed up the situation best: "Mrs. Oswald claimed at certain points that her son was an American espionage agent. She claimed at other points that, if her son shot the President, he was part of a conspiracy involving Marina, Ruth Paine, two Secret Service agents, and a 'high government official' who she refused to identify."[167] As author Fred Newcomb reported,[168] "Secret Service agents Howard and Kunkel made certain claims to gain the confidence of the Oswald family. When Howard interviewed Robert Oswald on Nov. 23, 1963, he asserted that personal details of the family would be of special interest to Mrs. Kennedy. Robert thought this meant that Howard was close to Mrs. Kennedy.[169] Also on November 23rd, Kunkel told Oswald's mother, Marguerite, that he was sure Oswald killed the President. Marguerite objected. Howard replied that Kunkel was upset because he had guarded Mrs. Kennedy[170] ... Marguerite came to be 'deathly afraid' of both Kunkel and Howard. On May 12, 1964, she told the FBI in Fort Worth she not only refused to allow Kunkel in her home but did not want anything further to do with them both.[171] Marguerite stated, 'I have had documents stolen from me. I have had newspaper clippings stolen from my hand by the Secret Service.'[172] Marguerite also said: '... I thought that we have a plot in our own government and that there is a high official involved. And I am thinking that probably these Secret Service men are a part of it.'" It's funny how Marguerite picks out Howard and Kunkel over all the agents who guarded her and her family.

"On December 4, 1963, Special Agent James M. Howard, assigned to the Dallas, Texas office, and who assisted in the advance arrangements at Fort Worth, Texas,[173] advised that he was on duty at the Texas Hotel from the time the President arrived until 4:00 A.M. on November 22, 1963; that he was representing the Dallas Office and had occasion to meet and to talk to many of the Special Agents accompanying the President from Washington in the lobby, at the President's suite and in the Agents' rooms. He stated that at no time did he ever see any Special Agent of this Service in an intoxicated condition; that he himself was not at the Press Club [how about

---

167   *The Secret Service Story* by Michael Dorman, p. 213; 1 H 169-170.
168   *Murder From Within*, pp. 291-292.
169   CD 75, p. 356; *Lee: A Portrait of Lee Harvey Oswald by His Brother* by Robert L. Oswald (New York: Coward-McCann, 1967), p. 149.
170   CD 1066, pp. 532, 533, 539; 1 H 169.
171   CD 1066, pp. 532, 533.
172   1 H 129.
173   The Secret Service's Final Survey Report for the Fort Worth leg of the Texas tour lists Agent's Bill Duncan, Ned Hall, and Howard as assisting in the advance arrangements. However, Howard is listed as "James M. Harwood."

the Cellar?]. This Special Agent's remarks are worthy of comment, as it is known that he does not drink intoxicants of any kind, and it is believed that any remarks by him would be unbiased [!]."[174]

So, where was Dallas agent Howard at 12:30 p.m. on 11/22/63? Why did he wait until a 1999 lecture to state his location at that specific time? Allegedly he was cleaning President Kennedy's room at the Hotel Texas in Fort Worth.[175] He did not mention exactly where he was during the assassination to either the *Fresno Bee* or the *Houston Post*, in 1993; his only known pre-1999 interviews. During the period of his 12/4/63 statement, Howard was temporarily assigned to Lynda Bird Johnson's detail (from 12/1/63-1/24/64). Howard, along with his partner Kunkel, allegedly on an unspecified assignment on 11/22/63 in Washington D.C. (another 1999 Howard statement), were the only Dallas office agents connected to the Dallas trip not to have reports made available to the Warren Commission. Howard became a member of the White House Detail 4 months later, on 3/29/64.

Mike Howard and his brother Pat also planted the story that a janitor saw Oswald pull the trigger.[176] That said, according to author Harrison Livingstone, "Retired Secret Service agent Mike Howard ... has repeatedly hinted at LBJ's involvement in the plot."[177] As for Kunkel, the agent was involved in the investigation of a very obscure yet deadly threat to JFK's life: one Russell W. McLarry, as the following newspaper account makes clear. From the *New York Times*, 12/20/63: A 21-year-old Dallas machinist was arrested by the Secret Service today on charges of threatening to kill President Kennedy. The machinist, Russell W. McLarry, said the threat had been made in jest Nov. 21, the day before Mr. Kennedy was assassinated here. Two women to whom Mr. McLarry allegedly made the statement reported it to the police in Arlington, about 15 miles west of here, soon after they heard of the assassination. At a preliminary hearing in Fort Worth today, the Secret Service agent who apprehended Mr. McLarry testified that the machinist had said he was "proud – no glad" that the President had been

---

174   18 H 675.

175   Interestingly, Ira David Wood III reported on page 20 of James Fetzer's *Murder in Dealey Plaza*, "While showering this morning [11/22/63, Hotel Texas, Fort Worth], JFK takes off his Saint Jude and Saint Christopher medals and leaves them hanging on the shower head. When later "sweeping" the room, Secret Service agent Ron Pontius finds the medals and puts them in his pocket, with the intentions of returning them to JFK after the Dallas motorcade. Pontius eventually gives the medals to Marty Underwood who, at last report, still retains them." Not only is there no mention of Agent Howard, Pontius did not refute this account when contacted by the author in October 2000.

176   25 H 721-722,725: Lane-Rankin correspondence; 25 H 844-850: The Howards' side of the story.

177   *Stunning New Evidence*, 2000 (online publication: Secret Service chapter).

killed. Mr. McLarry attends night classes at the Arlington State College in Arlington as a freshman. The alleged threat was made on the campus to two women students. Mr. McLarry was alleged to have told the women that he would be working near the Trade Mart the next day and would be waiting with a gun to "get" the President. Works Near Trade Mart: Charles E. Kunkel, of the Dallas office of the Secret Service testified that he had confronted Mr. McLarry with this report and that, in substance, the student had admitted it. Mr. McLarry works at the Dahlgren Manufacturing Company, which makes lithographic printing equipment in a plant three blocks north of the Trade Mart. President Kennedy was driving to the mart to make a luncheon speech when he was killed, apparently by rifle shots from a sixth-floor window of a downtown Dallas building in the other direction from the mart. United States Attorney Barefoot Sanders said here today that he had no evidence of any connection between Mr. McLarry and Lee H. Oswald, the alleged assassin.... The authorities said they had found no connection between Mr. McLarry and anti-Kennedy leaflets that appeared on the Arlington campus the day before the assassination. The leaflets bore the heading: "Wanted for Treason." Mr. McLarry was interviewed by the Secret Service Tuesday night and was arrested this morning. The agency indicated that the case had not been pursued immediately after the assassination because there had been more pressing things to do.[178]

The *(Washington D.C.) Evening Star*, 12/19/63, noted, "The Complaint was signed by Charles E. Kunkel, special agent for the Secret Service."[179] *Newsweek* added this important detail to the mix: "McLarry, who is unmarried, lived in the Oak Cliff section of Dallas, where Lee Harvey Oswald, the President's accused assassin, and Jack Ruby, Oswald's killer, also lived."[180] With agent Kunkel now dead and agent Howard incommunicado, it will probably be difficult to unravel these mysteries further.

These agents were to make sure that Marina Oswald portrayed the "patsy," Lee Harvey Oswald, as a lone nut killer. They were to tie up untidy loose ends. Two of them cannot be ruled out as the unidentified agent in Dealey Plaza that day. Interestingly, just moments before he died on 1/22/73, former President Johnson asked that Agent Mike Howard come to his room "immediately."[181]

178   *New York Times*, 12/20/63 p. 19.
179   *Evening Star*, (Washington, D.C.) 12/19/63 [this newspaper article photocopy was found in DNC advance man Jerry Bruno's JFK Library Texas trip files].
180   *Newsweek*, 12/30/63, p. 15 [courtesy of researcher Bill Adams].
181   *LBJ: A Life* by Irwin Unger (John Wiley & Sons, 1999), p. 536. Howard wasn't there, but agents' Ed Noland and Harry Harris rushed in with a portable oxygen machine

In recent years, former agent Mike Howard has done several media interviews and videotaped presentations. In one such interview, Howard said: "Marguerite was as looney as a fruitcake!" he said. In his testimony to the Warren Commission, Peter Gregory described Marguerite Oswald "as being not necessarily rational.... She demands public attention." Of Marguerite and Oswald, he said, "I felt they both craved public recognition or ... attention or publicity or whatever you wish to call it." Howard tells his stories often, especially lately, surrounding the 50th anniversary of the assassination. His goal is not to change the minds of skeptics, but rather to tell them what he witnessed. "Look," he tells them in his thick Texas drawl, "I'm just telling you what it was. You can take it or leave it."

Howard continued: "If I can get up and explain that to people and tell them what happened, then I feel like I've done a service, not only for the Secret Service, but for the country."[182] In another press interview, Howard revealed the following: Soon after President John F. Kennedy and his wife departed from their Fort Worth hotel for Dallas that morning, Howard and other agents faced a monumental duty – meticulously collecting the half-used cologne, scraps of paper, bars of soap and even left-behind pieces of thread from the Kennedys' hotel suite into two trash bags. By the time we got everything into those bags we heard over the TV that there had been a shot fired in Dallas," Howard, 82, recalled Monday afternoon at the Carrollton Senior Center. The retired agent spoke there during an event to commemorate the 50th anniversary of Kennedy's assassination. Immediately after the shooting, Howard's duties quickly changed. Soon he would be questioning suspects and in time, he would guard the family of Lee Harvey Oswald, but first he had to get to Dallas. After hearing of the shooting, Howard got into the Tarrant County sheriff's new Ford Crown Victoria. The car could go as fast as 150 mph, which Howard said he thought was "kind of funny – until we got in and took that drive to Dallas."[183] In yet another press interview, Howard talked about 11/22/63: "Howard said he has had a lot of time to think about that day. He has even asked himself lots of "What if's?" and "How's?" on the procedures and events that led to that tragic moment in American history. "You think what could have been done or what should have done and what wasn't done and did everybody do what they needed to be doing," Howard said..."(President Kennedy) was really

instead. It was too late: LBJ had passed away.

182   *Dallas Morning News*, 11/22/2013.

136 183   *Dallas Morning News*, 6/3/2013.

a nice fellow," Howard said. "He liked the agents. He always spoke to us. He spoke to everybody. He was very congenial, a good man to work with."[184]

In another press interview, Howard reveals the dubious side of his personality and why some of the things he says should be taken with a grain of salt: "Of course, any Secret Service agent that ever guarded the Kennedy family is always asked if he ever met Marilyn Monroe. Howard says certainly … at a pool party. But that meeting came later when Howard was assigned to protect Lynda Bird Johnson. Miss Johnson happened to be dating a fellow by the name of George Hamilton and there was a pool party on the West Coast. Marilyn Monroe was there. Everyone was watching Elvis Presley's movie *Acapulco*. "She was wearing a swimsuit," Howard said, "and that's as far as I'm going with that."[185] Marilyn Monroe died in 1962, well over a year before this was even possible to have happened.

More dubious tales from Howard continue, this time with some alarming results: "Secret Service agent Mike Howard had been in charge of security for the Fort Worth leg of the JFK trip. As he told me in 1993, there was coincidentally a "grassy knoll" on the way to the Fort Worth Airport. These kinds of topography were clear security risks, says Howard, who adds, "We placed two deputies there. This is routine. Sorrels [Forrest Sorrels, the Secret Service agent in charge of the Dallas motorcade] did the same thing in Dallas." Howard was told by the now deceased Sorrels that, like Howard, he had placed security people in all the obvious areas. Howard elaborated: "We deputized everybody we could get our hands on – including agents from ATF [the Bureau of Alcohol, Tobacco and Firearms], customs, border patrol, reserve police, deputy sheriffs, etc. The motorcade route in Dallas was crawling with these people, especially in Dealey Plaza and the overpass." Howard adds that many of these security reinforcements were technically off-duty and wouldn't appear on any "official" listing of posted officers. In addition, many of these agents had standard ATF IDs, which were virtually identical to Secret Service cards, both being issued by the Treasury Department. Compounding the confusion is the fact that the ATF and Secret Service were often perceived as interchangeable in 1963. Frank Ellsworth, a Dallas ATF agent at the time of the assassination, told me, "In 1963, if you would have asked me if I was a Secret Service agent, I most likely would have answered yes – our roles overlapped that much." Robert Gemberling, the FBI agent in Dallas who investigated Oswald after his arrest, told me that he remembers being told that two Customs Agents

---

184 *McKinney Courier Gazette*, 11/28/2010.
185 Former Secret Service agent gives personal account of Kennedy assassination - North Texas e-News (ntxe-news.com)

who worked at the Post Office building across Dealey Plaza were, in fact, spending their lunch break helping with security in the knoll area."[186]

Finally, Howard gave a videotaped talk on 11/14/2013 that is lambasted with dislikes and negative comments from many viewers – they are not fooled, either.[187] A sampling of the comments: "His narrative is full of untruths and distortions as well as pure speculation." "This was hard to watch. The facts in the case are at odds with what this former agent says." "I suppose his pension depends on proselytizing and repeating the blatant lies told by the Warren Commission, and other nonsense. Not one witness, not even a team of witnesses – could corroborate his version of the J.D. Tippit slaying, for example. Couldn't watch the remaining 20 minutes after that.

CHARLIE KUNKEL   MIKE HOWARD

Sorry to be so harsh, but this is simply hearsay from a vested establishment shill. A library should know better. File under fiction."

Secret Service agents Charlie Kunkel and Mike Howard.

White House Detail Secret Service agent Chuck Zboril, scheduled to be on the 11/2/63 Chicago trip and was later on the 11/18/63 Tampa, Florida trip riding on the rear of the limousine: While doing research for author T.C. Elliott, I decided to peruse a document only released in 1998, the official Marine Corps Unit Diaries, RG 127, Camp Pendleton, CA 1957-01-20 to 1957-02-26. As most people know (so common I grabbed this from an online encyclopedia) "Lee Harvey Oswald was sent to Camp Pendleton for advanced infantry combat training. Oswald completed his training between 20th January 1957 and 26th February 1957 as a member of QUA

186   Gus Russo, *Live by the Sword* (Baltimore: Bancroft, 1998), p. 473.
187   Secret Service Agent Mike Howard, Ret. - JFK, Oswalds, LBJ (youtube.com)

Company, 1st Battalion, 2nd Infantry Training Regiment, Marine Corps Base, Camp Pendleton, California."

Guess who else was a member of the very same QUA Company, 1st Battalion, 2nd Infantry Training Regiment, Marine Corps Base, Camp Pendleton, California at the very same time and never told anyone, at least not in public for books, articles, or the television interviews he has done: JFK White House Detail Secret Service Agent Charles T. "Chuck" Zboril! "Although he wasn't present, Zboril still agonizes about that fateful day in Dallas. After being at the President's side in Tampa, Zboril was sent to Atoka, VA, where the president was to be following his trip to Dallas. "I drove to

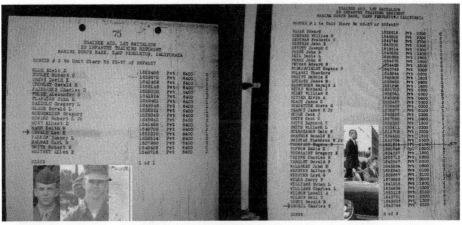

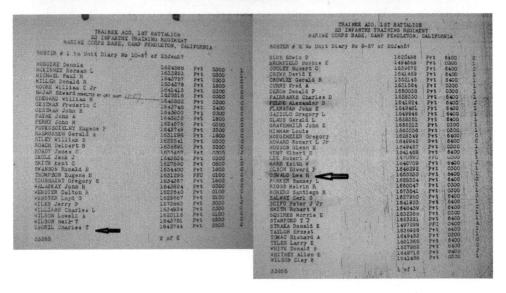

```
                        WHITE HOUSE DETAIL
                      REGION 1, OFFICE #16
                       MIDDLEBURG DETAIL

Special Agent in Charge: Gerald A. Behn
                                            DATE: November 22, 1963
                                                    Friday
                                            IN:   Middleburg, Va.

                                            WEATHER: Overcast

                                            HOURS TODAY: 12m  12m
```

AGENTS	REGULAR DUTY	EXTRA DUTY
Zboril ⇦	12-8	
Kollar	8-4	
Coughlin	4-12	
Rodham	8-4	4-6

```
                      ACTIVITY OF SECTION

Routine activity
President assassinated in Dallas, this Detail on standby




                          TRAINING

                                          Special Agent (in charge)
                                          Wade J. Rodham
```

Atoka and spent the night thinking "If only I had been there, maybe things would have been different," Zboril recalls."[188]

Agent Zboril on 11/22/63.

─────────────

188   2014 interview for Bonita Springs, *Florida Retirement Home* magazine article "The President's Man."

Chapter Six:

Interlude II – Building Rooftop Security Would Have Negated Both 11/2/63 and 11/22/63

A major discovery of mine occurred just in 2020 during the Covid lockdown. A fellow You Tuber had hours of ABC video from 11/22/63 on their channel (the channel and user are now gone). Although most of the footage I already had, there were several gems I had never seen before, including ABC report Ron Gardner telling the world that normally building rooftops were guarded during motorcades and that this occurred for years before Kennedy was president.[189] In addition, I also came across a valuable passage in a January 1960 (Ike era) book entitled *The United States Secret Service*, written by Walter Bowen and Secret Service agent Harry Neal, in which it is stated that" If the President is to lead a parade, agents and policemen patrol the roofs of buildings along the parade route."[190]

NEW DISCOVERY OF SOMETHING OLD-The book *The United States Secret Service* by Walter S. Bowen and Harry Edward Neal. With a foreword by JFK Secret Service Chief U. E. Baughman (January 1960/paperback January 1961/modern kindle edition 11/22/2019)

---

189   UPDATED: Building rooftops WERE guarded before and during the JFK era! 11/22/63 (youtube.com)
190   *The United States Secret Service* by Walter S. Bowen & Harry E. Neal (New York: Chilton, 1960), page 131. See also *The Lone Star Speaks: Untold Texas Stories about the JFK*

Chief Inspector Michael Torina was about as important and influential an agent or official that the Secret Service could ever boast about, for it was he that actually wrote the Secret Service manual itself.[191] Torina contributed significantly to a book about the Secret Service in 1962 which used almost the same words: "If the President is to appear in a parade, agents and policemen are assigned posts atop buildings and on the street along the parade route."[192] I corresponded with Torina on 12/5/97 and 2/23/04, respectively, and the former agent confirmed the veracity of what was written in that book, although he took pains to not say too much more: "I am not in a position to comment on our concerns in dealing with Presidential security matters." That said, he did contribute significantly to the aforementioned book about the Secret Service written in 1962, in which it is plainly stated, "Agents of the White House Detail ride in the same car with the President. Others will walk or trot alongside, while still others ride in automobiles in front of and behind the Presidential car ... if exceptionally large crowds are expected ... the Secret Service may call upon the Armed Forces to station troops along the line of march."[193] Torina also told author William Manchester in 1961 that wherever a Presidential motorcade must slow down for a turn, the entire intersection must be checked in advance.[194] Needless to say, none of these security measures were used for the fateful Dallas trip of 11/22/63.

Written during the Ike era [modern kindle edition]:

If the President is to lead a parade, agents and policemen patrol the roofs of buildings along the parade route. If unusually large crowds are expected, the Secret Service may call on the Armed Forces to station troops along the line of march.

The United States SECRET SERVICE

WARREN S. BOWEN and HARRY EDWARD NEAL

Assassination (2020) by Sara Peterson and K.W. Zachry, page 285.

191   The United States Secret Service by Walter S. Bowen & Harry E. Neal (New York: Chilton, 1960), page 209.

192   What Does A Secret Service Agent Do? By Wayne Hyde (New York: Dodd, Mead, and Co., 1962), p. 28 (and acknowledgments).

193   What Does A Secret Service Agent Do? by Wayne Hyde (1962), page 28 (and acknowledgments) On the same page is a picture of agents walking beside JFK's car in 1961.

194   The Death of a President by William Manchester, page 32. See also The Lone Star Speaks: Untold Texas Stories about the JFK Assassination (2020) by Sara Peterson and K.W. Zachry, page 285.

During my extensive research for my prior books, I came across much corroboration for this buried in documents and old newspapers.

Official Getty Images caption: "McKeesport High School marching band lining up preparing to march, with sharpshooters on roof tops and billboard for Union Clothing Co., during President Kennedy campaign stop, McKeesport, Pennsylvania, October 13, 1962. (Photo by Charles 'Teenie' Harris/Teenie Harris Archive/Carnegie Museum of Art/Getty Images)."

The Age (Australia), 6/1/61 and photo with police on rooftops- President Kennedy's trip to Paris, France.

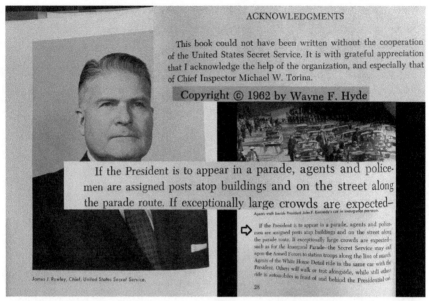

ACKNOWLEDGMENTS

This book could not have been written without the cooperation of the United States Secret Service. It is with grateful appreciation that I acknowledge the help of the organization, and especially that of Chief Inspector Michael W. Torina.

Copyright © 1962 by Wayne F. Hyde

If the President is to appear in a parade, agents and policemen are assigned posts atop buildings and on the street along the parade route. If exceptionally large crowds are expected—

James J. Rowley, Chief, United States Secret Service.

From the 1962 book *What Does a Secret Service Agent Do?* By Wayne Hyde, written with the help of the Secret Service, Chief James Rowley and Chief Inspector Michael Torina who wrote the Secret Service manual.

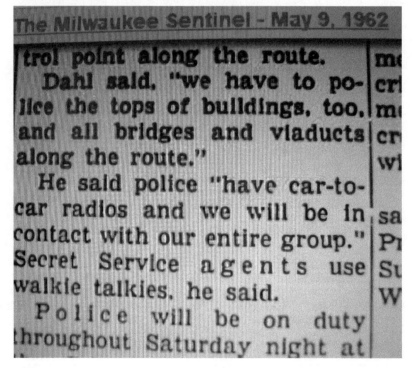

The Milwaukee Sentinel – May 9, 1962

trol point along the route.

Dahl said, "we have to police the tops of buildings, too, and all bridges and viaducts along the route."

He said police "have car-to-car radios and we will be in contact with our entire group." Secret Service agents use walkie talkies, he said.

Police will be on duty throughout Saturday night at

The Milwaukee (Wisconsin) Sentinel, 5/9/62 regarding President Kennedy's trip to Milwaukee.

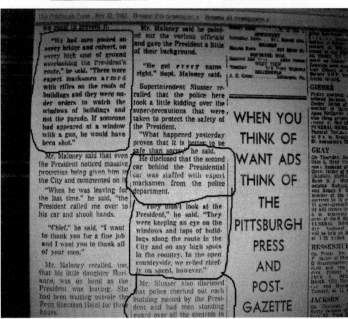

2 CORPUS CHRISTI TIMES, Friday, June 21, 1963

President Will Have Plenty Of Protection While Abroad

By DOUGLAS B. CORNELL.

WASHINGTON. (AP)—When President Kennedy visits Europe, he's going to be just about as safe as if he stayed home.

They ask local authorities to put police on top of buildings and along the streets. Bridges get special attention. Servants, waiters palace or embassy abroad as it does at the White House in Washington.

In this country, the Secret Service has the sole responsibility for safeguarding the Chief Executive, although it also calls on local and state police and occasionally the military for assistance. On trips to other countries, the foreign counterpart of the Secret Service is responsible technically for the security of the President. But actually it is the Secret Service that sets forth the security requirements, working in close cooperation with its opposite number abroad.

WHEN a president travels in other lands, the sharp-eyed, well-built young men constantly by his side draw exclamations from the crowds. Foreigners always figure they are FBI men or G-men. But the FBI has no specific authority for guarding the president. Congress put this power in the hands of the Secret Service years ago. The Secret Service is an agency of the U.S. Treasury Department, and one of its other major duties is running down counterfeiters.

A Special Secret Service detail is assigned to the White House

under Gerald A. Behn, a young-looking, gum-chewing veteran who goes back to the days of the late President Franklin D. Roosevelt. As on all presidential trips, the

PROBABLY a flying trouble-ter will take along a huge, specially built and equipped car for the Secret Service, as well as Kennedy's limousine with a removable metal or plastic top.

The Secret Service car has running boards and hand grips. In a motorcade, agents are hopping on and off constantly and racing ahead to run alongside Kennedy's car. The two cars travel almost bumper to bumper. Usually each is driven by an agent. Now and then there are exceptions, as when a turbaned, d-coated Indian was at the heel of the president's car when rmer President Dwight D. Eisenhower visited New Delhi. At the airports, along the roads d streets, at public buildings, at all other places the President ill visit. Secret Service and local security agents will have combed over the entire route in advance.

They ask local authorities to put police on top of buildings and along the streets. Bridges get special attention. Servants, waiters and other employes in places the President visits will be checked. So will kitchens.

ALL THIS doesn't mean that crowds won't get a good look at the President or the photographers and reporters won't be able to cover his activities.

At ceremonies, representatives of the press probably will be no more than 30 feet away. And at times even closer. The general public may not be much farther away. In fact, some people are likely to see Kennedy close up. He is a gregarious kind of person who seldom passes up the chance to wander over to a crowd behind a fence or other barricade and walk along with a smile and outstretched hand, offering handclasps and sometimes yielding to requests for autographs.

Or he might get right into the crowd and mingle. This rather worries the Secret Service, because it never knows for sure what the President is going to do about joining the crowd. That's the kind of man he is.

San Francisco To Be Site of U. S. World Trade Fair

SAN FRANCISCO. (AP) — San Francisco will host the seventh United States World Trade Fair Sept. 19-20 — the first time the event has been held outside New York City — Mayor George Christopher announced yesterday.

More than 60 nations in Europe, Asia, Africa, the Middle East, and Central and South America have exhibited at the international trade event in the past.

We go to prevent it—

"We had men posted on every bridge and culvert, on every high spot of ground overlooking the President's route," he said. "There were expert marksmen armed with rifles on the roofs of buildings and they were under orders to watch the windows of buildings and not the parade. If someone had appeared at a window with a gun, he would have been shot."

Mr. Maloney said that even the President noticed massive protection being given him in the City and commented on it.

"When he was leaving for the last time," he said, "the President called me over to his car and shook hands.

"Chief," he said, "I want to thank you for a fine job and I want you to thank all of your men."

Mr. Maloney recalled, too, that his little daughter Marianne, was on hand as the President was leaving. She had been waiting outside the Penn Sheraton Hotel for three hours.

Mr. Maloney said he pointed out the various officials and gave the President a little of their background.

"He got every name right." Supt. Maloney said.

Superintendent Slusser recalled that the police here took a little kidding over the super-precautions that were taken to protect the safety of the President.

"What happened yesterday proves that it is better to be safe than sorry," he said.

He disclosed that the second car behind the Presidential car was staffed with expert marksmen from the police department.

"They didn't look at the President," he said. "They were keeping an eye on the windows and tops of buildings along the route in the City and on any high spots in the country. In the open countryside, we relied chiefly on speed, however."

Mr. Slusser also disclosed that police checked out each building passed by the President and had men standing guard over all the controls in

WHEN YOU
THINK OF
WANT ADS
THINK OF
THE
PITTSBURGH
PRESS
AND
POST-
GAZETTE

The Pittsburgh (PA) Press 11/22/63 regarding President Kennedy's trip to Pittsburgh:

JFK IN NASHVILLE

⇨ Other officers were assigned to stations atop the Municipal terminal and other buildings along the route.

⇨ These men took their posts at 8 a.m. and remained at their rooftop stations until the President and his party had passed.

⇨ The same was true at Vanderbilt stadium where Metropolitan officers and state patrolmen were assisted by members of the Metropolitan fire department and members of the armed forces.

The Nashville (TN) Banner released an official book entitled JFK in Nashville on 5/18/63 based on the newspaper's actual articles.

The Tampa, FL motorcade of 11/18/63 was a textbook example of what usually happened. Officer Russell Groover recalled that there were police or military stationed on the roof of every multistory building along the motorcade. As we know, this was not done on 11/22/63. Chief Inspector Michael W. Torina told author William Manchester back in 1961 that wherever a Presidential motorcade must slow down for a turn, the entire intersection must be checked in advance[195], which sounds a lot like Elm Street in Dallas.

Russell Groover

8/27/13, 5:47 PM

Russell Groover

Worked at Tampa Police Department
Went to Hillsborough Senior High School
Lives in Brooksville, Florida

8/30/13, 12:42 PM

I would say the fastest we ever ran was between 25 and 35 in the sparsely populated area just before Mac Dill AFB close to the end of his trip. Remember there were 5 other people with him in the vehicle.

⇨ Vince, yes, every building along the route was manned on every floor and the roof with either law enforcement or military. All armed. We traveled only about 25 mph in the sparsely populated area just before we got to Mac Dill AFB . The highest speed could have gotten up to 35.. Did you know the Black Ops man in charge was changed before they got to Dallas. He was sent to escort a group of Senators on a fact finding tour of Alaska. They had different security. It was a known fact back then. I don't know how you can verify it now The only reason we have photos at all is they didn't think to confiscate Tony Zapponi's because he was only a 16 year old kid ? Remember history changes and memories fail.

men were reinforced by motorcycle escort intersection control. The sheriff's office secured the roofs of major buildings in the downtown and suburban areas.

---

195 *The Death of a President* by William Manchester, page 32.

Mr. James J. Rowley   -2-   1-16-602.111

along the route were controlled by uniformed police officers and these
men were reinforced by motorcycle escort intersection control. The
sheriff's office secured the roofs of major buildings in the downtown
and suburban areas.

All underpasses were controlled by police and military units. The police
department secured all rail traffic during the visit as the motorcade
passed over rail arteries enroute.

From the Secret Service Final Survey Report regarding 11/18/63 Tampa, Florida:

Congress passed the JFK Act of 1992. One month later, the Secret Service began its compliance efforts. However, in January 1995, the Secret Service destroyed presidential protection survey reports for some of President Kennedy's trips in the fall of 1963. The Review Board learned of the destruction approximately one week after the Secret Service destroyed them, when the Board was drafting its request for additional information. The Board believed that the Secret Service files on the President's travel in the weeks preceding his murder would be relevant.

It took many years-decades-to compile this valuable information, as much of it was buried and many documents were destroyed by the Secret Service. From the ARRB's Final Report.

A SUMMARY OF THE RECORDS DESTROYED BY THE SECRET SERVICE IN JANUARY OF 1995[196]

The Protective Survey Reports destroyed by the Secret Service in January 1995 were part of a group of records transferred by the Secret Service to the General Services Administration's Washington National Records Center in Suitland, Maryland on August 7, 1974 under accession number 87-75-4. The instructions on the SF-135 ("Records Transmittal and Receipt" form) were: "Retain permanently for eventual transfer to the

---

196   Special thanks to researcher William Kelly for help with this listing.

National Archives or a Presidential Library." There were six boxes transferred under the accession number, and the two that were destroyed in January of 1995 contained the following files:

Box 1 Protection of the President (John F. Kennedy)
Andrews Air Force Base 1961 (Arrivals and Departures)
Andrews Air Force Base 1962 (Arrivals and Departures)
Andrews Air Force Base 1963 (Arrivals and Departures)
Arlington National Cemetery
Camp David
The Capitol
Churches
D.C. National Guard Armory
D.C. Stadium
Departures from South Grounds
Dulles International Airport
Embassies
Executive Office Building
Golf Clubs
Griffith Stadium
Homes of Friends
International Inn
Mayflower Hotel (three folders, for 1961-63)
National Press Club
Other Places Folders (#s 1-4, from January 1961-December of 1962)
Box 6 Protective Survey Reports for the following trips:
Duluth, Minnesota (9-24-63)
Ashland, Wisconsin (9-24-63)
Billings, Montana (9-25-63)
Grand Teton National Park, Wyoming (9-25-63)
Cheyenne, Wyoming (9-25-63)
Grand Forks, North Dakota (9-25-63)
Laramie, Wyoming (9-25-63)
Salt Lake City, Utah (9-26-63)
Great Falls, Montana (9-26-63)
Hanford, Washington (9-26-63)
Tongue Point, Oregon (9-27-63)
Redding, California (9-27-63)
Tacoma, Washington (9-27-63)
Palm Springs, California (9-28-63)
Las Vegas, Nevada (9-28-63)

Heber Springs, Arkansas (10-3-63)
Little Rock, Arkansas (10-3-63)
University of Maine (10-19-63)
Boston, Massachusetts (10-26-63)
Amherst, Massachusetts (10-26-63)
Philadelphia, Pennsylvania (10-30-63)
Chicago, Illinois (11-2-63): Three Folders [TRIP CANCELLED]
New York City (11-8-63)

In addition, one folder of vital records was missing from Box 2 in this accession, titled: "Other Places Folder #6" (for the period July-November 1963).

The Secret Service, in the form of future Director Ralph Basham, tried to downplay the significance of the missing Chicago protective survey reports for the cancelled November 2, 1963 trip (during which conspirators had planned to assassinate President Kennedy) to the ARRB by writing: "The folder concerning the canceled trip to Chicago would only have contained a preliminary survey report, if any document at all, since final reports are not conducted when a trip is cancelled. This report, if in fact it was even in the prepared folder, would have been of limited scope." However, there were 3 folders on the cancelled Chicago trip, not one, and this attempt to portray the Chicago file as one folder was duplicitous. Furthermore, how did Basham presume to know that any reports written about the cancellation of the Chicago trip would have been "of limited scope?" It is easy to make such a claim after evidence is destroyed, because there is no way you can be challenged.

Professor Jim Fetzer summed up the situation nicely with his comments in the documentary *The Men Who Killed Kennedy: The Smoking Guns* which aired on the History Channel in 2003: "The Secret Service deliberately destroyed records that would have revealed that the motorcade in Dallas was a travesty, a violation of at least 15 different Secret Service policies for Presidential protection. This behavior on their part raises the most serious and deserving questions about their complicity in the entire affair- which of course, is the reason why the Secret Service destroyed the records of its own motorcades when they were asked for them by the Assassination Records Review Board."

Doug Horne, the chief analyst for military records of the Assassination Records Review Board (ARRB), wrote more extensively about the deliberate destruction of Secret Service records in his book *Inside the ARRB* (2009, Volume V, p. 1451): "The destruction of key documents by the Se-

THE PLOT TO KILL PRESIDENT KENNEDY IN CHICAGO

cret Service in 1995 suggested that the Secret Service cover-up of its own malfeasance continued, more than 30 years after the assassination. In 1995, the Review Board Staff became aware that the U.S. Secret Service had destroyed protective survey reports related to John F. Kennedy's Presidency, and that they had done so well after the passage of the JFK Records Act, and well after having been briefed by the National Archives (NARA) on the Act's requirements to preserve all Assassination Records from destruction until the ARRB had made a determination that any such proposed destruction was acceptable I reported to work at the ARRB on August 7, 1995, and I still distinctly recall that this controversy was raging full force during the first two weeks I was on the job. I recall both General Counsel Jeremy Gunn and Executive Director David Marwell being particularly upset; they were seriously considering holding public hearings in which the Secret Service officials responsible for said destruction would be called to account and castigated, in an open forum, with the media present. The thinking at the time was that doing so would: (a) cause the Secret Service to take the Review Board and the JFK Act seriously; and (b) send a warning to other government agencies, such as the FBI and CIA, to also take the Review Board and the JFK Act seriously, lest they, too be dragged into public hearings that would cause great discomfiture and professional embarrassment. Eventually – and unfortunately – tempers cooled and no public hearings were held. I suspect that Board Chair Jack Tunheim played a major role in finessing the matter; presumably, the Board Members believed that since the ARRB was still in its first year of its three-year effort to locate and review assassination records, that we would get more out of the Secret Service in the future with honey, than with vinegar. Stern official letters levying charges and countercharges were exchanged; a face-to-face meeting between high-level officials of the ARRB and Secret Service was held; tempers cooled; and no public hearings were ever held. Relations with the Secret Service remained testy throughout the remainder of the ARRB's lifespan. It was my impression, during my ongoing discussions with my fellow analysts on the Secret Service Records team for the next three years (from September 1995 to September 1998), that the Secret Service never "loosened up" and reached a comfortable working accommodation with the ARRB like the FBI, the CIA, and the Pentagon (or, at least the Joint Staff Secretariat) did. The Secret Service and the ARRB remained wary adversaries for four years. The Review Board itself consciously soft-pedaled the dispute in its Final Report, devoting only one paragraph (and virtually no details whatsoever) to the incident, on page 149: "Congress passed the

JFK Act in 1992. One month later, the Secret Service began its compliance efforts. However, in January 1995, the Secret Service destroyed Presidential protection survey reports for some of President Kennedy's trips in the fall of 1963. The Review Board learned of the destruction approximately one week after the Secret Service destroyed them, when the Board was drafting its request for additional information. The Board believed that the Secret Service files on the President's travel in the weeks preceding this murder would be relevant."

And that was it – that was the only mention of the entire imbroglio in the Final Report of the Assassinations Records Review Board."

CHAPTER SEVEN:

THE CHICAGO PLOT

POWERFUL LEADER–Technically, U.S. Secret Service Chief James J. Rowley is the most powerful man in the United States. He can forbid the President to take a walk or a trip to Mexico, and make any other decisions regarding the chief executive's personal safety. The law charges the Secret Service with the protection of the President, and, in reverse, the President is charged with obeying the Secret Service (UPI).

Secret Service Chief James Rowley, head of the Secret Service at the time of the plot.

O n 11/1/63 South Vietnam's President Ngo Diem is assassinated in a CIA backed coup.[197] The very next day, 11/2/63, JFK's trip to Chicago, Illinois is canceled at the last minute due to threats against his life:[198] apart from subjects Thomas Arthur Vallee[199], Thomas Mosely, and Homer Echevarria, there was a team of four Cuban gunmen,

---

197   *Triangle of Death* by Brad O'Leary & L.E. Seymour (Nashville, TN: WND Books, 2003). On that same day, the *Chicago Sun-Times* ran a page one headline story "1,300 Policemen to Guard Routes of Kennedy Here."
198   *The JFK Assassination* (2016/2018) by James DiEugenio, pages 271-278.
199   The Chicago Threat – Part 1 | Larry Hancock (wordpress.com)

two of whom eluded surveillance and escaped. Former Secret Service agents Sam Kinney, Bill Greer, Robert Kollar, J. Lloyd Stocks, Gary Mc-Leod, Robert J. Motto, Edward Tucker, David Grant, James Griffiths, Abraham Bolden[200], and Chicago SAIC Maurice Martineau told the HSCA that this trip was cancelled at the last minute – the excuses were varied: JFK had a cold (a repeat of the Cuban Missile Crisis alibi that turned out to be a false pretense), Diem's death (refuted by Salinger)[201], the Thomas Arthur Vallee arrest[202], and others. When the author asked former agent Walt Coughlin why the trip was cancelled, he responded, "I have not a clue!"[203]

David Grant told the HSCA, "President Kennedy canceled his appearance, but had requested that the trip continue, despite his absence, 'as though he were still there.' Consequently, the trip was carried out exactly as planned with the exception that President Kennedy did not attend. Mr. Grant was informed that the President canceled his trip because of illness."[204] Joseph Noonan, a Chicago office agent, told the HSCA that he "participated directly in surveillance involving Tom Mosely and Homer Echevarria ... he and [the] other agents were uneasy that the Cubans might have some ties to the CIA ... a little later they received a call from Headquarters to drop everything on Mosely and Echevarria and send all memos, files, and their notebooks to Washington and not to discuss the case with anyone."[205] On November 21, 1963, Thomas Mosley was negotiating the sale of machine guns to a Cuban exile named Homer Echevarria. In the course of the transaction, Echevarria said that "we now have plenty of money – our new backers are Jews" and would close the arms deal "as soon as we [or they] take care of Kennedy." The next day, Kennedy was assassinated in Dallas. Mosley, an ATF informant, reported his conversation to the Secret Service, and that agency quickly began investigating what it termed "a group in the Chicago area who may have a connection with the JFK assassination." Echevarria was a member of the 30th November group, associated with the DRE with whom Oswald had dealings the previous summer. Mosley said the arms deal was being financed through Paulino Sierra Martinez

---

200   Abraham Bolden - Wikipedia
201   *Chicago Independent* by Edwin Black November 1975.
202   The Chicago Threat – Part 2 | Larry Hancock (wordpress.com)
203   E-mail to author dated 2/25/04.
204   2/3/78 HSCA interview with Grant [RIF# 180-10082-10451].
205   4/13/78 HSCA interview with Noonan; RIF#'s: 180-10104-10331; 180-10087-10191; 180- 10099-10491; 180-10078-10493; 180-10082-10453; 1541-0001-10174: Secret Service shift report.

and his J.G.C.E. – Sierra interestingly was connected to Bobby Kennedy's effort to unite various exile groups, through Harry Ruiz Williams.206

Secret Service Agent Abraham Bolden wrote the author, "I arrived in Washington on November 8, 1963, and left November 11, 1963, eleven days before Kennedy was assassinated. It was during this time that I discussed the breakdown in security with Chief Rowley in person and it was also at this time that I found out that Chief Rowley had written an article for Reader's Digest November issue stating and outlining how easy it would be to assassinate a President using a high-powered rifle."207

Abraham Bolden inside Chicago office of the U.S. Secret Service (June 1961)   *Photos courtesy of Abraham Bolden*

President Kennedy 11/1/63, the day the President of Vietnam was assassinated in a CIA-backed coup and one day before the 11/2/63 Chicago plot.

206   Secret Service report- Commission Document (CD) 87.
207   Letter to author dated 10/30/93.

When JFK was scheduled to be in Chicago on 11/2/63 for the Army–Air Force game at Soldier Field, Secret Service agent Abraham Bolden, the first African American to serve on the White House Detail, was a member of the Chicago office of the Secret Service handling security. As Warren Swindall noted, "The visit had political implications as JFK has 'stood up' Mayor Daley on a similar scheduled visit the previous year, and the President was most anxious to mend his fences before the next year's election."[208] The eleven-mile parade from O'Hare Airport to Soldier Field caused considerable misgivings to the Secret Service:

> 1. JFK's limousine "would pass through a warehouse district – which Secret Service advance men consider ten times more deadly than any building corridor."[209]
>
> 2. Involve a "slow, difficult left-hand turn."
>
> 3. "A difficult 90 degree turn that would slow (JFK) to practically a standstill."

However, prior to the scheduled visit, Chief James J. Rowley himself phoned SAIC Maurice G. Martineau with word that, via J. Edgar Hoover and the FBI, they had wind of an assassination plot involving a four-man team of gunmen. According to Bernard Fensterwald's memo from his interview with Mr. Bolden, "Martineau called in all men in his charge in Chicago and told them of Rowley's call. He also informed them of the following as to this matter: (1) there were to be no written reports; any information was to be given to Martineau orally; (2) Nothing was to be sent by TWX (interoffice teletype); he (Martineau) was to report only by phone to Rowley, personally; (3) no file number was to be given to this case. All Secret Service agents in Chicago (including Bolden) were shown four photos of the men allegedly involved in the plot (of the four, Bolden remembers two names: Bradley and Gonzalez)."[210]

---

208   AARC files provided to the author in 1993 by Jim Lesar.

209   *Chicago Independent*, article by Edwin Black, November 1975. During Bolden's 1/9/78 HSCA interview, he stated that he was the unnamed informant who supplied information for Black's article. He was not, however, the only source used [i.e. HSCA interview of former Chicago Agent Robert J. Motto, etc.]. Inspector Thomas Kelley also noted the Secret Service's concern regarding warehouses, even those that were partially occupied [3 HSCA 335]. Of course, the Texas School Book Depository was a partially occupied warehouse. *JFK And The Unspeakable*, page 433: Chicago court investigator Sherman Skolnick was another major source for Black.

210   Memo dated 3/29/68 via AARC; Bolden letter to Congressman Louis Stokes, 1/26/92 (obtained by the author from Bolden).

Mr. Bolden named six other agents involved in the meeting with Martineau: James S. Griffiths, Joseph E. Noonan, Jr., Steven B. Maynard, Robert J. Motto, Thomas D. Strong, and J. Lloyd Stocks.[211] Former agents Sam Kinney, Bill Greer, Robert Kollar, J. Lloyd Stocks, Gary M. McLeod, Robert J. Motto, Edward Tucker, David Grant, and James Griffiths, as well as Bolden and Martineau[212], told the HSCA that the 11/2/63 Chicago trip was canceled at the last minute.[213] David Grant was the advance agent for the aborted Chicago trip.[214] Robert L. Kollar assisted Grant in the advance preparations, arriving in Chicago a week before the start of the trip.[215] One of the Secret Service Shift Reports for 11/2/63 reads, "(Note: Above SA's [ATSAIC/Shift Leader Emory P. Roberts, Lubert F. "Bert" deFreese, J. Frank Yeager, Donald J. Lawton, Charles T. Zboril, and William T. McIntyre] departed Wash., DC 8:40 a.m. via AAL enroute to Chicago-while in air approx. 20 minutes from Chicago, advised that Pres. cancelled trip-returned to Wash. DC 12:15 p.m.)."[216] The report also notes that, in addition to Roberts, deFreese, Yeager, Lawton, Zboril, and McIntyre, ASAIC Floyd M. Boring and William R. Greer departed the White House with President Kennedy via two helicopters at 6:05 P.M. for Atoka, Middleburg, VA, the

211   The last three were named and contacted by the *Chicago Independent*.

212   2/26/78 HSCA interview with Kinney [RIF # 180-10078-10493]. 2/28/78 HSCA interview with Greer [RIF# 180-10099-10491]. 3/1/78 HSCA interview with Kollar [RIF# 180-10071-10163] At the time of the HSCA hearings, Kollar was the ASAIC of the Ford Protective Division [12/14/77 letter from Secret Service Legal Counsel Robert O. Goff to the HSCA's G. Robert Blakey, [RIF #180-10112-10218]. 4/12/78 HSCA interview with Stocks [RIF #180-10104-10326]. 3/6/78 HSCA interview with McCleod [RIF # 180-10071-10164]. 12/30/77 HSCA interview with Motto [RIF # 180-10087-10190]. 1/19/78 HSCA interview with Tucker [RIF # 180-10070-10276]. 2/3/78 HSCA interview with Grant [RIF # 180-10082-10451]. 2/1/78 HSCA interview with Griffiths [RIF # 180-10082-10453]. 1/19/78 HSCA interview with Bolden [RIF # 180-10070-10273]. 2/1/78 HSCA interview of Martineau [RIF # 180-10087-10191].

213   Strangely, SAIC Jerry Behn told the HSCA on 1/30/78 that he was "unable to recall anything about the President's cancellation of his planned appearance on 11/2[63]. He did not remember hearing about either the trip or its political purpose." And yet, "He did remember that SA Dave Grant was the advance agent from the WHD to Chicago for the 11/1 [sic] trip ... he [also] did remember that Maurice Martineau was the acting SAIC of the Chicago office at the time of the trip," to which one of the HSCA investigators appropriately handwrote in a "?" to end the sentence.

214   2/3/78 HSCA interview of Grant [RIF# 180-10082-10451] USSS Record # 1541000110182; 1541000110175.

215   3/1/78 HSCA interview of Kollar [RIF# 180-10071-10163] USSS Record # 1541000110183; 1541000110176.

216   In a letter to the author dated 1/24/04, Yeager wrote, "I do not remember a cancellation of a trip to Chicago; I only remember a cancellation of a trip to Seattle from Chicago during the Cuban missile crisis when we returned to Washington [October 1962]. I don't remember who was in charge that day." USSS Record # 1541000110174: ATSAIC Emory P. Roberts' report.

Kennedy residence, arriving at 6:40 p.m. Another Secret Service Shift Report notes that Samuel A. Kinney "arrived Wash. D.C. Andrews AFB 4:50 p.m. via USAF Plane C-130-2368 from Chicago, Ill."[217]

Authors Lamar Waldron and Thom Hartmann thank me for getting them in touch with Bolden, which led to information the former agent provided to them ending up on several pages of their book *Ultimate Sacrifice*[218] and the 2006 television documentary *Conspiracy Files: The JFK Assassination*.[219] Likewise, author Jim Douglass contacted me in 1998 (and again in 2005) regarding getting a hold of Bolden for his masterpiece book *JFK And the Unspeakable*.[220] (My work is also prominently featured in Mark Lane's 2011 book *Last Word*. Lane had also sought me out to use my work for his book).[221] However, Abraham Bolden and Nemo Ciochina are far from the only sources for the Chicago plot. Bolden wrote to the author: "I do not believe Oswald acted alone because evidence is that there were at least 3 riflemen following the President just 3 weeks before he was assassinated in Dallas."

Direct and indirect corroboration for Mr. Bolden's accounts of threats to JFK's life in Chicago, in general, and the 11/2/63 plot in Chicago, in particular, comes from the following sources:[222]

> 1. "[Maurice] Martineau said that he was in Chicago when President John F. Kennedy made a visit prior to November 1963. He could not recall the precise date. "We got a telephone threat. The caller was not identified, that Kennedy was going to be killed when he got to Jackson Street. We adjusted the routine to rely on the Chicago Police to cover the area. The threat did not materialize," he said. ... We asked Martineau about threats against JFK in [the] Chicago area [for] November 1963. Martineau visibly stiffened. "I can recall no threat that was significant enough to cause me to recollect it at this time" he

217   USSS Record # 1541000110173. Mrs. June Kellerman told the author on 3/2/92 that Roy's only television appearance was during the Army-Air Force game, presumably the same one held on 11/2/63 in Chicago (based on the context of the conversation). This is the only documentation for Kellerman's presence on that day; the shift reports do not mention him at all.
218   *Ultimate Sacrifice* by Lamar Waldron and Thom Hartmann (2005), various.
219   *Conspiracy Files: The JFK Assassination* 2006 (youtube.com)
220   *JFK And the Unspeakable* by James Douglass (2008), various.
221   *Last Word* (2011) by Mark Lane, pages 168-171, 185-186.
222   From *Chicago Independent* article by Edwin Black, November 1975: Stocks, Coll, Linsky, Coffey, and Vallee himself. See also *Last Word* (2011) by Mark Lane, pages 162-163, and 2022 book *JFK Revisited* by James DiEugenio (and the documentary with the same name), pages 69-70.

said. In contrast to the wealth of detail which flooded his earlier recollections, his answers became vague and less responsive."[223]

```
Martineau memo to Chief 11/26/63 re call from
2-1-266 pertaining to a group of anti-Castro
Cubans possibly involved in assassination - copy
```

Interesting item from Martineau.[224]

2. Col. George J. McNally, WH Signal Corps and former Secret Service agent: "But during the Chicago visit [3/23/63], the motorcade
was slowed to the pace of a mounted Black Horse Troop, and the
police got a warning of Puerto Rican snipers. Helicopters searched
the roofs along the way, and no incidents occurred."[225] Please note
McNally calling the suspects "Puerto Rican."

3. "A postcard was received in the Saturday morning mail of the Chicago office threatening the life of the President during the [3/23/63]
motorcade from O'Hare Field to the Conrad Hilton Hotel."[226]

4. FBI agent Thomas B. Coll: "I remember that case. Some people
were picked up. And I'm telling you it wasn't ours. That was strictly
a Secret Service affair. That whole Soldier Field matter was a Secret
Service affair ... You'll get no more out of me. I've said as much as
I'm going to on that subject. Get the rest from the Secret Service."
Note Coll using the plural "people."

5. Captain Robert Linsky, security liaison between the Chicago Police and the Secret Service, remembered the Vallee arrest.[227]

6. Lloyd Stocks remembered, "something about a guy called Vallee."[228] This was Thomas Arthur Vallee, a man arrested apart from
the four-man team.[229] Vallee's sister Mary Vallee-Portillo told author

223   2/1/78 HSCA interview with Martineau [HSCA RIF# 180-10087-10191].
224   docid-32277356.pdf (archives.gov)
225   A Million Miles of Presidents by Col. George McNally (1970/1982), p. 204.
226   RIF #154-10003-10012: Chicago, Il trip 3/23/63 Secret Service survey report.
6 motorcycles surrounding limo, Lawton riding on (JFK's side of) rear of limo, Mayor's
follow-up car with four detectives in addition to SS follow-up car, police facing crowd
(not JFK) on the route, no-one permitted on overpasses except four policemen guarding them, press/photographers close to JFK, Hatcher with Kilduff. PRS: one threat (the
postcard). WHD agents on trip: Grant (advance agent), Burke, Pontius, Lilley, Johnsen,
Chandler, Giannoules, Lawton, Blaine, Lawson, Olsson, Burns, Paolella, Godfrey, Boring,
Greer, Shipman, O'Leary;Chicago office agents: Hanly, Tucker, Martineau, Plichta, Bold-
en, Cross, Maynard, Stocks, Gorman, Noonan, Griffiths, Motto, McLeod, Russell, Strong.
227   Backed up by government reports on file at the AARC.
228   Chicago threats Part 3 | Larry Hancock (wordpress.com)
229   Chicago Police Officer Peter Schurla was interviewed 1/18/78 by the HSCA
pertaining to surveillance and early morning arrest of Thomas Arthur Vallee on 11/2/63

James Douglass: "My brother probably was set up. He was very much used."[230]

7. Sergeant Lawrence Coffey: "Naturally, I remember every detail ... How often is anyone involved in a threat against the President's life?"

8. Thomas Arthur Vallee himself[231]: "Soldiers Field. The plot against John F. Kennedy." Mr. Vallee claimed he was framed by someone with special knowledge about him, such as his "CIA assignment to train exiles to assassinate Castro." Vallee told Edwin Black that he had been assigned by the Marines to a U-2 base in Japan, Camp Otsu, which came under the control of the CIA, just as Oswald came under similar control of the CIA at another Marine U-2 base in Japan.[232]

Vallee answered quickly and curtly: "Soldiers Field. The plot against John F. Kennedy."

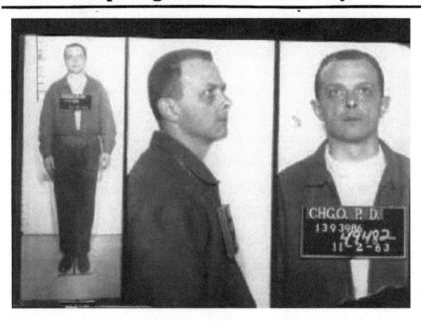

Thomas Arthur Vallee.

[HSCA RIF #180-10070- 10277]; also, Stocks told the HSCA on 4/12/78 that he remembered the Vallee incident but did not take part in the investigation (agents Thomas Strong and Ed Tucker handled the case) [HSCA RIF # 180- 10104-10326].

230   *JFK And the Unspeakable*, page 204.

231   Vallee's arrest record and mug shots can be found on p. 406 of *November Patriots*. See also HSCA Report, pp. 231-232.

232   *JFK And the Unspeakable*, page 205.

9. PRS Agent Glen A. Bennett told the HSCA: "[He] remembers the name Vallee but does not recall why."[233]

10 Agent Joseph E. Noonan, Jr.: As previously noted, Noonan "participated directly in surveillance involving Tom Mosely and Homer Echevarria ... he and [the] other agents were uneasy that the Cubans might have some ties to the CIA ... a little later they received a call from Headquarters to drop everything on Mosely and Echevarria and send all memos, files, and their notebooks to Washington and not to discuss the case with anyone." Noonan also knew about the Vallee case.[234] In addition, the administrative assistant of the Intelligence Division (formerly known as PRS) made an interesting observation to Agent Bob Ritter soon after the Reagan assassination attempt (3/30/81), "She [unnamed] came to me later in the day and said she wanted to 'warn me' ... She's been around a long time. She started in the Chicago Field Office and worked there during the JFK assassination [This had to be either Charlotte Klapkowski or June Marie Terpinas]. She told me that 'funny things' went on back then and she has the same feeling again ... she wouldn't elaborate on that. She did say that SAIC Richards told her to type only the original of my report. No copies were to be made, not even the standard agent's copy. And she was ordered to shred my original handwritten submission! She knew how strange that was. She warned me to look out for myself."[235]

11. Agent James S. Griffiths: "Griffith[s] stated that the name of Thomas Vallee was familiar and remembers a case concerning Vallee but does not remember any of the details."[236] In the Fall of 1963, shortly before the ill-fated Chicago trip, Chicago Police Lieutenant Berkeley F. Moyland's son, Moyland Junior, told author James Douglass that his father counseled Vallee after hearing his threatening remarks about JFK, warning him that this kind of talk could lead to serious consequences. Moyland Senior took the extra step of phoning the Secret Service with a warning about Vallee. However, it was not

---

233   1/30/78 HSCA interview of Bennett [HSCA RIF #180-10082-10452]. See also *JFK Revisited* by James DiEugenio (and the documentary with the same name), pages 372-373.

234   4/13/78 HSCA interview of Noonan Re: Mosely and Echevaria – 12/19/63 USSS report [HSCA RIF # 180-10087-10136], 11/27/63 USSS report (Martineau to Paterni) [HSCA RIF # 180-10087- 10137], 12/13/63 USSS report [HSCA RIF # 180-10087-10138]. See also HSCA Report, p. 236.

235   *Breaking Tecumsah's Curse* by Jan and Bob Ritter (2013), p. 414.

236   2/1/78 HSCA interview of Griffiths; At the time of the HSCA hearings, Griffiths was the SAIC of the Special Investigations & Security Division [12/14/77 letter from Secret Service Legal Counsel Robert O. Goff to the HSCA's G. Robert Blakey, RIF #180-10112-10218].

Moyland but an FBI informant named "Lee" whose alert disrupted the four-man rifle team and potential patsy Vallee as well. The Treasury Department (with jurisdiction over the Secret Service) swore Moyland to secrecy over the matter, although Moyland confided in his son in his final years.[237] One wonders if the "Lee" was Lee Harvey Oswald.[238]

12. Chicago's *American*, 11/26/63: "Daly Diary" by Maggie Daly: "The word is that the assassination of President Kennedy was planned at a meeting on Chicago's west side in the early part of February.... That a dissident Cuban group financed Lee Harvey Oswald and that he lived on occasional money from the members and occasional money from his mother."[239]

13. Agent Edward Z. Tucker: told the HSCA the details of his involvement in the Thomas Arthur Vallee investigation.[240] From the HSCA interview:" Tucker told us that for security reasons, on or about October 30, 1963, he recalls going to interview a subject named Vallee, who was supposed to represent a threat to the President. This was a customary practice prior to Presidential visits. Accompanied by Agent Tom Strong, he visited Vallee at his rooming house on the north side of Chicago. He was troubled by his conversation with Vallee, who he says had one or more rifles in his possession. Absent any Federal sanctions, Tucker reported back to the Secret Service office about his misgivings. The next day Vallee's landlady, whom Tucker suspects was the informant, called the Secret Service office and said that Vallee had told her that he was not going to work on Saturday, November 2nd, the day JFK was coming to Chicago. Tucker said it was this information which caused the Secret Service to alert the Chicago Police Department to place surveillance on Vallee. He is aware that they did, and that Vallee was

237   *JFK And the Unspeakable*, pages 206-207. *Burying the Lead: The Media and the JFK Assassination* by Mel Hyman (2019), pages 354-355.
238   *The JFK Assassination Chokeholds* (2023) by Jim DiEugenio, Paul Bleau, Matt Crumpton, Andrew Iler, and Mark Adamczyk, pages 206-212. *The JFK Assassination* (2016/2018) by James DiEugenio, pages 273-274. *JFK Revisited* by James DiEugenio (and the documentary with the same name), pages 202-203.
239   As reproduced in HSCA RIF #180-10087-10137; In this same HSCA collection, there is a reproduction of a *Chicago Daily News* article dated 11/26/63. In the article, Mrs. Ruth Paine, the woman who was instrumental in getting Oswald the Book Depository job, while lodging Marina Oswald & the two children in her house, is quoted as saying: "I understand there are people in the Chicago area who are talking of helping [Marina], too.
240   1/19/78 HSCA interview of Tucker [HSCA RIF # 180-10070-10276]. Fellow Chicago office agent Conrad Cross told the HSCA "the name Thomas Arthur Vallee was familiar and he remembers it was Ed Tucker's case." [HSCA RIF# 180-10104-10324]. *Daily Herald*, 2/3/75: interview with Tucker.

arrested by two Chicago Police officers on November 2nd before the President was due in Chicago. On that Saturday morning, Tucker's assignment had been to go to the airport (O'Hare) and meet the President. He did not recall that he was to ride in the Pilot car in the motorcade, but he said he did not go into the Secret Service office downtown and was therefore unaware of any other subjects that the Secret Service might have had in custody at the time. If this happened, he was not informed about it, he said. When he reached the airport in the morning of November 2, 1963, he was told that the President had canceled his trip to Chicago but that several Members of Congress had arrived, and the Secret Service was told to escort them to the Army-Air Force Academy game at Soldier Field. He thinks he went home instead."[241]

14. Agent Gary M. McLeod: told the HSCA that he did recall the name Thomas Arthur Vallee and that Agent Ed Tucker was assigned to the Vallee case that involved guns but does not remember any involvement with the Chicago Police. Here, McLeod is dead wrong.[242]

15. HSCA Report: "One agent [Robert Motto] did state there had been a threat in Chicago during that period, but he was unable to recall details."[243] Specifically, Robert J. Motto told the HSCA: "The trip was cancelled. I think they told us at the [Air Force/ Army game at Soldier's Field], but we decided to watch it anyway ... When I got back to the office, someone said there had been threats."[244] Please note Motto confirming a threat and actually using the plural "threats" in his actual interview, not the summary.

16. Agent Louis B. Sims: told the HSCA: "He could not remember dates but he recalls it could have been any time up to a year prior to the assassination, he was assigned to conduct a surveillance on a subject that was either Puerto Rican or Cuban. He does not remember any specific details other than it involved gun running and it appeared to be a very sensitive investigation. He stated the names Echevarria and Manuel Rodriquez were familiar, but he couldn't

---

241   Tucker wrote a positive review of fellow agent Gerald Blaine's book *The Kennedy Detail* on Amazon (in sharp contrast to Bolden's negative review) and also did a Sixth Floor Museum oral history on 5/6/2015.

242   Chicago Police Officer Peter Schurla was interviewed 1/18/78 by the HSCA pertaining to surveillance and early morning arrest of Thomas Arthur Vallee on 11/2/63 [HSCA RIF #180-10070- 10277]; also, fellow agent Ed Tucker mentions the Chicago police surveillance of Vallee during his 1/19/78 HSCA interview [HSCA RIF # 180-10070-10276].

243   HSCA report, pp. 231 & 636. 12/30/77 HSCA interview with Robert Motto (JFK Document 008482).

244   12/30/77 HSCA interview with Motto [HSCA RIF# 180-10113-10038].

place them."[245] Please note Sims stating that the subject was "Puerto Rican" as his first thought. Mr. Bolden told the HSCA[246] that Mr. Vallee was independent of the four-man team, and he told the author the same thing, adding that the confusion was "done intentionally by the government agencies." Sims later became involved in the Watergate investigation:

LEAVES COURT — Louis Sims, head of the technical services division of the Secret Service, reaches to open the car door as he leaves United States District Court in Washington Thursday. Sims gave testimony before U.S. District Judge John J. Sirica on the White House tapes related to the Watergate affair.
—(AP Wirephoto)

Apparently living in a parallel universe, David Grant, advance man for the 11/2/63 Chicago trip, conveyed to the HSCA that " ... no information about a threat ever came to his attention from any source including PRS, the local Chicago SS office, and the Chicago P.D. Specifically, Mr. Grant was 'not familiar' with the name of Thomas Arthur Vallee, a person who was suspected by the Chicago SS to be involved in a threat and who was detained by the SS. Nor could Mr. Grant 'recall' in the context of this trip other instances of the investigation of a threat or the detention of a person."[247]

---

245   5/22/78 HSCA interview with Sims [HSCA RIF # 180-10093-10022].
246   HSCA Report, pp. 231-232.
247   2/3/78 HSCA interview with Grant [RIF# 180-10082-10451].

Secret Service agent Abraham Bolden (far right) with JFK June 1961.

Likewise, Robert Kollar, who assisted in the advance, also let it be known to the HSCA that "he has no recollection of any subject named Thomas Arthur Vallee nor does he remember ever being told of Thomas Arthur Vallee being considered a 'threat' to the President or being told that Vallee had been taken into custody by the Chicago Police Department. He also stated that he had never heard of any other possible threat to the President in the Chicago area during his advance trip to Chicago."[248]

Agent Louis B. Sims,[249] while telling the HSCA about some tantalizing information regarding surveillance (see above), also told them: "He had no recall of any threat relative to the Presidential visit to Chicago in April [sic: March] 1963."[250] However, nothing was said about the 11/2/63 trip.

248   3/1/78 HSCA interview with Kollar [RIF# 180-10071-10163].
249   Agent Lawson, Agent Louis Sims (Chicago office, later of Watergate tape 'fame'), and a CIA operative who knew Oswald and was also allegedly privy to the assassination plot, Richard Case Nagell, all served at Fort Holabird, MD in the 1950's. Louis B. Sims, 1950's: served three years with U.S. Army Intelligence at Fort Holabird, MD [HSCA RIF# 180-10093-10022: 5/22/78 interview]. Entered Secret Service in 4/61 and assigned to Chicago office until 1/64; 1/64-12/65: Washington Field Office [See also 26 H 726-727]; 12/65-7/69: Intelligence Division; 7/69-11/72: Liaison Section; 11/72-9/74: Technical Security Division; 9/74 until at least 5/78: Chief of Interpol. A member of the Chicago office with Bolden; also attended Bolden's trial (Bolden was in a cell across from Nagell for a time: The Man Who Knew Too Much by Dick Russell, p. 635).
250   5/22/78 HSCA interview with Sims [RIF# 180-10093-10022].

Agent John Ready told the HSCA: "He stated that to his knowledge no trip had ever been cancelled because of a threat." Recalling a 1972 trip with Dr. Henry Kissinger involving a threat, Ready stated, "the only thing changed was the route."[251] Likewise, Agent Gary McLeod told the HSCA that he has heard of trips being altered but has never heard of one being canceled because of a threat.[252] However, as author Philip Melanson wrote, "[President] Nixon was scheduled to visit New Orleans in late August 1973, where he was planning to ride in an open car motorcade through the city's French Quarter. The Service uncovered a purported assassination plot and asked Nixon to cancel the motorcade; reluctantly, Nixon did so, issuing the order personally."[253]

In any event, the motorcade was cancelled at the last minute, ostensibly for two reasons:

> 1. JFK had a cold. This is the same made-up excuse JFK gave Salinger in reference to the Cuban Missile Crisis the year before in the same city of Chicago.[254]

> 2. The Diem assassination. However, Salinger himself "announced at 9:30 a.m. that a special communications facility would be rush constructed under the Soldiers Field bleachers to keep the President informed on up-to-the-minute developments in coup-torn South Vietnam. He reiterated Kennedy would not cancel the trip."[255]

Since Mr. Vallee was arrested and off the streets, it appears obvious the real reason for the cancellation of the trip was the threat of the four-man team, two of which eluded surveillance and escaped. Mr. Bolden did manage to get information about the plot into the public domain: Before any conspiracy book footnoted his testimony, the *New York Times* issue of 12/6/67 documented it for the record.

---

251   3/1/78 HSCA interview with Ready [HSCA RIF # 180-10071-10165].

252   3/6/78 HSCA interview with McLeod [HSCA RIF# 180-10071-10164].

253   *The Secret Service: The Hidden History of an Enigmatic Agency* by Philip Melanson, p. 104 (see also pp. 105-109).

254   *Johnny, We Hardly Knew Ye*, pp. 371-372; Agent Gary McLeod said JFK having a cold was the reason for the cancellation of the 11/2/63 trip (3/6/78 HSCA interview), while Agent David Grant called it an "illness" (2/3/78 HSCA interview). Agent Bill Greer could not recall why (2/28/78 HSCA interview). SAIC Jerry Behn could not even recall the trip itself! (1/30/78 HSCA interview) Agent Sam Kinney said the reason for the cancellation was the "Cuban Missile Crisis," obviously confusing the 11/2/63 trip with the 10/62 Chicago trip (2/26/78 HSCA interview). Finally, when the author asked former agent Walt Coughlin why the trip was cancelled, he responded: "I have not a clue!" [E-mail to author dated 2/25/04].

255   *Chicago Independent*, November 1975.

Before continuing with Mr. Bolden's plight, it is important to look at Maurice G. Martineau. Martineau was the SAIC of the Chicago field office, and served some 32 years with the agency, from 1941 to 1972.[256] He was a member of the White House Detail during the FDR years, and on temporary assignments during the Eisenhower administration. Mr. Martineau stated, "Any time they [the White House Detail] came thru Chicago, [he] worked very close with the advance team from Washington." Importantly, Mr. Martineau confirmed that the motorcade was cancelled "at the last minute – I was already out at the airport" to meet JFK's plane when this occurred, he said. Mr. Bolden was a touchy subject: "As far as Bolden is concerned, I'd rather not discuss it. He was a blight on the agency." Interestingly, Mr. Martineau revealed that he "was subpoenaed to testify before" the HSCA, which he declared "a lot more valid than the Warren Commission."[257] He believed "there was more than one assassin" on 11/22/63, stemming from the HSCA's report, his own role in the investigation, his extensive experience with firearms, and his own gut feelings on 11/22/63, "As soon as I learned some of the details." When the author conveyed to him agent Sam Kinney's own beliefs of conspiracy, including Kinney's qualification that his own "outfit was clean," Mr. Martineau stated: "Well ... ah ... (long pause) ... I've got some theories, too, but, ah ... without any actual data to back them up, I think I'll keep them to myself."

Abraham Bolden was adamant that Mr. Martineau knew about both the plot to kill JFK on 11/2/63 and the internal "top secret" investigation of the Secret Service Commission books, one of which was "lost or stolen" in Dallas on the Texas trip of November, 1963: "I recalled that in January, 1964, the Secret Service recalled all commission books all over the United States. We were told they were to be redesigned ... to me, the redesign of the commission books was for one purpose and that purpose was to render the lost or stolen commission book a counterfeit when the persons bearing the lost or stolen commission book were found." Mr. Bolden wrote the author: "When Inspector Kelley of the Secret Service came to Chicago in 1961, I discussed with him the fact that during a conversation between SAIC Maurice Martineau and two other agents who were discussing Kennedy's push for racial balance and equal justice in America, Mr. Martineau blurted out angrily, 'The bastard should be killed.' This coming from an agent was dangerous."[258]

256   Author's interviews with Martineau, 9/21/93 & 6/7/96.
257   Executive Session testimony of Martineau, HSCA, 3/15/78 [RIF# 180-10116-10084].
258   See also *Burying the Lead: The Media and the JFK Assassination* by Mel Hyman

Bolden continued: "The prevailing attitude of the Caucasian agents, the majority of whom were southern born, was that Kennedy was moving too fast on Civil Rights and in the Chicago office of the Secret Service, I heard the term 'nigger lover' applied to President Kennedy by more than one or two agents." Mr. Bolden added that "all (this) information … was discussed with Inspector Kelley, John Hanley (SAIC), Harry Geghlein, and John [sic?] Burke (Assistant SAIC) in the Chicago office to no avail."

Regarding Inspector Kelley, ASAIC Martineau told the HSCA on 2/1/78: "He did remember SA Tom Kelley calling from Dallas on 11/23/63-regarding Oswald's rifle ordered from Klein's in Chicago. He said in those days the Secret Service in Chicago was not open on weekends so Kelley called him at home. He then called SA Tom Strong and asked him to check Klein's Sporting Goods for information on the rifle. Strong told him that the FBI had beaten them to Klein's and got the records."[259]

Bolden had more to say about Mr. Martineau: "My mind flashed back to the day Kennedy was assassinated whereupon returning to the Secret Service office, June Marie Terpinas (secretary) approached me with tears in her eyes. She had gone into the office of SAIC Maurice G. Martineau upon hearing a radio flash concerning the shooting of the President. She told me that upon hearing that the President was shot and relaying that report to Mr. Martineau, his reply was 'So what else is new?' I remembered rushing into Mr. Martineau's office and confronting him about his attitude and having been thrown out of his office with a warning to mind my own business."

Bolden told Bud Fensterwald that, after the assassination, both Martineau and Inspector Kelley (who came straight from the investigation in Dallas) personally visited the North side landlady in Chicago with whom the four suspects stayed prior to 11/2/63. Also, "shortly after the assassination, Martineau called all agents into his office and showed them a memo from Washington to the effect that the Secret Service was to discuss no aspect of the assassination and investigation with anyone from any other federal agency now or any time in the future. Every agent, including Bolden, was made to initial this memo. Bolden believes this took place on Wednesday, November 27th. When asked why, he stated, "FBI wanted to get role of Presidential protector away from Secret Service and thought this was [the] ideal opportunity."[260]

(2019), page 354.
259   2/1/78 HSCA interview with Martineau; see also 3 HSCA 339.
260   AARC file.

There is no question that the prior trip to Chicago on 3/23/63 offers tantalizing hints at what was planned for 11/2/63 and beyond: As mentioned above, and it is definitely worthy of repeating, Colonel George Mc-Nally wrote: "But during the Chicago visit [3/23/63], the motorcade was slowed to the pace of a mounted Black Horse Troop, and the police got a warning of Puerto Rican snipers. Helicopters searched the roofs along the way, and no incidents occurred."

A very rare photo discovered by the author: Bolden[261] (far right) with JFK and Chicago Mayor Daley 3/23/63 (agent Art Godfrey next to Kennedy).

The following Secret Service documents about the 3/23/63 Chicago trip only came to light in the mid-1990's thanks to the ARRB. Please note the postcard threat, the heightened security, and Bolden's involvement with the security. Also note that this is another trip the SAIC of the White House Detail, Gerald Behn, was absent from (as he was scheduled to do for the 11/2/63 Chicago trip and as he did do for the Florida trip of 11/18/63, Behn's immediate assistant, ASAIC Floyd Boring, went in his place. As

261   Bolden enthusiastically confirmed that this was indeed a photo of himself when the author contacted him after discovering the photo at an online auction house in 2019. Inexplicably, he tentatively recanted the identity the next day, although he was definitely a part of the security of the trip and others beside myself also believe it is a photo of Bolden.

noted in my prior books, although third-stringer Roy Kellerman made the Texas trip in place of both Behn and Boring, Boring was still the agent in charge of planning):[262]

262   RIF #154-10003-10012: Chicago, IL trip 3/23/63 Secret Service survey report. 6 motorcycles surrounding limo, Lawton riding on (JFK's side of) rear of limo, Mayor's follow-up car with four detectives in addition to SS follow-up car, police facing crowd (not JFK) on the route, no-one permitted on overpasses except four policemen guard-

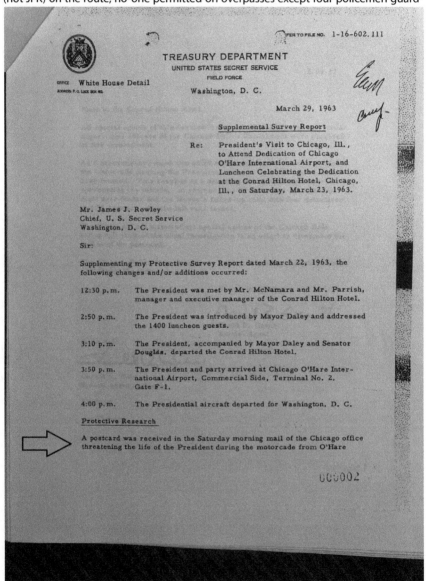

ing them, press/photographers close to JFK, Hatcher with Kilduff. PRS: one threat (the postcard). WHD agents on trip: Grant (advance agent), Burke, Pontius, Lilley, Johnsen, Chandler, Giannoules, Lawton, Blaine, Lawson, Olsson, Burns, Paolella, Godfrey, Boring,

- 2 -   3-29-63

Field to the Conrad Hilton Hotel.

All special agents of this Service involved in the movement and senior supervisory officers of the Chicago Police Department were apprised of this development.

As a precautionary move two additional motorcycles were employed in the motorcade flanking the President's limousine at the right and left rear fenders. This resulted in a shielding effect with six motorcycles surrounding the vehicle. In addition, the SS follow-up car rode the right rear fender and the Mayor's follow-up car, with four detectives, and SA Lawton, rode the left rear fender.

The threat did not materialize; special agents of the Chicago field office will conduct the usual investigation in an effort to determine the author of the postcard.

The Chicago Police Department was requested to keep the information concerning the threat confidential.

Very truly yours,

David B. Grant

David B. Grant
Special Agent

Approved:

Gerald A. Behn

Gerald A. Behn
Special Agent in Charge

DBG:ebd

cc: Chicago

Greer, Shipman, O'Leary; Chicago office agents: Hanly, Tucker, Martineau, Plichta, Bolden, Cross, Maynard, Stocks, Gorman, Noonan, Griffiths, Motto, McLeod, Russell, Strong.

Mr. James J. Rowley   - 4 -

1-16-602.111
March 22, 1963

Members of the Chicago Police Department, both detectives and uniformed officers, will be strategically placed in and around the South Imperial Suite, the Grand Ballroom, the Normandy Lounge, the elevator landings, stairways, and halls.

The Chicago Fire Department will have officers strategically positioned throughout the hotel.

Routes

A motorcycle escort will be employed on this occasion. All intersections of traffic, underpasses, and overpasses will be controlled by uniformed officers of the Chicago Police Department.

At Jackson Boulevard and Franklin Street a group of 26 horsemen, the Black Horse Troop, will join the motorcade and fall in between the pilot car and the lead car for the remainder of the parade route to the Conrad Hilton Hotel.

POST ASSIGNMENTS

Chicago-O'Hare International Airport, Chicago, Illinois

1. Point where the President deplanes	SAIC Hanly ASAIC Martineau SA Grant 6 detectives 15 uniformed officers
2. Front ramp - Air Force 1	SA Tucker 4 detectives 10 uniformed officers
3. Down escalator, upper level, Terminal 2	SA Plichta 2 detectives 6 uniformed officers
4. Down escalator, lower level, Terminal 2	SA Cross 2 detectives 6 uniformed officers
5. Exit to street, lower level, Terminal 2	SA Stocks 4 detectives 12 uniformed officers

000907

Mr. James J. Rowley   - 6 -

1-16-602.111
March 22, 1963

5. Entrance to Normandy Lounge, check point ⟹ SA Bolden
     2 detectives
     2 uniformed officers

6. Stairway to Grand Ballroom, check point   SA Lawson
     2 detectives
     2 uniformed officers

7. Balcony, Grand Ballroom, north side (press area)   SA Lawson
     2 detectives
     4 uniformed officers

8. Balcony, Grand Ballroom, south side (above   SA Olsson
    speakers table)   2 detectives
     4 uniformed officers

9. Head table, east end, check point   SA Burns

10. Head table, west end, check point   SA Paolella

11. Seated - table directly in front of President   ASAIC Godfrey

⟹ ASAIC Boring will ride in the Presidential limousine and remain close to the President at all times. SA Greer will drive the Presidential limousine.

⟹ SA's Pontius, Lilley, Johnsen, Giannoules, Chandler, and Lawton will work the Secret Service follow-up car, with SA Shipman driving, from Chicago-O'Hare International Airport to the Conrad Hilton Hotel.

⟹ ASAIC Godfrey and SA's Blaine, Lawson, Olsson, Paolella, and Burns will work the Secret Service follow-up car, with SA Shipman driving, from the Conrad Hilton Hotel to Chicago-O'Hare International Airport.

ASAIC Martineau will ride in the Chicago Police Department pilot car. SAIC Hanly and SA Grant will ride in the Chicago Police Department lead car. SA O'Leary will ride in the Chicago Police Department tail car.

The general supervision of all activities and post assignments will be under the direction of ASAIC Boring and SA's Grant and Burke, office 1-16, and SAIC Hanly and SA Tucker, office 2-1.

To properly establish their identities, all special agents will wear their permanent lapel buttons. Chicago Police Department detectives will wear yellow

000209

1-16-602.111
March 22, 1963

Mr. James J. Rowley   - 7 -

lapel buttons. Chicago-O'Hare International Airport employees will wear gray lapel buttons. Conrad Hilton Hotel employees will wear green lapel buttons. Communications personnel will wear lilac lapel buttons. Chicago Fire Department and Bureau of Streets employees will wear orange lapel buttons.

PROTECTIVE RESEARCH

SAIC Bouck, Protective Research Section, has been apprised of this movement. If it develops that there are any active protective research subjects at large in this area, all pertinent information concerning them will be given to the personnel participating in the security measures.

With reference to the recent rash of bombings that have occurred in Chicago, Sergeant Edward Neville, Chicago Police Department, Bomb and Arson Squad, was interviewed and advised this Service that the bombings his department has investigated for the past few years, which have occurred in local restaurants and taverns, were the result of black powder confined in pipes and dynamite sticks, all of them hand ignited. There have been no exotic explosives or time devices used in these bombings. All of the bombings have occurred when the businesses have been closed, and no persons have been injured or killed as a result.

Sergeant Neville advises that it appears these bombings have been in the way of a warning to the owners of the businesses, and appear to be labor or crime syndicate oriented. He further advised that it is his opinion that there is not a "mad bomber" involved; also, that none of the approximately 30 bombings in the past two years appear to be the work of a crank.

As mentioned earlier in this report, a bomb squad will thoroughly sweep Chicago-O'Hare International Airport and the Conrad Hilton Hotel prior to the President's arrival and will be available in the event of an emergency.

INSTRUCTIONS TO AGENTS

Saturday, March 23, 1963

SAIC Hanly, ASAIC Martineau, and SA's Grant, Tucker, Plichta, Cross, Stocks, Noonan, Griffiths, Motto, McLeod, and Russell will report to Chicago-O'Hare International Airport at 9:30 a.m. to set up security arrangements prior to the President's arrival.

SA's Burke, Strong, and Bolden will report to the Conrad Hilton Hotel at 9:30 a.m. to prepare advance security measures.

1-16-602.111
March 22, 1963

Mr. James J. Rowley   - 9 -

The Chicago Fire Department is supplying the drivers for the automobiles in the motorcade. The Airline Association will supply drivers for the busses.

A list of car assignments in the motorcade is attached to this report.

PRESS AND PHOTOGRAPHERS

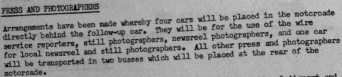

Arrangements have been made whereby four cars will be placed in the motorcade directly behind the follow-up car. They will be for the use of the wire service reporters, still photographers, newsreel photographers, and one car for local newsreel and still photographers. All other press and photographers will be transported in two busses which will be placed at the rear of the motorcade.

Press facilities have been set up at Chicago-O'Hare International Airport and the Conrad Hilton Hotel for press and photographers.

All press activities will be under the supervision of Assistant Press Secretaries Andrew Hatcher and Malcolm Kilduff.

COMMUNICATIONS

Communication facilities were arranged by the White House Communication Agency and consist of the following.

Telephone service will be provided to Washington and all local facilities. Direct telephones are available to the Presidential aircraft, speech sites, security post, advance personnel's quarters, and press areas. The Chicago White House switchboard dial number is 427-2608.

Charlie channel radio will be utilized to control all aircraft, motorcades, and arrival locations. The Presidential motorcade will have radios in the pilot car, lead car, President's car, follow-up car, and tail car.

A communication center for classified traffic will be in operation and service may be obtained by calling the Chicago White House switchboard.

All Presidential remarks will be recorded by WHCA personnel.

CONCLUSION

The following number of personnel will participate in the overall security measures:

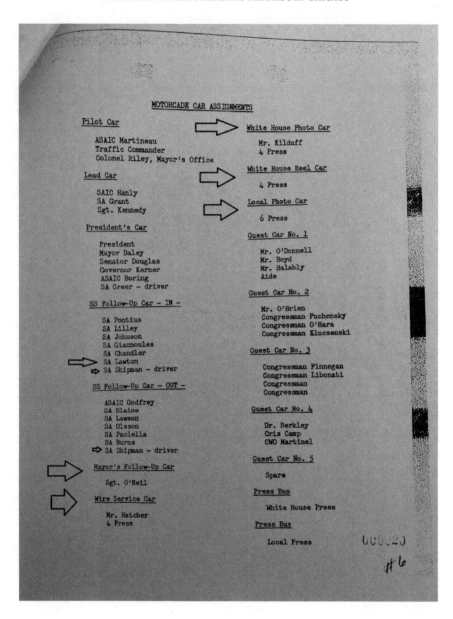

MOTORCADE CAR ASSIGNMENTS

Pilot Car

ASAIC Martineau
Traffic Commander
Colonel Riley, Mayor's Office

Lead Car

SAIC Hanly
SA Grant
Sgt. Kennedy

President's Car

President
Mayor Daley
Senator Douglas
Governor Kerner
ASAIC Boring
SA Greer – driver

SS Follow-Up Car – IN –

SA Pontius
SA Lilley
SA Johnson
SA Giannoules
SA Chandler
SA Lawton
SA Shipman – driver

SS Follow-Up Car – OUT –

ASAIC Godfrey
SA Blaine
SA Lawson
SA Olsson
SA Paolella
SA Burns
SA Shipman – driver

Mayor's Follow-Up Car

Sgt. O'Neil

Wire Service Car

Mr. Hatcher
4 Press

White House Photo Car

Mr. Kilduff
4 Press

White House Reel Car

4 Press

Local Photo Car

6 Press

Guest Car No. 1

Mr. O'Donnell
Mr. Boyd
Mr. Halably
Aide

Guest Car No. 2

Mr. O'Brien
Congressman Puchensky
Congressman O'Hara
Congressman Kluczenski

Guest Car No. 3

Congressman Finnegan
Congressman Libonati
Congressman
Congressman

Guest Car No. 4

Dr. Berkley
Cris Camp
CWO Martinel

Guest Car No. 5

Spare

Press Bus

White House Press

Press Bus

Local Press

Rare photos of JFK's motorcade in Chicago 3/23/63.

And, without further ado, valuable documents related to the ill-fated 11/2/63 trip to Chicago. Chicago Special Agent in Charge Maurice Martineau's 1978 HSCA interview:

> Martineau said that he was in Chicago when President John F. Kennedy made a visit prior to November 1963. He could not recall the precise date. "We got a telephone threat. The caller was not identified, that Kennedy was going to be killed when he got to Jackson Street. We adjusted the routine to rely

Maurice Martineau Interview

Page 4

on the Chicago police to cover the area. The threat did not materialize," he said. Martineau said that if a threat came to SS field offices, even if it came anonymously, it was reported to Headquarters in Washington. Protective Research Service (PRS) would be notified. They are now called Protective Research Division (PRD). If the threat came by letter it was sent to PRS for fingerprint analysis and phraseology studies.

We asked Martineau about threats against JFK in Chicago area November 1963. Martineau visibly stiffened. "I can recall no threat that was significant enough to cause me to recollect it at this time" he said. In contrast to the wealth of detail which flooded his earlier recollections, his answers became vague and less responsive.

Chicago Secret Service agent Lois Sims 1978 HSCA interview.

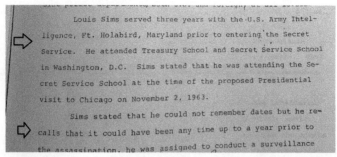

Louis Sims served three years with the U.S. Army Intelligence, Ft. Holabird, Maryland prior to entering the Secret Service. He attended Treasury School and Secret Service School in Washington, D.C. Sims stated that he was attending the Secret Service School at the time of the proposed Presidential visit to Chicago on November 2, 1963.

Sims stated that he could not remember dates but he recalls that it could have been any time up to a year prior to the assassination, he was assigned to conduct a surveillance

Chicago Secret Service agent Joseph Noonan's 1978 HSCA interview:

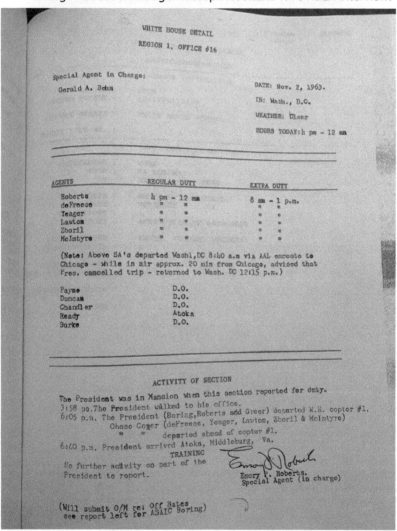

The Secret Service shift report for 11/2/63, released in the late 1990's thanks to the ARRB, duly notes the cancelled Chicago trip (note Agents Tim McIntyre and Bert de Freese listed for trip).

Louis B. Sims Interview
Page 2.

on a subject that was either Puerto Rican or Cuban. He does not remember any specific details other than it involved gun running and it appeared to be a very sensitive investigation. He stated that the names Echevarria and Manuel Rodriquez were familiar; but he couldn't place them. Sims also stated that he believes there may have been a grocery store involved in his surveillance. He stated that all of the details would be in his reports. He believes agents Tucker and Strong had helped him on the case.

Sims stated that he had no recall of any threat relative to the Presidential visit to Chicago in April 1963.

Interview: Joseph Noonan

Page 4

Noonan said he and other agents were uneasy that the Cubans might have some ties to the Central Intelligence Agency and they called Assistant Chief Paul Paterni in Washington and asked him to check on this possibility. Paterni assured them shortly thereafter that it was all right to proceed with their investigation.

A little while later they received a call from Headquarters to drop everything on Mosely and Echevarria and send all memos, files and their notebooks to Washington and not to discuss the case with anyone.

Chicago Secret Service agent Joseph Noonan's 1978 HSCA interview.

McIntyre had heard of Abraham Bolden but did not
know him.

The name Conrad Cross sounded familiar.

He did not know the names Vallee and Moseby.

He stated that he does not believe that he was
assigned to either the Miami trip or the Chicago trip,
both scheduled for November 1963.

section on duty Miami. (See survey report to SA deFreese for details)

9:50 p.m. Roberts, Lawton, Zboril, McIntyre, Bennett, Blaine and Kollar
departed Miami, Fla. via USAF 6972 and arrived Wash.,D. C. 11:50 p.m.

Like Secret Service agent Glen Bennett, agent Tim McIntyre lied to the HSCA about not being scheduled for the Chicago and Florida trips as the shift reports bear out.

deFreese interview...page 6

IV. Chicago

Mr. deFreese did not participate as an agent in any aspect of the November 2, 1963 Presidential trip to Chicago. He does not now recall whether the trip was cancelled, and for that matter, does not even recall that it was scheduled. Hence the name of Vallee did "not ring any bells."

His contact with Agent Bolden was limited -- he had met Bolden only "on one or two occasions." However, Mr. deFreese knew of Bolden's conviction and stated that "he was infamous."

Like Secret Service agent Tim McIntyre, agent Bert DeFreese seems to have amnesia regarding the 11/2/63 trip, as he was scheduled for the trip.

DRAFT

April 15, 1997

Ms. Jane E. Vezeris
Deputy Assistant Director
Office of Administration
United States Secret Service
1800 G Street, N.W.
Washington, D.C. 20223

Re: Request for Information (SS-15): Files on Individuals

Dear Jane:

This letter constitutes our fifteenth formal request for additional information and records under the President John F. Kennedy Assassination Records Collection Act of 1992, 44 U.S.C. § 2107 (Supp. V 1994).

I am writing to ask that you make available for our inspection files that are listed in the Abraham Bolden file. I have enclosed a memorandum from SAIC Boggs to Assistant Director Peterson dated December 12, 1967, which explains Bolden's Protective Intelligence activities for October and November, 1963. Included in this memo are the following individuals whose files we ask you to make available to us:

Frances Welsing:	CO-2-33,804
Brady Hugh Fonden:	CO-2-28,894
Mrs. Jena McFarlen:	CO-2-33,958
NPPR:	J-CO-2,2271, as follows:

Armando Diaz-Matos	Document #2775
Julio Cesar Acosta Negron	Document #2209
Julio Flores Medina	Document #2012

In addition, this memo indicates (on page 2) that Bolden spent 8 hours on November 25, 1963, doing PRS check-ups on "Cuban subjects." If possible, please provide the names of these subjects of Bolden's check-ups.

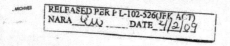

RELEASED PER P L-102-526(JFK ACT)
NARA ____ DATE 4/2/09

Ms. Jane E. Vezeris
April 11, 1997
Page 2

Also, Bolden's Monthly Activity Report, which Assistant Director Peterson summarizes in this memo, stated that Bolden spent 2 hours on November 1, 1963, in a conference with White House Detail agents on President Kennedy's November 2, 1963 visit to Chicago. We ask that you provide us with any notes or reports resulting from this meeting.

By making this request, we are not designating these materials "assassination records." To the extent that this request presents logistical or other difficulties that we may not have anticipated, or to the extent that these records may be located in the National Archives at a place other than the JFK Collection, we will be happy to discuss with you ways in which the request might be amended.

We ask that you make these records available by May 14, 1997.

We appreciate your assistance.

Sincerely yours,

David G. Marwell
Executive Director

cc: Mr. Donald Personette

Enclosure

We can all thank the ARRB and the file releases just in the last few years (2017-2018) for the following gems. The current Secret Service was requested to basically check on Bolden's claims regarding the Chicago plot and they hit pay dirt: Bolden was credible after all. It is only a shame that it took so very long to see these releases see the light of day, but at least they are out now. It turns out (as if anyone should have doubted him in the first place) that Bolden was doing exactly what he said he was doing: checking out potential threats to JFK's life and possible participants in the plot to kill Kennedy in Chicago planned for 11/2/63:

RELEASED PER P L-102-526(JFK ACT)
NARA ⟨⟨⟩ DATE 5/2/09

OPTIONAL FORM NO. 10
MAY 1962 EDITION
GSA FPMR (41 CFR) 101-11.6

UNITED STATES GOVERNMENT   U. S. SECRET SERVICE

Memorandum   J-CO-1-9513

TO   :   Assistant Director Peterson - Investigations   DATE: December 12, 1967

FROM :   SAIC Boggs - Chicago

SUBJECT: Abraham W. Bolden

This will confirm long distance telephone calls to and from
Assistant Director Peterson on December 7.

As requested, I reviewed the daily reports of Abraham Bolden for
the months of October and November 1963 relative to any Protective
Intelligence activities conducted by Bolden during that period,
with the following results:

Bolden's Monthly Activity Report, Form 1659, listed five hours
for Protection, Investigative Surveys, for the month of October
1963:

10/28/63	Frances Welsing, PRS 00-2-33,804	2 hours - both at office and in field. No breakdown shown.
10/29/63	Frances Welsing, PRS 00-2-33,804	1 hour in field 1 hour at office
10/30/63	Frances Welsing, PRS 00-2-33,804	1 hour in field
10/31/63	Frances Welsing, PRS 0042-33,804	Listed in narrative. No hours shown in distribution.

Bolden's Monthly Activity Report, Form 1659, for the month of November
1963 listed 31 hours for Protection, Investigative Surveys and five
PRS check-ups:

11/1/63	PP re conference with White House Detail agents (office meeting re visit of 11/2/63)	2 hours
11/2/63	9 am to 12 noon at Soldiers Field re Presidential visit	3 hours

Buy U.S. Savings Bonds Regularly on the Payroll Savings Plan

- 2 -

11/4/63	Frances Welsing, PRS CO-2-33,804	Mentioned in narrative. No hours shown in distribution
11/12/63	Brady Hugh Fonden, PRS CO-2-28,894	4 hours total in office and field surveillance. Breakdown not shown.
11/13/63	Mrs. Jena McFarlen, PRS CO-2-33,958	2 hours in field
11/19/63	Brady Hugh Fonden, PRS CO-2-28,894	2 hours at office
11/20/63	Brady Hugh Fonden, PRS CO-2-28,894	2 hours at office and in field. No breakdown shown.
11/21/63	Brady Hugh Fonden, PRS CO-2-28,894	2 hours at office
11/25/63	PRS check-ups - Cuban subjects	8 hours in field

A review of the 1639-s under file J-CO-2-2271 (NPPR) revealed that Bolden made check-ups on 11/25/63 on the following subjects:

Armando Diaz-Matos	Document #2775
Julio Cesar Acosta Negron	Document #2209
Julio Flores Medina	Document #2012

I was unable to locate any other 1639-s showing Bolden making check-ups on 11/25/63. It is possible that the other two NPPR's have returned to Puerto Rico and their files transferred to San Juan.

I also mentioned two persons that Bolden may have named in his recent interviews at Springfield, Missouri, one being Thomas Arthur Vallee, file CO-2-33,991, and Thomas Mosley, who is mentioned in file CO-2-34,104 entitled Homer S. Echevarria.

Those were the ARRB- initiated inquiries from 1997 (released 2009 but, for some strange reason, did not come to my attention until 2017-2018). Here are the actual blockbuster 1967 Secret Service documents generated by Chicago Special Agent in Charge Lilburn "Pat" Boggs and former Inspector and later Assistant Director Burrill Peterson regarding Bolden.

As we know from the previous pages, the three names at the very bottom of page two of the document, Thomas Arthur Vallee, Thomas Mosley and Homer Echevarria are actual persons and suspects. The other three near the bottom of the document but above the previous three – Armando Diaz-Matos, Julio Cesar Acosta Negron,[263] and Julio Flores Medina[264]--are new names to us all now. These names immediately remind one of what Colonel George McNally, former Secret Service agent and then head of WHCA, the White House Communication Agency, wrote in his book regarding "the police got a warning of Puerto Rican snipers" during the prior trip to Chicago on 3/23/63. Indeed, it is noted that at least two of the three persons of interest may have returned to Puerto Rico and their files transferred to the Secret Service office in San Juan. Please note that the other names on the upper part of the two-page document – Frances Welsing, a well-known psychiatrist and Black Supremacist[265], Jena McFarlen, and Brady Hugh Fonden – as well as the unnamed "Cuban subjects", are new.

Left: Armando Diaz-Matos. Right: Julio Flores Medina.

Armando Diaz-Matos and Julio Flores Medina were Puerto Rican Nationalist Party members accused of conspiracy to overthrow the government of the United States. Diaz-Matos was convicted of sedition and sen-

263   Julio César Acosta in the 1940 Census | Ancestry®

264   Julio Flores Medina, Puerto Rican sedition trial: 1955 | Flickr

265   Frances Cress Welsing - Wikipedia

tenced in 1954 to six years in prison.[266] For his part, Medina was convicted of sedition and sentenced in 1955 to 18 months in prison for sedition.[267] On 3/1/54, four Puerto Rican Nationalists fired upon and attempted to assassinate U.S. Congressman in the U.S. House of Representatives, wounding five members in the process.[268] Diaz-Matos and Medina were among the 17 indicted Puerto Rican Nationalists charged with "seditious conspiracy to overthrow the United States government by force" and the indictment alleged that the defendants were "active members, leaders, officers or persons in control of the Nationalist Party of Puerto Rico, which is charged to be an organization dedicated to bringing about the political independence of Puerto Rico from the United States by force of violence or armed revolution." They even had plans to assassinate President Eisenhower.[269] From the *Chicago American*, 11/23/63: "Hagerty Tells 2 Plots Against Ike New York (AP) – James C. Hagerty, former press secretary to President Eisenhower and now an American Broadcasting company executive said there were two plots against Eisenhower's life during his term. Hagerty said both plots had been traced to the Nationalist party of Puerto Rico. That group was accused of the abortive attempt earlier on the life of President Truman. Hagerty explained that in the spring of 1958 secret service agents learned an attempt would be made to toss grenades into Eisenhower's car during a trip thru a Midwest city. He said two grenades were found in the mail sent from outside the country to a fictitious name in care of a post office in a southwest city. The cities were not named. The second plan to assassinate Eisenhower, he said, was reported to the secret service in the spring of 1959 on word that Puerto Rican nationalists had met and decided to kill the President. Security measures were tightened and the reported attempt failed. Hagerty said no one was arrested in either plot."

Keep in mind, two Puerto Rican Nationalists, Oscar Collazo and Griselio Torresola, attempted to assassinate President Harry Truman at Blair House on 11/1/50.[270] Several Secret Service agents who protected Truman and who went on to protect JFK – Stu Stout, Floyd Boring, and Vince Mroz – served with Bolden.

266   United States of America, Respondent-appellee, v. Julio Pinto Gandia, Juan Francisco Ortiz Medina, Jose A. Otero Otero, Rosa Collazo, Juan Bernardo Lebron, Carmelo Alvarez Roman, Armando Diaz Matos, and Manuel Rabago Torres, Petitioners-appellants, 255 F.2d 454 (2d Cir. 1958) :: Justia
267   Julio Flores Medina, Puerto Rican sedition trial: 1955 | Flickr
268   1954 United States Capitol shooting - Wikipedia
269   *New York Times*, 9/15/54.
270   Attempted assassination of Harry S. Truman - Wikipedia

These documents also demonstrate Bolden's vigilance in doing protective intelligence and related duties between 10/28/63 and 11/2/63 for the proposed 11/2/63 Chicago trip, including a meeting on 11/1/63 with White House Detail agents (some of whom Bolden served with on the same White House Detail in June 1961 and who he also worked with whenever President Kennedy came to Chicago in 1962-1963) and actually being stationed at Soldiers Field on 11/2/63. They also demonstrate the work Bolden did in this regard between 11/4/63 and 11/21/63 in the days leading up to the 11/22/63 assassination in Dallas, as well as the investigation of unnamed Cuban subjects 3 days after the murder.

Again, please recall what Col. George J. McNally, WH Signal Corps and former Secret Service agent, reported: "But during the Chicago visit [3/23/63], the motorcade was slowed to the pace of a mounted Black Horse Troop, and the police got a warning of Puerto Rican snipers. Helicopters searched the roofs along the way, and no incidents occurred."

Security for JFK exactly 4 months before the Chicago plot- 7/2/63 Rome: President Kennedy's limousine is surrounded by an excellent motorcycle formation as Secret Service agents David Grant (Clint Hill's brother-in-law) and Gerald Blaine ride the rear of the limo. Press photographers in front of the limo in a flatbed truck (including a LIVE TELEVISION FEED!), military aide in limo, SAIC Behn in limo (Greer driving), close follow-up car, etc.

> In October 1963 the Service consulted with a retired Army colonel with long experience in this field; in mid-November 1963 this officer furnished the Service with names of two commercial concerns which might be helpful and advised the Service that he was procuring a sample of a plastic material which could be used for firearms penetration tests.

Interestingly, around the time of the Chicago plot, the Secret Service was trying to come up with a bulletproof bubble top for the presidential limousine (from Commission Document 3).

CHAPTER EIGHT

ABRAHAM BOLDEN: AMERICAN HERO

Bolden when he was an Illinois State Trooper.

8 9-year-old Former Secret Service agent Abraham Bolden[271] was the first black member of the Secret Service White House Detail, whose "appointment came at the very instigation of President John F. Kennedy when he appeared in Chicago at a fundraiser in 1961."[272] Mr. Bolden was also, as Sam Kinney told the author, the first agent "dishonorably discharged," which took place not long after the Kennedy assassination. Kinney added, "We never got any bad publicity until Abe Bolden came

271   *The JFK Assassination* (2016/2018) by James DiEugenio, pages 275-278.
272   Letter from Bolden to the author, 9/10/93; The author made a lot of contacts with Bolden: 9/16/93, 4/10/94, 8/8/03: calls; 9/10/93, 10/30/93, 12/13/93, 12/31/93, 8/94 (including court documents re: Bolden's Petition to Expunge), and 1/97 (re: Bolden's Petition for Writ of Certiorari): letters and correspondence; 7/04, 8/04, 9/04, Spring/ Summer 2005: e-mails, as well as many Facebook connections. Also, the author made several online/internet contacts with Bolden's two sons and his daughter.

along."[273] As Chief Rowley told the Warren Commission: "This is the first time I remember anything like this happening since I have been with the Secret Service."[274] Former agent and Chief of White House Signal Corps Col. George J. McNally wrote in his book, "The Secret Service for the first time in its long history had an agent indicted for attempting to sell a government investigative report to a defendant in a counterfeiting case."[275] In the first of several letters to the author, the former agent described JFK as, "a sincere, dedicated president who because of his long sufferings was able to feel the agony of others," and his treatment by his fellow agents: "I was personally told by SAIC[276] Harvey Henderson, 'You're a nigger. You were born a nigger. You're going to die a nigger. So act like a nigger.'"

Bolden elaborated, "You may ask, why was I not present in Dallas on that fatal day of darkness. It is because the Secret Service White House Detail of the '60's was composed basically of new service recruits and entrenched senior agents, five of whom you named in your letter to me, who ran the Secret Service Detail, under James Rowley, as if their job was not to protect the President, but to 'look good' by putting up a front that protection was being afforded. The senior agents were "party people" (not so with Clint Hill, Ed Z. Tucker, or Bob Foster) who reported for assignment after consuming large quantities of alcohol, and attended lavish sex parties during off duty hours ... agents in Hyannis Port drank heavily the night before, the morning of, and during their Presidential guard assignments with some agents carrying liquor in their tote bags and drinking on duty.... Prior to May 21, 1964, no evidence or inquisitions had been made into the conduct of the Secret Service in Dallas on November 22, 1963."

Bolden continued: "As I spoke with the newspaper writers and T.V. newsmen on May 20, 1964, I knew from experience that the lax attitude concerning protective assignments, the deep disrespect for Kennedy prevalent within the Service, and the propensity to consume hard liquor prior to assignment were the actual murderers of our president. Oswald did not

---

273   Author's interviews with Kinney; During agent LuBert de Freese's 2/2/78 HSCA interview, de Freese said that Bolden "was infamous," while Agent Robert Kollar told the HSCA on 3/1/78, "like any other agent he was aware of Bolden because of the trouble he had gotten into." Agent Gerald Blaine denigrates Bolden in his inferior book *The Kennedy Detail* (2010), pages 334-336, 356-359.

274   5 H 458.

275   *A Million Miles of Presidents*, p. 225.

276   According to former Agent Art Godfrey, "Harvey Henderson was a shift agent-never a boss or shift leader." [Letter to author dated 11/24/97] That said, the recent ARRB releases vindicate Bolden: Henderson was indeed a temporary boss/shift leader.

kill Kennedy … the attitudinal violence of the Secret Service did! No one could have killed our President without the shots of omission fired by the Secret Service. Observe the feet of [four] Secret Service agents glued to the running boards of the follow-up car as bullets [sic?] pierce the brain of our President!!![277]

"If any person had the ability, love, and compassion to better the condition of all peoples of America, it was John F. Kennedy. Oft times during my assignment at the White House, he would approach me and ask, 'How are they treating you?' or 'How do you like the detail?' He introduced me to every member of his cabinet saying, 'This is Mr. Bolden. I brought him here to make history and to open a door for his people.' "Before I left the White House Detail [June 1961], I sought an audience with the then Chief of the Secret Service [U.E. Baughman]. I told him, in no uncertain terms that (1) the Secret Service Detail was not protecting President Kennedy properly by agents reporting for work in a drunken condition and (2) when the President was assassinated it would be the direct result of laxity by agents around the President. The reply to my assertions … was that the Secret Service had not "lost" a President in over 20 years and that to a new agent (me) it might appear that security was lax, but everything was covered."

In a follow-up letter, Bolden wrote, "In November 1963, I was in Washington, D.C. on a super-secret mission involving an Internal Revenue Investigation of members of the House of Representatives. My contact when I arrived was Mr. Joiner, Chief of Intelligence then for the I.R.S. I arrived in Washington on November 8, 1963, and left November 11, 1963, eleven days before Kennedy was assassinated. It was during this time that I discussed the breakdown in security with Chief Rowley in person and it was also at this time that I found out that Chief Rowley had written an article for *Reader's Digest* ['s] November issue stating and outlining how easy it would be to assassinate a President using a high-powered rifle. Some of the copies of the *Reader's Digest* had already been distributed when Kennedy was assassinated. After the assassination, all copies of that issue were withdrawn and new November issues were printed, deleting the 'essay' by Chief Rowley. In the essay, Chief Rowley contended that the weakness within the security of the President was 'an assassin perched in the window firing a high-powered rifle.' You can see how such an article was extremely detrimental to the safety of President Kennedy."[278]

---

277   *Washington News* and *San Francisco Chronicle*, both dated 5/21/64, document Mr. Bolden's claims to the media.
278   Letter to author dated 10/30/93.

Mr. Bolden, who was imprisoned on trumped-up charges of trying to sell a government report on a counterfeiting case, is adamant that he was innocent and framed by the Secret Service. A fellow agent from the Chicago office, Conrad Cross, told the HSCA "he believes Bolden was set up" but did not know by whom.[279]

Bolden wrote, "I surmised that the actual reason for my arrest was due to the fact that Kennedy was assassinated and that I could not be depended upon to keep quiet about my complaints [of laxity, etc.] regarding the Secret Service." Keep in mind, the assassination was the darkest day in Secret Service history and the agency was fearful of losing their position as protector of future presidents.

In reference to Chief Rowley, Mr. Bolden told the author, "You know what I could never understand? I talked to Jim Rowley several times after I left Washington, D.C.; it always puzzled me as to why he let this thing happen to me in Chicago. That bothered me because he impressed me as a fairly decent guy, a fair man – it seemed ... I just can't – I don't know if this thing that happened (to me) was over his head or he couldn't stop it or didn't want to stop it because he was the Chief of the Secret Service ... I just can't believe that Chief Rowley would let this thing happen." Mr. Bolden also wished that his fellow agents had attended his trial or at least read the transcript.

As it turns out, one agent was at both of Bolden's trials: Louis B. Sims, who, as we know, was later one of two agents in charge of maintaining the elaborate eavesdropping operation in the Nixon White House and changing the tapes.[280] Bolden was unaware that Rowley testified at some length about his case to the Warren Commission. J. Lee Rankin asked Rowley, "Chief Rowley, have you had any other complaints similar to this in regard to the conduct of the Secret Service agents on the Presidential or White House detail?" Rowley responded, "We had one in the last month. We had charges leveled at us by an agent of the Secret Service – Who is currently under indictment, and who will be brought to trial on criminal charges on the 29th of June. And, for that reason, while I have no reluctance to discuss it, I think we should go off the record, because I don't want to in any way prejudice the case ... [Bolden] said he was framed. Now, he said he was framed because he was prepared to go before your Commission, sir, to testify about this thing that happened 3 years ago, and in the charges he said he advised me, as well as others, and

---

279   HSCA interview of Conrad Cross [HSCA RIF# 180-10104-10324].
280   RIF# 180-10093-10022: HSCA interview with Sims, 5/22/78.

nothing was done. He said he was framed for this reason ... He had never made any complaint to me. It came as a complete surprise."[281] Considering the charges made in 1961 were addressed to then Chief Baughman, it is easy to see why.

Rowley makes no mention of Bolden's claim to have spoken to him in early November 1963. In any event, Rowley continued, "Now, in order to determine their ability and fitness for assignment, since some people are better criminal investigators than they are in protection work, we have an orientation program which includes duty on the White House detail. Mr. Bolden was one of the men selected to come in the summer of 1961. He was also a replacement for some regular agent on the detail who was on leave. It was a 30-day assignment. This afforded us an opportunity to observe him, determine whether he was equipped and so forth. And he was on the White House detail for this short period of time. "The time that he describes was a 5-day weekend up in Hyannis Port ... Before he left his detail assignment, you see, he alleges that he told me about the condition that was going on up in Hyannis.... When he left to return to his office in Chicago.... The fact is he never informed me. He never informed any of his supervisors or anyone on the detail ... I found out there was no truth to the charges of misconduct. There were 11 charges lodged against us. One charge, the ninth charge, a part of it was true. The boys did contribute for food. In other words, up there in Hyannis, when they are up there for a week, or a weekend, they would be assigned to a house, which economically was beneficial to them. One shift, and some of the drivers would be in this house. This house was in a remote area from the shopping area and so forth. So they agreed when they arrived there to contribute, to buy food for breakfast, it being an 8 to 4 shift. Eight to four meant they would have breakfast there and dinner ... One of the agents who enjoyed it as a hobby cooked the meals for them, while the others took care of the dishes ... when they went shopping they bought two or three cases of beer which they had available in the icebox when the men came off duty in the evening."[282]

Both in his letters and in his interviews with the author, Mr. Bolden expressed much interest in and suspicion of Harvey Henderson, his "boss" during his time on the White House Detail: "While in New York on a protective assignment, Harvey Henderson countermand [ed] a direct order from the President. This act occurred in September or October 1963 [Mr.

---

281   5 H 454-455, 457-458.
282   5 H 455-457.

Bolden may be mistaken:[283] the time period may have been mid-November 1963, a mere week or so before Dallas]. The President subsequently had Henderson removed from the detail and this act by the President was very unpopular with Jerry Behn, Emory Roberts, and others on the detail." Mr. Bolden elaborated during a telephone interview with the author: "Do you know what happened to Harvey Henderson? I heard that he had been relieved of his Detail by President Kennedy himself ... Harvey had made some threats like, 'We'll get you' ... I understand that he told the President "I'll get you, or something to that effect ... (it was) no secret that Kennedy wanted him removed from the detail ... Harvey was a quick-tempered guy who couldn't take the heat. ... Where is Harvey Henderson at? I think that you would do well if you could find out where Harvey Henderson was on November 22-can you track him down?" In reference to the illicit Secret Service credentials present in Dealey Plaza on 11/22/63, Mr. Bolden said, in reference to Harvey Henderson, "that's the first thing that crossed my mind – he would have the nerve, the guts, the anger, the craziness, the instability ... I'm not saying he was in Dallas, but I'm saying that ... it would be something to look at."

Unfortunately, Henderson died in 1994 before the author could locate and contact him for comment. Interestingly, information regarding a plot to kill Martin Luther King was furnished to Henderson, the ASAIC of the Birmingham Secret Service office, on 3/11/65, over three years before MLK's murder. [284] During interviews with two other agents, Maurice Martineau (Mr. Bolden's superior in Chicago) and Robert Lilley, the name Harvey Henderson struck a nerve. Mr. Martineau said nervously, "I knew him – not very well ... I didn't have too much contact with him" (More on Martineau later.) When asked when Mr. Henderson "left" the White House Detail, Lilley said he "would have left ... (pause) ... probably 1962."[285] Former agent Walt Coughlin wrote, "Harvey (The Birmingham Baron) Henderson had left the Detail when I arrived [6/62] but I recall he was there thru most of the 1950's."[286] Walt later added in a 2004 e-mail to the author, "Harvey Henderson he [Bolden] is probably rite (sic) about."[287]

283   *One Scandalous Story* by Former CBS newsman Marvin Kalb, p. 4, relates a September 1963 JFK trip to NY.

284   *Martin Luther King, Jr.: the FBI File* by Michael Friedly and David Gallen (New York: Carroll & Graf, 1993), pp. 366-367.

285   Henderson, along with Blaine and Boring, made the security arrangements for a JFK vacation at Bing Crosby's home in Palm Desert, CA in early 1962: *Looking Back And Seeing The Future: The United States Secret Service 1865-1990*, p. 77.

286   Undated letter to author received 2/21/04.

287   See also *Last Word* (2011) by Mark Lane, pages 156-163.

In contrast, former agent Gerald Blaine, who falsely claims to have been on Bolden's temporary shift at the White House, wrote the author on 6/12/05: "I don't remember anybody on the detail that was racist. Merit was perceived by a person's actions, their demeanor, reliability, dependability and professional credibility – not race! Harvey was not even on the shift that Bolden was during his thirty day stay. Even though Harvey Henderson was from Mississippi, I never heard of him discriminating nor demeaning anyone because of race." Blaine's best friend, Clint Hill, later said, "Now there were certain individuals in the service, I won't deny that, who were very, very bigoted. Most of them came from Mississippi or Alabama or somewhere in the South. Sometimes we had problems with them. They didn't want to work with a black agent."[288]

Darwin Horn wrote, "Harvey Henderson was on the Detail from about 1952 to about 1960 and then went to Birmingham."[289] Finally, former V.P. LBJ agent Jerry Kivett wrote the author, "I knew Harvey Henderson but do not know when he served on the White House Detail. Probably late 50's to early '60's."[290]

A rare photo of Secret Service agent Harvey Henderson next to Roy Kellerman.

---

288   Butler, Maurice. *Out From The Shadow: The Story of Charles L Gittens Who Broke The Color Barrier In The United States Secret Service.* KY: Xlibris, 2012, pp. 125-126.
289   E-mail to author dated 2/22/04.
290   Letter to author dated 2/18/04.

Oliver Stone consultant Gus Russo told this author in 1992 that Mr. Bolden allegedly told him that Agent Robert Lilley "was either privy to the assassination or had foreknowledge." When the author asked Mr. Bolden if this was true, he equivocated nervously, "(pause) ... I don't recall right at this moment ... I don't recall right at this moment." Lawyers John Hosmer, Sherman Skolnick, Bernard Fensterwald, and Mark Lane were also convinced that Mr. Bolden was framed. In addition, Senator Sam Ervin (later of Watergate fame), Senator Edward Long, Assistant Attorney General Fred Vinson, and United States Attorney Edward Hanrahan were involved in the Bolden case. Mr. Bolden told the author, "The Secret Service office here in Chicago knows there was no crime committed – they absolutely know that there was no crime committed."

However, Secret Service agent Elmer Moore told researcher James Gouchenaur: "That goddamned lying nigger. We finally got him ... [Inspector Thomas] Kelley and the chief [Rowley] got 'em."[291] As Gouchenaur said, "I think that Moore and the rest of his crew were scared speechless that Bolden knew something."[292]

Mr. Bolden's attorney from Springfield, Illinois, John Hosmer, believes that "his client was imprisoned as a result of information he has about the assassination."[293] Mr. Bolden retained Attorney Hosmer because he "knew how the government worked." In a letter to Josiah Thompson dated 12/26/67, Attorney Hosmer outlined his case: "Some peculiar and remarkable things happened before and during the trial ... three Secret Service informers were the witnesses against Bolden. One of whom, Joseph Spagnoli, later in his own trial, admitted perjury at the behest of the Government, and Bolden's alleged co-conspirator, a man he had arrested twice (Frank W. Jones), was never brought to trial ... the 'shaft' was put to Bolden by the Secret Service and by my government." In a prison letter dated 3/14/68, Mr. Bolden summed up the situation to Senator Long: "I was kidnapped, denied an attorney, convicted on perjured evidence devised and suborned by the government, convicted by methods used by the trial judge that suppressed evidence favorable to the defense, and perjury admitted during the trial by government witnesses was suppressed from the jury."

---

291   *JFK Revisited* by James DiEugenio (and the documentary with the same name), pages 70, 204-205.

292   *JFK Revisited* by James DiEugenio (and the documentary with the same name), page 204.

293   AARC files provided to the author by researcher Bill Adams.

Bolden further added in his letter to the author, "U.S. District Judge J. Sam Perry instructed the jury, while that jury was in deliberation, that 'In my opinion, the evidence shows the defendant to be guilty of counts 1,2, and 3 in the indictment.' To give any personal opinion to a deliberating jury, by anyone, is clearly a violation of law called jury tampering. Yet, after a mistrial was declared in the 1st trial, this same judge (with opinion intact) heard the 2nd trial. Moreover, he was upheld by the 7th Circuit U.S. Court of Appeals who ruled that such opinions do not show prejudice on the part of the judge. Then what would he have to do to show prejudice? Lynch me? This charge by a judge has never been used by a Caucasian judge against a Caucasian defendant!" Fellow African-American Agent Charlie Gittens later wrote of his regret for having been used as a pawn by the prosecution team by having Charlie sit at the prosecution table "to circumvent any notion that Agent Bolden was being persecuted as a result of his race." Gittens was asked to sit at the prosecution table for Bolden's second trial, but he refused.

Bolden further wrote, "Then how did the government case against me initiate? On or about May 11, 1964, Frank W. Jones, a counterfeiter of U.S. currency who had been twice arrested by me and who at that time had a case pending in Federal District Court due to my investigations, called J. Lloyd Stocks (Acting Assistant Special Agent In Charge of the Chicago office). Jones wanted to talk to an agent about information he had concerning another counterfeiting ring. According to Stocks, Jones was afraid of going to jail and wanted to cooperate with the Secret Service. Stocks called me into the office on May 11, 1964 and assigned me to interview Jones. I vigorously protested to Stocks because (1) I had arrested Jones and was to be chief witness against him as the counterfeiting plant was discovered by me in his home during a set raid; (2) Jones could be setting me up to be killed or otherwise harmed and (3) I was leaving for Secret Service School on May 16, 1964 and there was no time to develop Jones as an informant. Both Acting Assistant Special Agent in Charge Maurice G. Martineau and Acting Assistant Special Agent in Charge J. Lloyd Stocks overruled my objections and I was told to meet with Jones or resign … I met Jones at his home at approximately 11:00 A.M. on May 11, 1964. Jones purported to have information concerning the 'Dagos' (Joseph Spagnoli et. al. counterfeiting band case) who was arrested on or about May 6, 1964. I was one of the arresting officers in that case also."

Bolden continued: "After speaking with Jones for about ½ hour while parked in a Secret Service vehicle in front of Jones' home, Jones and I went to a McDonald's restaurant where I exited the car leaving Jones seated inside. Later, I dropped Jones off at home and drove back to the Secret Service office, 219 South Dearborn in Chicago. I reported the conversation with Jones to ASAIC Martineau. Mr. Martineau stated, over my objections for the same reasons listed above, that Jones should be developed as an informant and Mr. Martineau issued Jones an informant number by which he was to be referred in any subsequent reports. "Jones called me at my home on the night of May 11, 1964 and told me that he had met with some Dagos and that these Dagos dealt in "a lot of suits." He stated that one of them, Joe, was to call him and that he would get a lot of good information from Joe. "The next day, May 12, 1964, I met Jones at his home about 10:00 a.m. Jones reiterated his confusing story stating that the counterfeiting plates for the $100.00 bonds were in the hands of "Slim" and we could buy them for $50,000. "I immediately drove to the Secret Service office and told ASAIC Martineau what Jones said. I also took that opportunity to dictate my reports on this matter to June Marie Terpinas, secretary for the Secret Service. Mr. Martineau agreed that it appeared that Jones was leading us on a wild goose chase and interested only in helping himself. I was instructed to stay away from Jones and discontinue the operation. "Jones called me at the Secret Service office around 2:30 p.m. on May 12, 1964. I told Jones that "Spagnoli called the boss and stop all contacts with him." Spagnoli was determined to be the "Joe" referred to by Jones as the Dago."

Bolden added: "When the Secret Service arrested me and brought me to Chicago, they charged me with (1) Solicitation of a bribe; (2) Conspiracy; and (3) Obstruction of Justice based upon allegations that I sent Jones to Spagnoli to solicit a $50, 000 bribe. For this bribe, Spagnoli was to receive an onionskin copy of a Secret Service report detailing the government's case against Spagnoli and 6 other defendants. "During the trial, it was brought out that I in fact was given an onionskin report to review and pass on to Agent Conrad Cross. Cross also worked on the Jones case with me. It was further affirmed that I in fact gave the Spagnoli onionskin report to Agent Cross while inside the Secret Service office on the morning of May 8, 1964. Cross further testified that he read and "lost" the onionskin report. "During the trial, no onionskin report was introduced into evidence. The only document introduced that pertained to the onionskin report was a passage from the report re-typed on bond paper. The name Vito Zaccagnini was misspelled (Zaggacnini) throughout the passage and this could have been the result of someone making a quick reading or writing of the paragraph and reproducing what he thought that he saw. According to Mr. Nason, who testified on behalf of the government concerning fingerprints lifted from the excerpt typed on bond paper, my fingerprints appeared nowhere on the paper. The fingerprints of both Jones and Spagnoli were clearly identified, but there was not one shred of evidence linking me to the excerpt introduced into evidence ... except the testimony of Jones who testified 'he removed the paper from his briefcase and handed it to me (on May 11, 1964).' There is no documented testimony as to how the onion skin paper changed to bond paper or how I could insert a paper in a typewriter, type the excerpt, remove the excerpt from my briefcase and give it to Jones (while not wearing gloves) and not one hint of my fingerprints were anywhere on the paper."

Bolden further wrote: "After I was charged by the Secret Service and U.S. Government on May 18, 1964 and subsequently released on bail on May 19, 1964, I felt betrayed and angry. Since a warrant had been issued and the decision made that I had in fact committed a criminal act, I knew that the agency had abandoned me and that I had been set up either by Jones and Spagnoli or the Secret Service itself. "I recalled how I had openly derided the agency for blowing the Chicago investigation of an assassination plot against [the] President in November 1963, two weeks before he was shot in Dallas. I recalled that I had been coerced to meet Jones by the Secret Service and now they were acting as if this was a secret deal between Jones and me outside of the agency.... On May 20, 1964, I decided to lash back at the Secret Service and hit back where it would hurt the most."

Bolden continued: "Shortly after November 22, 1963, rumors were circulating [which turned out to be true] within the agency that on the night before the assassination, agents of the detail were intoxicated in a teahouse [sic] in Dallas, Texas. Rumor was that a few agents became so intoxicated that one of them lost his U.S. Treasury Commission book. Stories within the agency persisted that the agency knew whose identification was lost or stolen but to admit that this occurred might place the agency in a bad predicament. In August 1964, an all-white jury returned a verdict of guilty on all counts against me and on September 4, 1964 [shortly before the issuance of the Warren Report], I was sentenced to serve 6 years in federal custody. "In January, 1965, Joseph Spagnoli, the counterfeiter contacted by Frank Jones on May 11,1964, was on trial in the court of J. Sam Perry, the same judge who had heard both of my trials. This was the same judge who had interrupted the deliberation of the jury in my first trial in order to coax that jury into returning a verdict of guilty.

Bolden added: "During the examination of Joseph Spagnoli by his attorney Frank Oliver, Spagnoli admitted in open court that he had committed perjury in "the Bolden trial." Spagnoli produced a yellow sheet of paper that he admitted stealing from the office of the U.S. Attorney during a pretrial conference. Judge Perry asked Spagnoli if he understood that he was admitting to perjury to which Spagnoli replied, 'Yes, sir.' He openly confessed that the government attorney Richard Sykes solicited the perjured testimony. The change of dates appearing on the stolen paper and the change of times of Jones' contact with Spagnoli were all in the handwriting of Assistant U.S. Attorney Richard T. Sykes. "Efforts to get a hearing on the perjury matter before Judge Perry by my attorney Raymond Smith proved unsuccessful and the case went to the 7th Circuit Court of Appeals in 1965. During the argument before the U.S. Court of Appeals the issue of Spagnoli's perjury was brought up. Judge Luther Swygert summoned Attorney Richard Sykes into the courtroom and point-blank asked Sykes if he had solicited perjury in the Bolden trial. Sykes' reply was, 'Your honor, I refuse to answer that question on the grounds that it may tend to incriminate me.'" "In June 1965, the 7th Circuit Court of Appeals affirmed the conviction noting in a footnote that Spagnoli was "less than forthright in his testimony."

Bolden continued: "In June 1966, the U.S. Supreme Court refused to grant Certiorari and on June 26, 1966[294] I commenced to serve a 6-year sentence in custody of the Federal Bureau of Prisons [in Springfield, Missouri]." Richard Case Nagell, an intelligence agent who both knew Oswald[295] and who had allegedly uncovered a plot to kill JFK in advance, was placed in a cell directly across from Bolden.[296] Former White House Detail and Chicago office agent Joseph E. Noonan, Jr. told the HSCA on 4/13/78 that "he briefly discussed the elements of the Spagnoli case and told us that there was no way that Bolden was going to be able to give Spagnoli files which would really help him with his case. He could only feed him office files and Spagnoli already knew that information. The Secret Service had 'turned' Spagnoli's girlfriend and she was the one who set him up. Bolden's case was a sad chapter in the Chicago office of the Secret Service [,] according to Noonan. He felt that Bolden got a stiff rap from the judge (6 years) and part of the problem he felt related to Bolden's personality. He talked a lot and angered many people in the Secret Service with allegations about

---

294   Incidentally, the day after the author was born!

295   WCD 197, regarding Nagell, says in its entirety: "For the record he would like to say that his association with Oswald was purely social and that he had met him in Mexico City and in Texas."

296   *The Man Who Knew Too Much* by Dick Russell, p. 635.

laxity in their presidential protection functions." Noonan also said, "Bolden was too gentle for this job. Abe never wanted to arrest anybody." However, former agent Bob Lilley said Bolden was "a good street agent."[297] Surprisingly, even former Secret Service agent Gerald Blaine wrote that Bolden "was no doubt a good investigative field agent."[298] The *Washington News* reported on 5/21/64: "Mr. Bolden who has graduated cum laude from Lincoln University in Jefferson City, Missouri, and won two commendations for cracking counterfeit rings after he joined the Secret Service, said the charge was a 'direct result' of his superiors' learning his intentions to testify before the Commission."

Bolden had attempted to contact the Warren Commission's General Counsel, J. Lee Rankin, in May of 1964 from a White House phone during his stay in Washington to attend a special Secret Service school. The next day, Mr. Bolden was charged with attempting to sell a government report. He should have known better; his earlier talks with both Chief Baughman in 1961 and Chief Rowley in 1963 went unheeded, and he was transferred out of the White House Detail to ordinary anti-counterfeiting duty in the Chicago office. This second request for an audience was a tragic mistake, but Mr. Bolden had information to tell the Commission far more important than laxity on duty and drinking by agents: the 11/2/63 Chicago plot to kill President Kennedy. Bolden wrote to the author: "I do not believe Oswald acted alone because evidence is that there were at least 3 riflemen following the President just 3 weeks before he was assassinated in Dallas."

Bolden asked this question in his letter to Ohio Congressman Louis Stokes, formerly Chairman of the HSCA: "Who is John Heard? If the name John Heard (Hurd) has not been documented in the files of the Warren Commission then the files of the United States Congress are far from complete regarding the assassination of the President. Less than 24 hours after the assassination of the President and while Lee Harvey Oswald was still in custody prior to his own assassination by Jack Ruby, all Secret Service offices across the nation were instructed to determine the whereabouts of a John Heard and any name phonetically sounding like Heard whose name was in the Secret Service files. At a time when the nation's attention was focused upon the name Lee Oswald, the Secret Service were investigating John Heard all across the nation."[299]

---

297   Author's interview with Lilley, 9/27/92.
298   *The Kennedy Detail* (2010), page 335.
299   1/26/92 letter to Congressman Stokes provided to the author. This information regarding "John Heard" was provided by Bolden to the HSCA during the agent's 1/19/78 interview.

Author Michael Benson wrote, "According to phone records, Lee Harvey Oswald attempted to make phone calls from the Dallas Police station following his arrest that are not mentioned in the Warren Report. Those records indicate that Oswald attempted to call (919) 834-7430 and (919) 833-1253. Both numbers are listed to John Hurt in Raleigh, North Carolina, at two separate addresses (415 New Bern Ave, and Old Wake Forest Road). The first was listed to a John D. Hurt and the second to John W. Hurt. A John D. Hurt from Raleigh, according to researcher Ira David Wood III, served with U.S. Military Intelligence during World War II. Wood contacted John David Hurt in Raleigh and discovered that he had been a U.S. Counterintelligence officer during World War II. Hurt said that he had worked as an insurance investigator ever since, employed by the state of North Carolina. He claimed to have no idea why Lee Harvey Oswald would have wanted to contact him from his jail cell."[300]

During a telephone conversation on 4/10/94, Bolden told the author that the statement attributed to him by author Paris Flammonde in *The Kennedy Conspiracy*, that Oswald said, "Ruby hired me!" and variations on that theme, is not true. He never made such a statement.[301] However, Mr. Bolden did confirm statements made to Ian Calder in 1968[302] that his wife was harassed, a brick was thrown into his home, and that "a shot [was] fired in the house," as well as his captivity in the "snake pit," a room for "incurable psychotics … [they] have killed four or five people … multiple murderers." Bolden also confirmed to the author that Richard Case Nagell was in a cell close to him. Mr. Bolden has since "filed for a pardon in Washington three times," to no avail. Finally, Mr. Bolden had this to say: "I think you're right on target … I heard of these things when I was an agent of the Secret Service … I really hope you can straighten it out … because there's a whole lot more than meets the public's eye." Indeed.

Bolden told the author, "I had heard that there was some conflict between Kennedy and the White House Detail, that he was trying to scale them back." Bolden later wrote to the author, "The facts are that the S.S. [Secret Service] and F.B.I. were not the cooperating organizations as portrayed by the media in the 1960['s]. The facts are that President Kennedy and Robert Kennedy made no bones about their dislike of the S.S. as an independent service. Early in 1961 there was great fear within the service that

300   *Encyclopedia of the JFK Assassination* by Michael Benson, p. 11. See also *Burying the Lead: The Media and the JFK Assassination* by Mel Hyman (2019), pages 441-442.
301   Author's article in the Feb-May 1994 *Investigator* research journal.
302   AARC file provided to the author in 1993 by Jim Lesar.

the duties of the S.S. would be given to the F.B.I. and that the S.S. would be made a part of the IRS investigators. The relations between the F.B.I. and the S.S. was a 'dogfight' with the F.B.I. oft times refusing to assist the S.S. in collateral investigations. "The facts are that most of the agents surrounding the President disliked the President for (1) his stand on civil rights and (2) his studies undertaken by Robert Kennedy to disband the S.S. as the protective agency. The detail was staffed by a core of southern-born agents and it was no surprise to me that, after the James Meredith Mississippi school incident, an attempt on the life of the President would be met by agents standing on the side of the follow-up car waiting for the final shot to hit … Simply put, the S.S. covered up evidence [and] lied to the Warren Commission and to the public for one reason and one reason only: to save the S.S. and not be branded with the taint of gross negligence and be therefore open to judicial proceedings … the attitude of the S.S. against the President and the attitude of the F.B.I. against Robert Kennedy caused these agencies to permit the assassination to occur."[303]

In a postscript, Abraham Bolden wrote the author in September 2004 with the following information regarding his arrest, the trumped-up charges against him, and more: "[Agent Gary] McLeod lied about the circumstances of my arrest. He was well aware of what was going on on May 18th while we were in Washington, D.C. When I started to go to the White House to get some info. on the Commission, McLeod was right on my heels, so much so that I had to change plans. He even walked with me to an all-black cafe on "P" Street. It was very unusual for a white man to be seen in that part of town in a restaurant. When I went to a pay telephone to call my wife in Chicago, McLeod entered the booth next to mine and pretended to make a call. The only problem was that I listened for his coin deposit to drop and it never did. "Later during the night at about 2:00 A.M., I was awakened by a loud thump against the walls of my room. I put a drinking glass up to the wall and placed my ear against it. There was a lot of commotion inside of McLeod's room adjacent to my room. We shared a common wall. I heard the sound of low voices and the movement of furniture but I could not make out what was being said. Cross had been a friend as well as a fellow agent. The Secret Service put a lot of pressure on him after I was arrested. He was under so much strain. He told a devastating lie against me at the trial when he testified that we talked about $50,000 in a conversation. That was the exact amount that the government charged that I was solicit-

---

303   Letter to author dated 12/31/93.

ing as a bribe. That one lie coming from a Negro agent was one of the most damaging statements made during the trial."

Bolden continued: "And Vince, I tell you before God, and I am a very religious man, that that conversation never took place. Agent Cross was the last person with the file that I was charged with trying to sell. A part of the file ended up in the hands of Spagnoli. I think that whoever set me up arranged it so that the file was stolen from Cross and used to implicate me. That way, if Cross did not go along with the program, he could be included as a defendant in the case. "The secret service is standing solidly behind their claim of a lack of knowledge about an investigation of a Cuban assassination attempt around November 2, 1963. Not only was there an investigation of a Cuban faction here in Chicago but after that, in Miami and Palm Beach around November 18 the secret service used decoy aircraft because of a major threat against the President there. They were afraid that a missile could be fired from Cuba into the United States so they used two planes for Kennedy to throw the assassins off. The use of the two planes is a matter of record. How any agent could not recall the change of identification is far beyond me. "The old Commission Books had printed across the top "United States Treasury Department" The new [Commission] Books said "The United States Treasury Department." Also, all agents had to submit new photographs for the books to Washington, D.C. The new Commission Books were engraved by the Bureau of Printing and Engraving on special order. I had my new photograph made at a passport processing studio across from the federal building on Jackson Blvd. Any agent that says that he doesn't remember that should resign especially since it was done during a time when it was alleged that a possible assassin on the grassy knoll showed a deputy sheriff a secret service commission book. "As well as I like some of the agents and am glad that many of them are happily retired and are living the 'good life', they are still stonewalling and being deceptive about what the truth is. After seeing what happened to me, there is little doubt that some of the details they knew during that time have been unconsciously repressed. What happened to me was a message to those who entertained the same idea and believe me, they got the message. Abraham."

Happily, Bolden found a major publisher for his outstanding book *The Echo From Dealey Plaza*.[304] In addition, due to the efforts of the present author, Bolden was featured in the book *Ultimate Sacrifice* by Lamar Waldron

---

304   *The Echo From Dealey Plaza: The True Story of the First African American on the White House Secret Service Detail and His Quest for Justice After the Assassination of JFK* (2008) by Abraham Bolden.

and Thom Hartmann in 2005, as well as, albeit briefly, on the Discovery Channel on 5/11/06, his first ever TV appearance, as well as Jim Douglass book *JFK And the Unspeakable* in 2008. Abe had this to say about myself on 4/10/12: "Vince Palamara is the foremost authority on the secret service in the 60s. He is a personal friend of mine and a very good researcher."

A review of the personnel file reflects that Special Agent Abraham Bolden was appointed on October 31, 1960, at Chicago. In accordance with policy, he was temporarily assigned to the White House Detail from June 6 to July 6, 1961. (It has been Secret Service policy to assign special agents to the Detail for orientation in protection methods and procedures which also serves to identify those agents who like this type of activity and whose attitude and demeanor to protective work indicates a potential replacement.)

Reports reflect that Bolden made one trip with the Detail to Hyannis Port from June 30, to July 5, 1961. He was assigned

- 4 -

to ATSAIC Stout's shift. Stout did not make this trip and the supervisor of the Shift was Acting ATSAIC Henderson.

The following agents who were assigned to this same shift were interviewed and statements obtained:

SA Harvey G. Henderson
SA William B. Payne
SA Edward Z. Tucker
SA Winston G. Lawson
SA Kenneth J. Wiesman
SA George V. Mesaros

These 1967 Secret Service document excerpts, opened by the ARRB in 2009 from an initial 1997 inquiry with the agency and only released 2017-2018, corroborate Bolden and his fine 2008 book *The Echo from Dealey Plaza* on several major points.

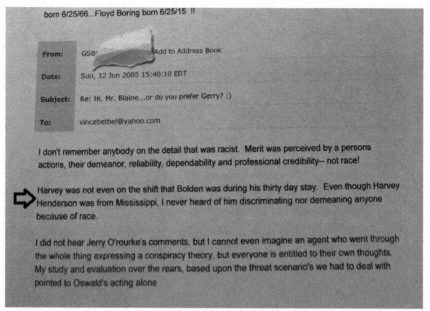

born 6/25/66...Floyd Boring born 6/25/15 !!

From:	GSB... Add to Address Book
Date:	Sun, 12 Jun 2005 15:40:10 EDT
Subject:	Re: Hi, Mr. Blaine...or do you prefer Gerry? :)
To:	vincebethel@yahoo.com

I don't remember anybody on the detail that was racist. Merit was perceived by a persons actions, their demeanor, reliability, dependability and professional credibility-- not race!

Harvey was not even on the shift that Bolden was during his thirty day stay. Even though Harvey Henderson was from Mississippi, I never heard of him discriminating nor demeaning anyone because of race.

I did not hear Jerry O'rourke's comments, but I cannot even imagine an agent who went through the whole thing expressing a conspiracy theory, but everyone is entitled to their own thoughts. My study and evaluation over the rears, based upon the threat scenario's we had to deal with pointed to Oswald's acting alone

Interestingly, Winston Lawson would go on to become the lead advance agent for the ill-fated 11/22/63 Dallas trip. In 1997 correspondence with the author, former Secret Service agent and White House Shift Leader Arthur Godfrey tried unsuccessfully to debunk the notion that Bolden's nemesis, Harvey Henderson, was a boss. Likewise, former Secret Service agent Gerald Blaine did much the same thing in both interviews and correspondence with the author.

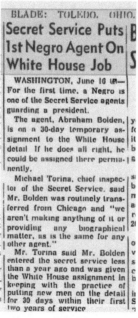

BLADE: TOLEDO, OHIO.

Secret Service Puts 1st Negro Agent On White House Job

WASHINGTON, June 16 (AP)— For the first time, a Negro is one of the Secret Service agents guarding a president.

The agent, Abraham Bolden, is on a 30-day temporary assignment to the White House detail. If he does all right, he could be assigned there permanently.

Michael Torina, chief inspector of the Secret Service, said Mr. Bolden was routinely transferred from Chicago and "we aren't making anything of it or providing any biographical matter, as is the same for any other agent."

Mr. Torina said Mr. Bolden entered the secret service less than a year ago and was given the White House assignment in keeping with the practice of putting new men on the detail for 30 days within their first two years of service

The Toledo (Ohio) Blade, 6/16/61.

Interview: C. Cross   2

same time as the Vallee incident.

We began discussing Abraham Bolden and Conrad Cross stated that he knew Bolden well, although they did not socialize too often. He stated that when Bolden was arrested, he (Cross) couldn't understand some of the allegations against Bolden regarding time and place, because he was with Bolden on some of those dates. Cross stated that he believes Bolden was set up, but he has no idea who would have done it. Cross stated that Bolden had a big mouth and did not think before he said things. He believes this was a contributing factor to Bolden's troubles. Bolden had a personality clash with ASAIC Maurice Martineau and they were always at each other.

Cross stated that the Bolden incident was the main cause of his resignation. Cross became very disillusioned with the Secret Service because he felt Bolden had been "shafted". He stated that he began to feel useless and lost faith in the Secret Service and felt it was time to get out. Cross stated his supervisors tried to dissuade him but he resigned. He stated that he holds no malice and had been proud to be an agent. He stated that he felt his training had been very good.

Excerpt from the 1978 interview with Secret Service agent Conrad Cross:

Bolden, Liggett & Myers representative William F. Stephenitch (c), and W. A. Blake Jr., of Ingersoll, beam about size of check.

Ex-Secret Agent Leads Drive To Get Smokes For GI's

"Ex-Secret Agent Leads Drive To Get Smokes For GIs". Jet. Chicago: Johnson Publishing Company. 29 (13): 8. January 6, 1966.

> of the...
> Abraham Bolden is the first African American Secret Service agent on White
> House detail. He was handpicked by JFK. He was not on duty the day of the
> assassination and is haunted by that to this day, knowing full well that he would
> have kept the young president from the sniper's bullets. (See "Chapter 10 Secret
> Service Abraham Bolden, A Real American Hero" for more information.)
>
> Holland: I had Minnie Jean Brown on this show, she was one of the
> original Little Rock Nine...I also had a fellow that used to work
> for your boss, on the show, his name is Abraham Bolden, do you
> remember him...?
>
> Sorensen: Oh the Secret Service agent?
>
> Holland: Yes sir, do you remember him?
>
> Sorensen: I remember that there was such a person, but, to be honest
> with you, I didn't pal around with the Secret Service agents, so I did
> not remember him personally.

Page 92 from Brent Holland's excellent book The JFK Assassination from the Oval
Office to Dealey Plaza (2014)- JFK's top aide Ted Sorensen remembered Abraham
Bolden.

The most amazing postscript happened for Abraham Bolden in April
2022 when President Biden pardoned him.[305] To say that many people were
delighted and shocked at the same time would be an understatement.[306]
This event was a major media happening. I am so very happy for Abe, as
we all are.

President Joseph R. Biden, Jr. is pardoning the following three
individuals:

Abraham W. Bolden, Sr. – Chicago, Illinois
Abraham Bolden is an 86-year-old former U.S. Secret Service agent and
was the first African American to serve on a presidential detail. In 1964,
Mr. Bolden was charged with offenses related to attempting to sell a copy
of a Secret Service file. His first trial resulted in a hung jury, and following
his conviction at a second trial, even though key witnesses against him
admitted to lying at the prosecutor's request, Mr. Bolden was denied a
new trial and ultimately served several years in federal custody. He has
steadfastly maintained his innocence, arguing that he was targeted for
prosecution in retaliation for exposing unprofessional and racist behavior
within the U.S. Secret Service. Mr. Bolden has received numerous honors
and awards for his ongoing work to speak out against the racism he faced
in the Secret Service in the 1960s, and his courage in challenging
injustice. Mr. Bolden has also been recognized for his many contributions
to his community following his release from prison.

Abraham Bolden, shown at his home, was pardoned Tuesday by President Joe Biden.
TERRENCE ANTONIO JAMES/CHICAGO TRIBUNE

Ex-Secret Service agent gets pardon from Biden

Chicagoan was first Black agent on a presidential detail

By Jason Meisner and Terrence James
Chicago Tribune

Nearly 60 years after his conviction on what he claimed were racist and retaliatory federal charges, the first Black U.S. Secret Service agent assigned to a presidential detail has been pardoned by President Joe Biden.

Chicagoan Abraham Bolden, 87, who served on the security detail for President John F. Kennedy, was among 78 people granted pardons or commutations of their sentences on Tuesday as part of Biden's first use of his executive clemency powers.

Bolden, who'd warned about lax security practices around the president, was charged in 1964 with attempting to sell a copy of a Secret Service file to a ring of counterfeiters. His first trial ended in a hung jury, and after he was convicted in

Turn to Pardon, Page 6

Bolden is briefed by lawyer, George C. Howard. Following the

209

OPTIONAL FORM NO. 19
5010—104

UNITED STATES GOVERNMENT

Memorandum

U. S. SECRET SERVICE
File No. 012.0
DATE: February 14, 1964

TO : Chief

FROM : Inspector Kelley

SUBJECT: HR 9958

Reference is made to the attached bill pending in the House of Representatives, a copy of which was furnished to you by Mr. Ranta for your information.

I consider this bill and similar bills to be a very dangerous piece of legislation. It would make the killing of the President or the Vice President of the United States a Federal offense under Section 1114, Title 18, USC. This would give the FBI sole jurisdiction over the investigation of an assassination. However, the FBI receives an appropriation for the protection of the President and are as concerned and involved with the protection of the President as we are. Therefore, they could be in a position of investigating their own dereliction in the event an assassination of a President or Vice President occurred.

This to me is another opportunity for a "Seven Days in May" situation. A venal Director of the Federal Bureau of Investigation could in the future bring about or allow the assassination of the President who he either felt was a poor President or a President unacceptable to him and so direct the investigation that the complicity would be unknown. To me it is much safer to have the State investigate the murder and have the Federal Government looking over its shoulder during the investigation.

This proposed bill would mean that the Federal Government would have sole jurisdiction over an investigation since the Federal law would take precedent over the State murder charge, therefore, there would be no one looking over the shoulder of the Federal Agency that is conducting this investigation and evidence could easily be suppressed. I think that this bill should be opposed by the Treasury Department and the American people, and especially by us who have the primary responsibility for the protection of the President. In other words, I do not think that even the Secret Service should have the sole jurisdiction over the investigation of the assassination of a President, and that the matter should be left as it now stands.

I believe that the present Director of the FBI had a reservation such as this in mind when he has insisted on having a small appropriation in the FBI's appropriation, "For the protection of the person of the President", i. e. if information was received that the Secret Service became suspected of plotting or became ineffective, the FBI could

Chief

step in. Mr. Hoover indicated this when in response to a question put by a Congressman during an appropriation hearing. "Why are we appropriating money for protection of the President when we appropriate money to the Secret Service for this purpose?" Mr. Hoover replied, "We have always had it – we believe we need it in the event we are called upon in an emergency."

This proposed legislation, however, would exclude any other Investigation Agency from any participation in an investigation. It should not be passed.

CHAPTER NINE

HOW IT WAS ALLOWED TO HAPPEN: A SUMMARY OF SECRET SERVICE MAL-FEASANCE
(ACTION THROUGH INACTION)

"Another opportunity"? An amazing Secret Service document written during the Warren Commission days by Secret Service Inspector (and later Assistant Director) Thomas Kelley, who had interviewed Oswald and would later rise to become Assistant Director and testify before both the Warren Commission and the HSCA:

"This to me is another opportunity for a 'Seven Days in May' situation. A venal Director of the Federal Bureau of Investigation could in the future bring about or allow the assassination of the President unacceptable to him and so direct the investigation that the complicity would be unknown. To me it is much safer to have the state investigate the murder and have the Federal Government looking over its shoulder during the investigation."

Was this Inspector Kelley's suspicion of what transpired after Dallas? The ARRB reported, "Mr. Boring was shown Inspector Kelley's 2/14/64 memo to Chief Rowley re: HR 9958 [USSS document No. 154-10002-10332], and stated that he had never heard Inspector Kelley speak in that manner of the inadvisability of allowing the FBI sole investigative jurisdiction over future assassination investigations; or of a Seven Days in May scenario [military intelligence coup]; or of a possible venal Director of the FBI bringing about or allowing an assassination under these new investigative guidelines; etc. He seemed somewhat surprised and speechless by the contents of this memo."[307]

Based on decades of research and Secret Service agent interviews comes the following summary:[308]

---

307   9/18/96 ARRB interview of Floyd Boring.
308   Please see the author's prior five books: *Survivor's Guilt, JFK: From Parkland to Bethesda, The Not-So-Secret Service, Who's Who in the Secret Service* and *Honest Answers.*

1) The Secret Service is the boss of the President, not the other way around – for example, an Associated Press story from November 15, 1963: "The (Secret) Service can overrule even the President where his personal security is involved." Shockingly, perhaps with an eye toward real history after he is long gone, Hill admitted in 2010 in his Sixth-Floor oral history, with Blaine right by his side: "[The president] can tell you what he wants done and he can tell you certain things but that doesn't mean you have to do it. What we used to do was always agree with the President and then we'd do what we felt was best anyway." Presidents Truman, LBJ, and Clinton are all on the record confirming this fact.

> The Secret Service, charged by law with protecting the person of the President, would say nothing. The service can overrule even the President where his personal security is involved.

2) Agents were frequently on or near the rear of JFK's limousine and Kennedy had nothing to do with their placement there or lack thereof – Kennedy-era White House Secret Service agents Gerald Behn, Floyd Boring, Art Godfrey, Sam Kinney, Bob Lilley, Winston Lawson, Abraham Bolden, and a host of others confirmed these facts.

3) Many motorcycles normally bracketed the limousine.

LAWSON, BELFORD 05/31/77
(e) Comparison of Dallas Motorcycle Security With That
of Previous Motorcade in The Same Texas Trip

The Secret Service's alteration of the original DPD
motorcycle deployment plan prevented the use of maximum possible
security precautions. The straggling of Haygood and Brewer,
on the right rear area of JFK weakened security that was already
reduced because of rearward deployment.

But in comparison with what the SS's own documents suggest
were the security precautions used in prior motorcades during
the same Texas visit, the motorcycle alteration in Dallas by
the SS may have been a unique occurrence.

The SS final report on security measures in San Antonio,
for example, indicates that there were 18 motorcycles that
"flanked the Presidential car as outriders." The SS final
report for Houston stated that in all motorcade movements,
"six motorcycles flanked the Presidential limousines and an
additional 33 motorcycles were used to flank the motorcade and
cover the intersections."

4) Multi-story building rooftops were normally guarded (FDR-JFK eras) – As both 1960 and 1962 vintage Secret Service books both stated: "If the President is to appear in a parade, agents and policemen are assigned posts atop buildings and on the street along the parade route."[309] The ARRB noted in their final report from 1998: "Congress passed the JFK Act of 1992. One month later, the Secret Service began its compliance efforts. However, in January 1995, the Secret Service destroyed presidential protection survey reports for some of President Kennedy's trips in the fall of 1963."

11/21/63 SAN ANTONIO- VIEW FROM POLICE HELICOPTER:

5) The bubble top was often used on the limousine – Agent Sam Kinney was adamant to me, on three different occasions, that he was solely responsible for the bubbletop's removal on 11/22/63. JFK had nothing to do with it. It was briefly on the car on 11/22/63 and was then removed. Although not bulletproof or bullet resistant in the traditional sense, many people thought it was, thus making it a psychological deterrent: would someone fire onto the car with it on? In addition, many agents thought it would deflect a bullet and/or shield

---

309   *The United States Secret Service* by Walter Bowen & Harry Neal (1960), page 131, and *What Does a Secret Service Agent Do?* By Wayne Hyde (1962), page 28.

the president via the sun's glare off the top. Many times, the top was on the car in either full or partial formations (meaning, just the front and rear pieces were used so the president could stand intermittently and offer some semblance of protection at the same time, similar to the famous Eisenhower bubble). In addition, the top was used in bright, no-rain conditions: I found it was used on approximately 25 good weather trips, roughly a third of all JFK motorcades.

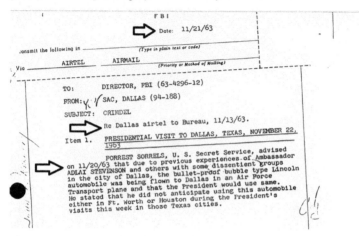

6) Press photographer's flatbed truck was normally in front of the Presidential limousine – Normally, a flatbed truck (sometimes two) carrying still and motion photographers from the press was used in motorcades and rode in front of the presidential limousine, as it was used on the prior trip in Florida and many other occasions. It was cancelled at the last minute by the Secret Service at Love Field.

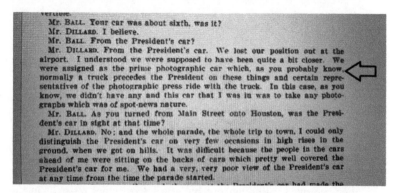

7) Behn and/or Boring always accompanied JFK on trips outside of the Capitol (D.C.) – For Behn, this was his very first vacation in over three years: the time period of both the Florida and Texas trips.[310] Boring was at home in Maryland but in charge of the Texas

---

[310]   See also *Last Word* (2011) by Mark Lane, pages 164-165.

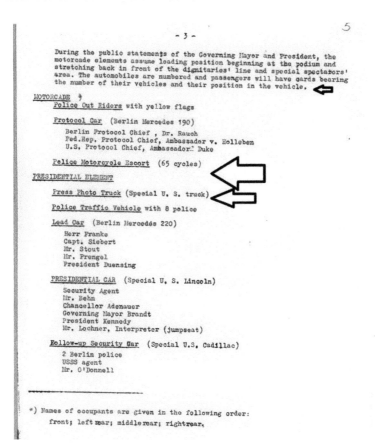

- 3 -

During the public statements of the Governing Mayor and President, the motorcade elements assume leading position beginning at the podium and stretching back in front of the dignitaries' line and special spectators' area. The automobiles are numbered and passengers will have cards bearing the number of their vehicles and their position in the vehicle.

MOTORCADE
    Police Out Riders with yellow flags

    Protocol Car (Berlin Mercedes 190)
        Berlin Protocol Chief , Dr. Rauch
        Fed.Rep. Protocol Chief, Ambassador v. Holleben
        U.S. Protocol Chief, Ambassador Duke

    Police Motorcycle Escort (65 cycles)

PRESIDENTIAL ELEMENT

    Press Photo Truck (Special U. S. truck)

    Police Traffic Vehicle with 8 police

    Lead Car (Berlin Mercedes 220)
        Herr Franke
        Capt. Siebert
        Mr. Stout
        Mr. Prengel
        President Duensing

    PRESIDENTIAL CAR (Special U. S. Lincoln)
        Security Agent
        Mr. Behn
        Chancellor Adenauer
        Governing Mayor Brandt
        President Kennedy
        Mr. Lochner, Interpreter (jumpseat)

    Follow-up Security Car (Special U.S. Cadillac)
        2 Berlin police
        USSS agent
        Mr. O'Donnell

*) Names of occupants are given in the following order:
    front; left rear; middle rear; right rear.

trip from the Secret Service's point of view. For third-stringer Roy Kellerman, this was only the second major trip he made on his own (the first appears to have been Nashville May 1963, a model of good security-helicopter, rooftops guarded, fast speed of cars, etc.).

8) Secret Service knew of prior threats to Kennedy's life – These include ones for Chicago 11/2/63 (cancelled) and Miami/Tampa 11/18/63. PRS agents Glen Bennett and Howard Norton were both on the Texas trip: Bennett rode in the follow-up car, as he had been on every trip since just joining the detail 11/10/63. For his part, Norton was in Austin, as he had also been on the Florida trip (the author only discovered his presence in late 1990's). These were obviously covert monitors of threats that were covered up afterwards. As mentioned earlier, former agent Jerry O'Rourke responded to all of this with the following: "I don't want to do it. I don't want to do it. I'm afraid for my agency." This is in addition to the presence (or lack thereof) of military intelligence operatives in Dealey Plaza, including James Powell, who took a photo of the Texas School Book Depository after the shooting.

9) Motorcade route was changed – SAIC Behn confirmed to me that the route was changed for the Dallas trip! He gave me no details other than to say, "I know it was changed but why– I have forgotten completely – I don't know." Needless to say, the Secret Service was responsible for the terrible route JFK took that fateful day in Dallas and there were alternate routes, as agents Sam Kinney, Win Lawson, and others confirmed, including the one going from Main to Industrial Boulevard, a route that would have bypassed Elm Street altogether and had the limo moving further away from the knoll and the Depository (and moving at a faster rate of speed, as well). Straight down Main Street is the route FDR took in 1936. It was also the ceremonial route, as Governor Connally admitted under oath. The route was changed between 11/18-/11/20- some even claimed 11/21-11/22.

10) Sheriff's Department and military stand down – Sheriff Bill Decker told his men to in no way participate in the security of the Dallas motorcade. There were not enough police guarding the route and no branch of the military augmented security, as was standard procedure (you see, agents weren't always on the back of the car and they were often short-staffed back then – this is why they relied on the local police and the military to help them out). Trained U.S. Army Intelligence Units were told their assistance was not needed in Dallas during the JFK visit. William McKinney, a former member of the crack 112th Military Intelligence Group at 4th Army Headquarters, Fort Sam Houston, Texas, has revealed that both Col. Maximillian Reich and his deputy, Lt. Col. Joel Cabaza, protested violently when they were told to "Stand Down" rather than to report with their units for duty in augmentation of the Secret Service in Dallas. McKinney said, "All the Secret Service had to do was nod and these units [which had been trained at the Army's top Intelligence school at Camp Holabird, Maryland] would have performed their normal function of Protection for the President in Dallas." The 315th, the Texas unit which would have been involved if its support had not been turned down, had records in its files, according to McKinney, on Lee Harvey Oswald. The 315th had a Dallas office and its records were up to date. McKinney added that, "Highly specialized classes were given at Camp Holabird on the subject of Protection. This included training designed to prepare this army unit to assist the Secret Service. If our support had not been refused, we would have been in Dallas."[311]

---

311   2003 internet news article: "JFK Stand Down" – Army Aid to Help Protect President Kennedy Was Refused." See also – RIF# 180-10093-10320: 5/31/77 Memorandum

11) Military aide riding in front seat of limousine (between driver and agent in charge of trip) – General Godfrey McHugh, who rode there 11/18/63, told Canadian radio in 1976, the HSCA in 1978 and an author in 1995 that he was asked for the first time in Dallas not to ride there. On 11/22/63, McHugh was asked to sit in a car farther back in the motorcade, rather than "normally, what I would do between the driver and Secret Service agent in charge of trip." He admitted that this was "unusual," as he had ridden there many times before, including 11/18/63 on the Florida trip. During a 5/11/78 interview with the HSCA's Mark Flanagan, it was conveyed that "Ordinarily McHugh rode in the Presidential limousine in the front seat. This was the first time he was instructed not to ride in the car so that all attention would be focused on the President to accentuate full exposure."[312] In regard to the preparations for the 11/22/63 Dallas trip, General Godfrey McHugh is also quoted as saying: "They'd asked me, for the first time, to please not ride in the President's car, because they want to give him full exposure. These are the exact words they used. Ken O'Donnell and the Secret Service said, 'the politicians here feel it's most important for the President to be given full exposure, to be seen coming and going. McHugh said he normally rode in the car in which JFK was a passenger "in the front, next to the driver, and [I] would take notes."[313]

12) Local police and detective cars – Dallas Police Chief Jesse Curry and Dallas Chief of Homicide Will Fritz each wanted a car full of policemen in the motorcade.

13) The overpass was not properly guarded and cleared of spectators.

14) 9 agents drank the morning of 11/22/63 – including 4 on the follow-up car: Hill, Ready, Landis, and Bennett.[314]

15) JFK/LBJ together for first time as President and Vice President in a motorcade: They rode together in September 1960 in Dallas, Texas when they were candidates. The next time? Dallas 11/22/63;

16) Fake or unauthorized "agents" in the plaza.[315]

---

from HSCA's Belford Lawson to fellow HSCA members' Gary Cornwell & Ken Klein (revised 8/15/77).

312   5/11/78 interview with the HSCA's Mark Flanagan (RIF#180-10078-10465 [see also 7 HSCA 14].

313   Ralph Martin's *Seeds of Destruction: Joe Kennedy and His Sons* (1995), p. 453.

314   *Last Word* (2011) by Mark Lane, pages 178-184.

315   *Last Word* (2011) by Mark Lane, page 163 and 188-192.

```
1-7                SELECT COMMITTEE ON ASSASSINATIONS


    NAME   J. M. Smith              Date 2/8/78    Time_____

    Address 733 Cliffview Lot #41    Place_____

           Dallas, Texas

   Interview:

       Officer J. M. Smith was asked about his testimony
    before the Warren Commission when he stated that he con-
    fronted a Secret Service Agent.

       Officer Smith stated that he remembers going back
    to the parking lot area in back of the knoll. He remem-
    bers walking there with a Deputy Sheriff but doesn't recall
    his name. Officer Smith had his revolver drawn and after
    getting to the parking lot area, had just started to holster
    his gun, when he observed a man on the parking lot near the
    railroad tracks. The man told Officer Smith that he was
    Secret Service and flashed his I.D. Officer Smith never
    examined the I.D. but continued searching the area. He
    did not notice the actions of the Secret Service man after
    that.
```

17) Secret Service agent driver Thomas B. Shipman – Passed away suddenly of an alleged heart attack at, of all places, Camp David on 10/14/63. He was buried quickly and no toxicology tests were given. One wonders what would have happened if Shipman – and not Greer – drove the presidential limousine in Dallas.

18) Secret Service agent driver Bill Greer – Effectively replaced the dead Shipman. Greer's inaction on Elm Street was a violation of training and common sense (two looks back, disobeyed Kellerman's order). Greer also withheld the president's clothes and effects (Dallas to Bethesda). Greer also harbored strange feelings toward JFK (According to his son Richard: "Well, we're Methodists and JFK was Catholic").[316]

19) Secret Service agent Floyd Boring – Boring was the planner of Texas trip (and many other trips) from the Secret Service's point of view.

20) Secret Service agent Emory Roberts – Roberts recall of agents Henry Rybka and Don Lawton at Love Field airport in Dallas as the motorcade began makes him infamous. Roberts also recalled agent Jack Ready and ordered the agents not to move during the shooting (according to agent Sam Kinney who sat right next to Roberts). Roberts also usurped agent Roy Kellerman, his boss, at Parkland. It was also his decision to take over Air Force One for LBJ's purposes. Incredibly, Roberts became the Appointment Secretary to LBJ while still an active agent!

21) **Motive** – It was a combination of a couple major factors: some of the agents (notably, follow-up car agents Tim McIntyre and Emory Roberts, among others) were angry and disgusted with President Kennedy's private life, while others, such as Forrest Sorrels and Elmer Moore, were angry at President Kennedy for his foreign policy views. Chief U.E. Baughman, like Allen Dulles, was fired by the Kennedy brothers – in Baughman's case, the reason was because he did not believe the Mafia existed, a view shared by J. Edgar Hoover of the FBI. Baughman was made the Chief on November 22 of 1948.

22) **The following agents believed or knew there was a conspiracy**- Abraham Bolden, Maurice Martineau, Sam Kinney, Bill Greer, Roy Kellerman, Robert Bouck, Gerald O'Rourke, John Norris, Marty Underwood, and John Marshall. A few other agents – Forrest Sorrels, Lem Johns and Paul Landis- believed at least one shot came from the front.

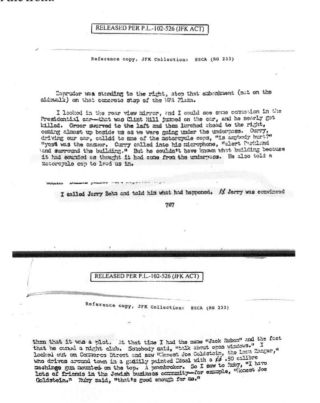

Secret Service agent Forrest Sorrels to William Manchester.

Sorrels was riding in the rear seat of the lead car. He recalls remarking on the number of people hanging out of the windows along the motorcade route. As the TSBD building came into view, he noticed several open windows and several people at the windows. A few of the people he saw were negroes. He saw no unusual motions; he has no recollection of seeing Oswald.

He heard a total of three shots. There was twice as much time between the first and second shots as there was between the second and third shots. He believes that the overall time for all three shots was something like six seconds. The shots sounded like gun-fire. They seemed to come more from the north slope of the bank of Elm Street than from the

- 4 -

TSBD building. All shots sounded like they came from behind and to the

Above: Secret Service agent Forrest Sorrels- Warren Commission "preliminary" interview. Below: *PRS Secret Service agent Max Phillips - Zapruder thought the shots came from behind him.*

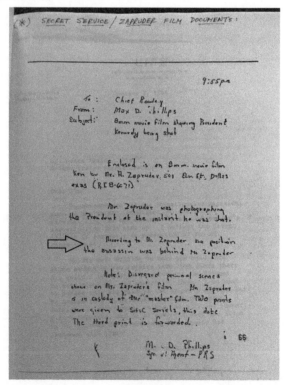

23) **Action thru inaction** – By not doing certain things (hitting the gas pedal, having agents on or near the rear of the limousine, and blaming JFK for the lack of security, among other items), the agency was made to purposely fail and, thus, had to run with the JFK-is-to-blame myth to cover up and hide their gross, purposeful negligence or face the consequences – Congressional hearings, press inquiries, loss of pensions, prosecutions, and the end of the agency, at least their role as protectors of our nation's highest officials. Furthermore, by covering up the drinking incident (as Rowley testified, he didn't want to stigmatize the agents, never mind that they broke a sacred rule that was grounds for dismissal and they lost a president) and giving out two awards (one arguably underserving – to Hill, the other dubious – to agent Youngblood, who allegedly covered LBJ a little sooner than even Youngblood believed was possible), the agents got away with a verbal slap on the wrist coupled with great praise for their heroism and courage. In the age before Watergate and true investigative journalism, with a dead president unable to defend himself and a naïve and trusting public, should we have expected anything else?

Puerto Rico Dec 1961--Secret Service agents Roy Kellerman and Bob Lilley on the rear of the limousine (bubble top on). Lilley told me several times that President Kennedy never ordered the agents off his limo and was very cooperative with the Secret Service: "whatever you guys want is the way it will be." He also remarked about this trip that they reached speeds of FIFTY MILES PER HOUR!

Find 2d JFK gunman, probers tell FBI

By JOSEPH VOLZ

Washington (News Bureau).— Rep. Louis Stokes (D-Ohio), chairman of the House Assassinations Committee, said yesterday that it was now up to the FBI to find the so-called "second gunman" who, the panel believes, took part in the Nov. 22, 1963, assassination of President Kennedy.

But Stokes, interviewed on "Face the Nation," held out little hope that the second gunman would ever be found. "It's difficult for the Justice Department to pick up the leads so many years after the assassination," Stokes said.

Thus, the committee, which spent $5.8 million in its two-year investigation — the most expensive congressional probe in history.— went out of business yesterday failing to answer a key question: If Lee Harvey Oswald was part of a conspiracy, who were the other conspirators?

Based mainly on acoustical calculations by Queens College Prof. Mark

Weiss, the committee findings said that there was a "high probability" that a second gunman fired one shot from a grassy knoll overlooking the Kennedy parade route in Dallas. Neither Weiss nor a committee report released Saturday gave any indication of who the gunman might be, what kind of weapon he fired or if he was aiming at Kennedy.

"We did leave some loose ends," said Stokes. "We're not perfect. I think the money was well spent. We have done what we were supposed to."

Stokes insisted that the "second gunman" theory, which directly contradicts the 1964 Warren Commission report that Oswald acted alone, was not based only on Weiss' findings.

178 interviewed

Stokes said that the Warren Commission had interviewed 178 persons who were near the grassy knoll and many of them thought they heard shots fired from the knoll. But the commission, which did not have the benefit of Weiss' acoustical tests, concluded that echoes were playing tricks with the listeners' ears. No one has ever report-

ed seeing a gunman on the knoll and no gun or any shells were found there.

The FBI which is severely criticized in the Stokes committee report for failing to investigate the possibility of a conspiracy, is now being asked by the committee to try to find the mystery gunman, even though no one has ever reported seeing him.

King assassination

The panel also probed the April 4, 1968, assassination of Dr. Martin Luther King Jr., the civil rights leader killed in Memphis by James Earl Ray.

Ray is serving a 99-year term for the murder, but Stokes said yesterday that "circumstantial evidence" linked him with two deceased white supremacists who had offered a $50,000 reward for King's murder. The two, John Kauffman and John Sutherland, had passed the word in prison circles in 1967 that they would pay a bounty for King's assassination, but there is no indication that Ray ever met the two men. The panel, however, received testimony indicating that Ray may have talked to underworld members who were aware of the offer.

Associated Press photo

Rep. Louis Stokes
Committee Chairman

The second government investigation came to the conclusion that a conspiracy took the life of President Kennedy.

Rule Violation Cited In JFK Assassination

Clearing Of Buildings On Parade Route Called Fundamental

By SETH KANTOR
Scripps-Howard Staff Writer

WASHINGTON, Dec. 1 The manager of the Texas School Book Depository Building in Dallas "should have been under firm instructions by the police" to keep people out of the upper stories of the building when President Kennedy passed by Nov. 22.

Mr. Baughman

Such instructions are "a basic, established rule," said U. E. Baughman, former chief of the U. S. Secret Service, the agency charged with protecting a President's life.

during presidential motorcade.

Rigid Rules Followed

According to Mr. Baughman, "it was always standard procedure for the Secret Service, through the local police, to insist that building managers follow rigid rules to protect the President."

This was true "in all buildings along Pennsylvania Avenue during presidential inaugural parades and in buildings along out-of-town motorcade routes" during Mr. Baughman's years from 1927 to 1961 with the Secret Service.

As the last building on the western edge of downtown Dallas, the Texas School Book Depository Building "certainly had to be considered a key building as a place from which to shoot the President," said Mr. Baughman

Upper floors of the seven-story orange brick structure were being used for storage purposes

Oswald Employe

Lee Harvey Oswald, charged with the murder of President Kennedy before he himself

Former JFK Secret Service Chief U.E. Baughman shocked the world on 12/1/63:

Detroit Free Press

DETROIT FREE PRESS SATURDAY, NOVEMBER 30, 1963

DREW PEARSON

Let's Probe Actions Of FBI, S. Service

BY DREW PEARSON

WASHINGTON—Three agencies sacrosanct as far as Congressional investigation is concerned are the FBI, the Secret Service, and Central Intelligence.

In the interest of protecting the life of the new President, however, it is my belief that a rigorous investigation should be undertaken regarding the first two.

* * *

SIX SECRET SERVICE men charged with protecting the President were in the Fort Worth Press Club the early morning of the day President Kennedy was shot. Some of them remained until 3 a.m.

They were drinking. When they departed, three were reported en route to an all-night beatnik rendezvous, "The Cellar."

It has been stated that it was an impossibility for the Secret Service to check the occupancy of every building along the route.

While this is true, it is also true that warehouse type buildings—such as that in which the assassin hid—should be searched. The extra time spent by Secret Service men at the Fort Worth Press Club could have been spent in so doing.

* * *

DALLAS POLICE stated that FBI agents had interviewed Lee Oswald but had not informed them about the interview. In Washington, the FBI denied its agents had interrogated Oswald recently.

Regardless of whether he was interviewed recently or a long time ago, it is the job of protective agencies to check on every suspect in any city which the President visits and make sure where he is at the time of the visit.

A man who had been working for the Fair Play for Cuba Committee, who had professed Marxism, and whose record showed a mixed-up, unsteady emotionalism, should have been kept under careful watch on the day the President entered this city—one of the most lawless and intolerant cities in the United States.

* * *

THE SECRET SERVICE keeps a file of people who have written threatening letters to the President or who are otherwise a suspect.

If Oswald was not on their list, the FBI should have communicated with the Secret Service after its agents interviewed him.

Since Oswald had been shown on TV passing out pro-Castro leaflets, certainly the FBI and the Secret Service should have been able to catalogue him without too much trouble.

* * *

AS FOR DALLAS police, newsmen on the scene inform me that it is inconceivable the police did not know Jack Ruby was inside the Police Department basement.

Most newsmen had to show their credentials to two police guards to enter the basement. It was more difficult to get in than into the White House.

Yet a strip-tease night club operator with a police record of arrests for assault and for carrying concealed weapons was let inside.

The Dallas police record shows Ruby was chiefly in trouble for having a violent temper and jumping on people. This is not the kind of a man normally allowed in police headquarters when the most important defendant in Texas history is being transferred.

How this happened may never be explained by the Dallas police. But a bipartisan, thorough-going Congressional committee should probe it to the bottom.

CONCLUSIONS

Based on the prior chapters in this book, the evidence for both a plot to kill Kennedy in Chicago and a conspiracy in his death is conclusive:

1. **The statements and beliefs of former Secret Service agent Nemo Ciochina** – he reached out to me (including thru a younger intermediary) adamantly telling me that there was a plot to kill JFK in Chicago and even gave me two strong leads: Lloyd John Wilson and Puerto Rican persons of interest (unnamed).

2. **Lloyd John Wilson** himself and the many reports related to his threats to both JFK and LBJ, his admitted connection to Oswald, his disturbing background, and the seriousness of the threats and the investigation, even including a member of the Secret Service White House Detail in Washington, D.C., Tony Sherman (who would be gone from the Detail in October 1963); the Special Agent in Charge of the White House Detail, Gerald Behn (who would be absent from Kennedy's trips to Chicago, Florida and Texas); the Chief of the Secret Service, James Rowley; the Secret Service Special Agent in Charge of the Protective Research Section (PRS), Robert Bouck; Bouck's deputies, Chester Miller and Walter Pine; a Secret Service agent who guarded President Kennedy in Hyannis Port, James Giovanetti; the Secret Service Special Agent in Charge of the Spokane, Washington field office, Norman Sheridan; Special Agent in Charge of the San Antonio Secret Service field office, Luis Benavides, who helped protect JFK in San Antonio on 11/21/63; the Acting Special Agent in Charge of the Chicago office, Maurice Martineau, Ciochina's (and Abraham Bolden's) boss in Chicago, as well as Chicago Secret Service agents Joseph Noonan and Ed Z. Tucker, both former White House Detail agents; Special Agent in Charge Fred Backstrom of the Springfield, Illinois Secret Service field office; The Special Agent in Charge of the San Francisco Secret Service office, Tom Hanson; FBI Director J. Edgar Hoover; and the Warren Commission's General Counsel, J. Lee Rankin.

3. **The many mortal threats to President Kennedy's life in the short years, months, weeks and even days before 11/22/63,** especially the written statement by Colonel George J. McNally, White House Signal Corps leader and former Secret Service agent, from his obscure 1970 book released in 1982 by his widow: "But during the Chicago visit [3/23/63], the motorcade was slowed to the pace of a mounted Black Horse Troop, and the police got a warning of Puerto Rican snipers. Helicopters searched the roofs along the way, and no incidents occurred."[317] Again, please note McNally calling the suspects "Puerto Rican."

4. **The sudden and unprecedented appearance of covert Secret Service threat monitors on trips in the month of November 1963,** including PRS agent Glen Bennett, PRS agent Howard K. Norton and PRS agent Dale Wunderlich.

5. **The disturbing background and statements of several Secret Service agents,** including former OSS man Paul Paterni, the Deputy Chief of the Secret Service, Elmer Moore (who called Kennedy a traitor), James Mastrovito (later a CIA agent), Roger Warner (also later a CIA agent), the CIA presence noted by Secret Service agent Andy Berger on 11/22/63, Chuck Zboril, a Secret Service agent on JFK's trip to Florida who rode on the rear of the limousine in Tampa and who served in the same Marine unit as Oswald, and other agents.

6. **The stunning security measures usually allotted to President Kennedy that were deficient or totally absent in Dallas on 11/22/63,** including rooftop security, a staple of Secret Service safeguards since at least the FDR era. Several prominent agents were well aware of threats to JFK's life, yet poor security dominated in Texas, a stark contrast to Florida, where security was superb, and in Chicago, where the trip itself was cancelled.

7. **The pro-conspiracy statements to the author from former Acting Special Agent in Charge of the Chicago office, Maurice Martineau** (Bolden and Ciochina's boss), as well as his 1978 admission to the HSCA about a telephone threat to JFK during a prior (pre-11/2/63) trip to Chicago (almost assuredly 3/23/63, as there was also a separate postcard threat to the president's life).

8. **FBI agent Thomas B. Coll's 1975 statement** that "some people were picked up" (people-plural) regarding 11/2/63.

317   *A Million Miles of Presidents* by Col. George McNally (1970/1982), p. 204.

9. **Suspect (some would say patsy) Thomas Arthur Vallee's 1975 admission** that there was a plot in Chicago for 11/2/63.

10. **Chicago Secret Service agent Robert Motto's 1978 admission to the HSCA** that there were "threats" (plural) regarding 11/2/63.

11. **Chicago Secret Service agents Lois Sims and Joseph Noonan's statements** regarding pre-11/2/63 Chicago trip Puerto Rican and/or Cuban threats to JFK.

12. **Chicago Secret Service agent Abraham Bolden's adamant statements to the author** and others concerning a plot to kill President Kennedy in Chicago on 11/2/63 (as also stated to journalist Edwin Black for the 1975 issue of the *Chicago Independent,* which also used Sherman Skolnick as a source).

13. **For the first time ever, several actual Puerto Rican suspects named** and how Puerto Rican Nationalists had threatened Presidents Truman, Eisenhower and Kennedy.

In addition, as noted in the prior chapter, Secret Service agents Sam Kinney (scheduled for the 11/2/63 Chicago trip and on the Florida and Texas trips), Robert Bouck, John Norris and Gerald O'Rourke (like Kinney, on the Texas trip) told the author their belief that a conspiracy took the life of JFK.[318] Also, Secret Service agents Bill Greer and Roy Kellerman harbored feelings and beliefs against official history, as conveyed to the author from author Harold Weisberg, as the respected writer had spoken to Kellerman's daughters at a book signing where these feelings were conveyed to him (and, as we know, both Greer and Kellerman made statements to both the Warren Commission and the HSCA that went against the single bullet theory and the official descriptions of the wounds, as well as the shooting itself). Fellow Secret Service agents Clint Hill and Paul Landis both stated that the right rear of Kennedy's head was gone, and Landis wrote in two reports that one of the shots came from the front, mirroring Forrest Sorrels and Lem John's beliefs.

History's verdict must be changed: there were mortal threats to President Kennedy's life and the eventual assassination that occurred in Dallas on 11/22/63 was the result of a moving crime that went thru Chicago and culminated in Texas.

---

318   Please see the author's prior books, especially *Survivor's Guilt: The Secret Service & The Failure to Protect President Kennedy, Who's Who in the Secret Service,* and *Honest Answers About the Murder of President John F. Kennedy,* numerous.

ACKNOWLEDGMENTS

Eternal thanks to the love of my life, my wife, Amanda Palamara, for her support and patience for yet another book, my sixth. All my love to my dad, my late mother, and my brother. I also wish to thank all the many former Secret Service agents, White House aides, Parkland Hospital personnel and Bethesda Medical Center personnel for their help. Although I have a tradition of working alone, I would also like to thank all the many dedicated authors and researchers who have worked diligently on this case.

Index